D0244556

4339501003098442772b012

Introducing Psychology

Abnormal Psychology

This edition published in 2005 by Grange Books
an imprint of Grange Books Plc
The Grange
Kingsnorth Industrial Estate
Hoo, Near Rochester
Kent ME3 9ND
www.Grangebooks.co.uk

ISBN: 1-84013-804-1

Printed in China

Editorial and design:
The Brown Reference Group plc
8 Chapel Place
Rivington Street
London
EC2A 3DQ
UK
www.brownreference.com

FOR THE BROWN REFERENCE GROUP PLC
Editors: Windsor Chorlton, Karen Frazer, Leon Gray,
Simon Hall, Marcus Hardy, Jim Martin, Shirin Patel,
Frank Ritter, Henry Russell, Gillian Sutton, Susan Watt
Indexer: Kay Ollerenshaw
Picture Researcher: Helen Simm
Illustrators: Darren Awuah, Dax Fullbrook, Mark Walker
Designers: Reg Cox, Mike Leaman, Sarah Williams
Design Manager: Lynne Ross
Managing Editor: Bridget Giles
Production Director: Alastair Gourlay
Editorial Director: Lindsey Lowe

PHOTOGRAPHIC CREDITS
Front Cover: Photodisc: National Cancer Institute (tr); Photos.com (br);
Mark Walker (l).
AKG London: 98; Albert Ellis Institute: 109; American Psychiatric Publishing
Inc.: 9; Jeff Bloom: 38; Brand X Pictures: Burke & Triolo 129; Bridgeman
Art Library: Geothe Museum, Frankfurt/Henry Fuseli 143; Citizens' Commission
on Human Rights International: 130; Corbis: 22, James L. Amos 112, Archivo
Iconograficoi 8, Bettmann 29, 31, 160, 162, Richard Bickel 64, Gianni Dagli Orti
163, Laura Dwight 75, ER Productions 151, Mitchell Gerber 66, 81, Richard
Hutchings 56, David Lees 157, Charles & Josette Lenars 7, Craig Lovell 92,
Stephanie Maze 23, Roger Ressmeyer 12, David & Peter Turnley 20, Underwood
& Underwood 158; Corbis Stockmarket: Jon Feingersh 94, Mark M. Lawrence
118, Rob Lewine 136; HOK: 154; Hulton Archive: 10b, 13, 99; Hutchison Picture
Library: J. G. Fuller 155; Image Bank: Sylvaine Achernar 35, Serge AEF Attal 144,
Barros & Barros 120, Derek Berwin 15, Jeff Cadge 6, Color Day Production 39, 65,
David Paul Productions 122, Britt Erlanson 86, Deborah Gilbert 123, Inc. Bokleberg
G&J Images 105, Vicky Kasala 43, Romilly Lockyer 47, 147, G. & M. David de Lossy
45, Zac Macauley 16, Marks Productions 146, Benn & Esther Mitchell 161, Kaz Mori
116, Nicki Pardo 101, Andrea Pistolesi 55t, Terje Rakke 55b, Marc Romanelli 28, 115,
Yellow Dog Productions 19; Imaging Body: 84, 127c, 127t; Kobal Collection:
United Artists 78, 97, United Artists/Fantasy Films 153; Mary Evans Picture
Library: 21, 25, 34, 95, 159; National Autistic Society, UK: 68, 70, 71, 72, 73, 74,
76, 77; NHPA: Daniel Heuclin 103; NIMH: 138; PA Photos: 11, 88, EPA 61
Photodisc: Alan & Sandy Carey 30l, Doug Menuez 51, Photolink 30r, Suza Scalora
48; Pictor: 27, 52, 67; Popperfoto: Reuter 46, 142; Robert Hunt Library: 10t, 40;
Ronald Grant Archive: 79; Science & Society Picture Library: DHA/NMPFT 42,
Science Museum 119; Science Photo Library: BSIP Mendil 58, Dr. Monty
Buchsbaum/Peter Arnold Inc. 33, Damien Lovegrove 125, Will & Deni MacIntyre
80, 100t, 125, 133, 141, Alfred Pasieka 59, Catherine Pouedras 62, James Prince 37,
Bo MI&I Veisland 87; Stone: Bruce Ayres, Jon Bradley 110, Mark Douet 140,
Zigy Kaluzny 36, 93, Tony Latham 148, Jonathan Nourok 41, David Harry Stewart
149, Ken Whitmore 91, David Young-Wolff 53; Sylvia Cordaiy Photo Library:
Anthony Reynolds 101b; TCL: Burgum Boorman 131; Travel Ink: 150;
TRH: Fairchild/Bud Shannon Photo Inc. 106; University of Pennsylvania
Health System: 108; University of Wisconsin: 126, 128; USHMM: 137;
World Health Organization: 18; p. 132 courtesy Pan Macmillan.

CONTRIBUTORS

Consultant:
Tom Heffernan, PhD
Senior Lecturer in Psychology,
Division of Psychology,
University of Northumbria, UK

Authors:
Robert F. Bornstein, PhD
Professor of Psychology,
Gettysburg College, PA
Mental Disorders in Society

Jennifer Gosselin, MA
Doctoral Student in Clinical Psychology,
George Mason University, VA
What Is Abnormality?

Nicola Kimber, PhD
Psychologist and Psychotherapist,
Division of Academic Psychiatry and Psychology,
Guy's Hospital, London, UK
Psychotherapies

James Maddux, PhD
Professor of Psychology,
George Mason University, VA
What Is Abnormality?

Peter D. Moxon, PhD
Lecturer in Psychology,
University of Huddersfield, UK
Abnormality in Development

Fiona Starr, PhD
Clinical Psychologist,
Insititute of Social Science Research,
University of Middlesex, UK
Mental Disorders

Graham Turpin, PhD
Director, Clinical Psychology Unit,
Department of Psychology,
University of Sheffield, UK
Physical Therapies

Malcolm Peet
Associate Professor of Psychiatry,
University of Sheffield, UK
Physical Therapies

Keith Woods, MSc
Clinical Psychologist,
New Zealand
Mental Disorders

Contents

About This Set

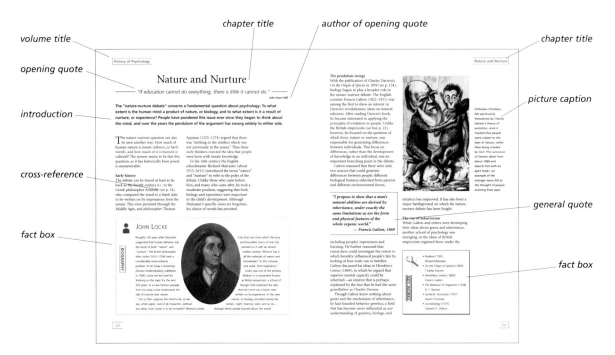

volume title — chapter title — author of opening quote — chapter title

opening quote

picture caption

introduction

cross-reference

general quote

fact box

fact box

The diagram above shows the typical elements found within a chapter in this set. The various types of fact box are explained more fully in the box shown opposite.

These pages explain how to use the *Psychology* encyclopedia. There are six volumes in the set, each one illustrated with color photographs and specially commissioned artworks. Each volume has its own contents list at the beginning and a glossary at the back explaining important terms. More information, such as websites and related reference works, are listed in the Resources section, also found at the back of each volume.

To find articles on a particular subject, look for it in the set index at the back of each volume. Once you have started to read a relevant chapter, cross-references within that chapter and in the connections box at the end of the chapter will guide you to other related pages and chapters elsewhere in the set.

Every chapter has several color-coded fact boxes featuring information related to the subject discussed. They fall into distinct groups, which are described in more detail in the box opposite (p. 5).

THE SIX VOLUMES

History of psychology (Volume One) takes a look at psychology's development throughout history. It starts in ancient Greece when concepts of "mind" existed only as a topic of philosophical debate, looks at the subject's development into a separate field of scientific research, then follows its division into various schools of thought. It also explores the effects of scientific developments, discusses recent approaches, and considers the effects of new research in nonwestern cultures.

The brain and the mind (Volume Two) analyzes the relationship between the mind and the brain and looks at how the brain works in detail. The history of neuroscience is followed by a study of the physiology of the brain and how this relates to functions such as thinking. Chapters tackle the concept of the mind as an intangible and invisible entity, the nature of consciousness, and how our perceptual systems work to interpret the sensations we feel. In a chapter entitled Artificial Minds the volume explores whether or not machines will ever be able to think as humans do.

Thinking and knowing (Volume Three) looks at how the brain processes, stores, and retrieves information. It covers cognitive processes that we share with animals, such as associative learning, and those that are exclusive to people, such as language processing.

Developmental psychology (Volume Four) focuses on changes in psychological development from birth, throughout childhood, and into old age. It covers theories of social and intellectual development, particularly those of Jean Piaget and Lev Vygotsky. It also covers social and emotional development and how they can be improved and nurtured.

Social psychology (Volume Five) studies people as unique individuals and as social animals. It analyzes the notions of personality and intelligence as well as considering how people relate to and communicate with each other and society, and the social groups that they form.

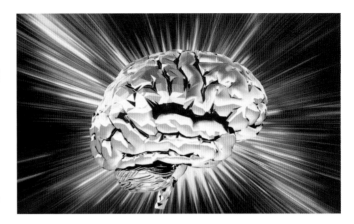

Psychologists using a variety of approaches work in different fields (developmental, social, or abnormal, for example), but all study the brain, trying to figure out how it functions and how it influences people's behavior, thoughts, and emotions.

Abnormal psychology (Volume Six) asks what is abnormality? It shows how the number and types of abnormalities recognized as mental disorders have changed over time and examines specific disorders and their causes. It also looks at diagnosis of disorders and treatments, which can be psychological (talking cures) or physical (drugs and surgery). The social issues associated with abnormality and how society deals with people who have mental disorders are also explored.

 KEY DATES
Lists some of the important events in the history of the topic discussed.

 KEY POINTS
Summarizes some of the key points made in the chapter.

 KEY TERMS
Provides concise definitions of terms that appear in the chapter.

 KEY WORKS
Lists key books and papers published by researchers in the field.

 FOCUS ON
Takes a closer look at either a related topic or an aspect of the topic discussed.

 EXPERIMENT
Takes a closer look at experimental work carried out by researchers in the field.

 CASE STUDY
Discusses in-depth studies of particular individuals carried out by researchers.

 BIOGRAPHY
Provides historical information about key figures mentioned in the chapter.

 PSYCHOLOGY & SOCIETY
Takes a look at the interesting effects within society of the psychological theories discussed.

 CONNECTIONS
Lists other chapters in the set containing information related to the topic discussed.

What Is Abnormality?

Investigating an indefinite concept

The scientific study of psychological disorders, or "psychopathology," is sometimes referred to as the field of abnormal psychology. One of the first major issues students of abnormal psychology encounter is that the answers to questions like "What is abnormal?" and "What is a mental disorder?" are constantly evolving. Guidelines have been established, however, that help psychologists and others diagnose and treat people suffering from mental disorders, which can cause distress, fear, and sometimes even physical pain in sufferers or those around them.

A young man in his first year at college feels sad and lonely as he tries to adjust to living away from home for the first time. A woman begins to panic when she drives over a bridge. A little boy has difficulty learning to speak. A grandmother feels disoriented and can't remember how to get home. Are these people having abnormal experiences? Do they have a mental disorder? The answers to these questions are complex and depend on who is answering them. That is because terms like "abnormal" and "mental disorder" are in part defined by social and cultural beliefs, which differ from culture to culture and change over time. This is not to say that some mental disorders might not have physical causes. Many are firmly based in biology, but it is not possible to diagnose or identify mental disorders with simple medical procedures, such as blood tests. In many cases (for example, phobias) there may be no biological cause to detect. Even if there is a biological cause, it is often difficult for a psychologist to determine whether or not a person needs treatment, and what sort of treatment that should be. In such cases a clinician's definitions of abnormality and mental disorders and their severity are crucial.

Whether or not someone is diagnosed as having a mental, or psychological, disorder has many important implications. For example, during a trial (below), if defendants are found to be mentally disordered, they might receive a different sentence than if they were considered psychologically healthy.

> *"nearly half of all Americans will experience a mental or emotional problem at least once during their lifetime that, if diagnosed, would be classified as a mental disorder."*
> —*R. C. Kessler and others, 1994*

Although there is no one definitive definition of psychological abnormality, a variety of definitions have been proposed and accepted. In the United States one official definition of mental disorders that is accepted by a large number of mental health professionals, despite some critics, can be found in the *Diagnostic and Statistical Manual of Mental Disorders*—or the DSM (*see* box p. 9). The DSM is published by the American Psychiatric Association (APA) to help psychologists, psychiatrists, and other medical professionals identify and diagnose psychological problems.

RELIGION VERSUS SCIENCE

Throughout history people have explained psychological abnormality mainly in terms of religion, magic, or—most recently—science. Ancient Egyptian writings indicate that in approximately the 16th century B.C. the Egyptians believed that the brain was responsible for mental functioning. While this might seem like the beginning of a scientific view of abnormality, other documents show that the ancient Egyptians, Chinese, Hebrews, and Greeks believed that abnormal behavior was caused by demons, spirits, or gods, depending on the religious beliefs of the people. For example, God might punish people for sinful acts by taking away their ability to think rationally and by making them behave in bizarre ways. Those who believed that abnormality was caused by an evil spirit that possessed a person's body might summon a priest to exorcise the spirit. Exorcisms could involve reciting chants, prayers, and performing rituals, such as whipping the evil spirit out of the person's body or making the person drink potions.

During the 18th and 19th centuries in Europe huge advances were made in science and the scientific method (see Vol. 1, pp. 30–39). Scientists increasingly emphasized rational thought and scientific discovery through careful observation and experimentation, rather than reliance on superstition, religion, or magic. Early psychologists, like the whole of western society, were greatly influenced by this development and worked to establish psychology as a separate discipline in its own right. They adopted scientific methodology as much as possible and began the long process of turning psychology into a science, which included diagnosing, classifying, and treating mental disorders.

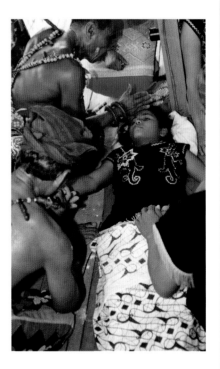

A traditional healer carries out an exorcism on a woman in Borneo, Indonesia, in an attempt to drive out an evil spirit. In some cultures people with psychological problems are just as likely to visit a nonmedical healer, such as this shaman, as they are likely to visit a physician. On occasion the treatment works.

Why define abnormality?
Defining psychological abnormality has many practical implications:
• It helps establish the subject matter covered by the field of abnormal psychology and so determines the patterns of human behavior that should become the subject of scientific study.
• It affects our criminal justice system: We might hold people less responsible for their crimes if we think that they have a mental disorder.
• It affects the way society thinks about and acts toward people whose behavior seems different or socially unacceptable. We usually hold people responsible for behavior that is within their control and

don't hold them responsible for behavior beyond their control. For example, a man who repeatedly shoplifts might not be held responsible if his behavior was judged to be the result of a mental disorder.
• It affects public policy: If we think people have mental disorders, we might view them as having disabilities that qualify them to receive special treatment. The Americans with Disabilities Act (ADA) was passed in 1990 for just such a purpose. Defining mental abnormality also helps the government and private organizations decide which problems are eligible for research funds.
• It affects the delivery of mental health services: Insurance companies and

government health services are more likely to pay for the cost of treating emotional and behavioral problems if the problems are officially classified as psychological disorders.

Defining criteria
In general, most definitions of psychological abnormality are based on one or more of the following criteria:
- deviation from statistical norms;
- maladaptiveness, meaning a difficulty in adapting;
- personal distress; and
- social acceptability.

DEVIATING FROM THE NORM
The word *abnormal* comes from the Latin *ab*, meaning "away from," and *norm*, meaning "average." So, abnormal literally means "away from the norm, or average." Deciding what is abnormal involves first deciding what is normal or average and then determining how far from that someone deviates.

For example, we might find that the average height for a woman is about 5 feet 4 inches (1.63m). If so, then women who are much taller or much shorter are of abnormal height.

To a certain extent we can apply this definition of abnormality to psychological functioning. First, psychologists try to determine what is psychologically normal and then try to determine what is psychologically abnormal. This might seem straightforward, but there are two important questions to answer:
- First, can we establish norms, or averages, for psychological functioning?
- Second, how far must someone's thoughts, feelings, or behaviors deviate from the average before they are abnormal?

The tremendous variety of people and behaviors makes determining what is normal very difficult. Some people enjoy skydiving, while others are too afraid to climb a ladder.

Austrian composer Wolfgang Amadeus Mozart (1756–1791) performed his first concerto at the age of three. By most people's standards that would be considered abnormal, but few would consider it undesirable. Below, Mozart (center) is shown at the age of 7.

THE DSM

The *Diagnostic and Statistical Manual* (DSM) is accepted by most mental health professionals as the standard and official classification of mental disorders, especially in the United States and the United Kingdom. First published by the American Psychiatric Association in 1952 and on its fourth revised edition by the year 2000, the DSM provides the organizational structure for almost every textbook and course on the study of abnormal psychology for undergraduate and graduate students. Plus, the DSM provides the basis for almost every professional book on the assessment and treatment of psychological problems.

The DSM basically groups psychological disorders into categories. Mental health professionals use the categories to agree on a common diagnosis, while researchers use them to guide them in their studies, and insurance companies use them to determine how to reimburse patients and providers for mental health services, such as psychotherapy and medication.

Supporters of the DSM argue that it provides a common language in which to describe and treat disorders and to conduct research. The authors of the DSM acknowledge that their manual has flaws; but they argue that until something better comes along, it is the best system available. Others argue that there are better ways of describing psychological problems, but they have not yet become widely accepted. There have been many debates within professional organizations such as the American Psychiatric Association and the American Psychological Association about how to define, describe, and classify psychological disorders.

Some are outgoing and love being around other people, while others are shy and prefer being alone. Some people seem to worry about every little thing, while other people always seem calm and relaxed no matter what happens to them. Most of us are somewhere in between these extremes. How do we determine who among us is normal and who is abnormal?

> *"abnormal: deviating from the norm or average; unusual, exceptional (behavior)"*
> *—Merriam-Webster's Dictionary*

Even if we could determine what is normal by developing a test of some kind, like an intelligence test, we would still have to decide how far from the average people's thoughts, feelings, and behaviors must be for them to be abnormal.

Another problem with defining psychological abnormality as deviating from the norm is that someone can greatly differ from the average in a way that is useful instead of harmful or desirable instead of undesirable. For example, people whose intelligence is much higher than average have advantages over those whose intelligence is much lower than average. Highly intelligent people might be abnormal, but their abnormality is of benefit to themselves and often also to society in general.

The DSM, published by the American Psychiatric Association, sets out widely accepted criteria for diagnosing various mental disorders. It provides mental health professionals with a common terminology for diagnosis.

CHANGING VIEWS OF ABNORMALITY

Most psychologists and psychiatrists strive to be as scientific as possible when they study abnormal behavior and psychological disorders. Many of the decisions about what is abnormal or disordered, however, have less to do with science and more to do with changing social norms and values.

In 1851 the American physician Dr. Samuel Cartwright invented a psychological disorder called drapetomania. This term was used to describe African-American slaves who resisted their condition by destroying the property of their owners or trying to escape. This behavior is now viewed as a rational response to slavery, not a disorder.

Because social and cultural standards continually change, definitions of psychological abnormality within society and the profession also continually change.

In the late 19th century masturbation was seen as a sign of psychological disturbance. Around this same time women who expressed an interest in sex were considered by some male psychiatrists to be abnormal. Today most people probably would agree that masturbation is a normal sexual activity and that it does not indicate mental illness. Most would also agree that sexual feelings are as natural and normal for women as they are for men.

Homosexuality has been accepted or tolerated by many societies and cultures throughout history. But in 1952 it became an official mental disorder in the first edition of the DSM, in which it was called sexual

A gay couple, poets Chester Kallman (1921–1975) and W. H. Auden (1907–1973), on Ischia, Italy. Their homosexual relationship would once have been considered a symptom of a mental disorder.

orientation disturbance. In 1973, however, homosexuality was removed from the DSM. This change of mind was mostly the result of changes in social attitudes toward gay people and protests from gay rights' groups and gay psychiatrists.

Psychologists have known for a long time that many soldiers develop severe anxiety problems, including depression, nightmares, and flashbacks, that can last years after experiencing combat. The condition was originally known as shell shock. But this problem did not become an official mental disorder in the DSM until 1980. Getting what is now called posttraumatic stress disorder into the DSM took several years of lobbying by U.S veterans of the war in Vietnam, their physicians, and other groups. They wanted the U.S. government to deal more seriously with the psychological problems many veterans were suffering as a result of having witnessed terrible events during the war. What removed homosexuality from the DSM and brought posttraumatic stress disorder into the DSM were principally changes in social norms and values.

Black slaves work in a cotton field in the United States while a white overseer on horseback watches them. If slaves tried to escape or rebel, they could have been diagnosed with the mental disorder of drapetomania.

ABNORMAL AS MALADAPTIVE

Since defining abnormal behavior in terms of deviance from norms can be problematic, many psychologists look at how a person's behavior affects their own well-being and that of the social group. Behavior is considered maladaptive or dysfunctional if it has a negative effect on society or on a person's ability to function in society. For example, a seriously underweight woman suffering from an eating disorder (*see* pp. 46–51) is behaving maladaptively since her behavior affects her health. A paranoid man who plots to kill random people is behaving maladaptively in a way that harms others, not himself.

People have to use different ways of coping in response to different situations. If your behavior helps you cope with stress, deal with challenge, or accomplish your goals, then your behavior is termed adaptive or functional. If, however, your behavior does not help you in these ways, or if it actually makes the problem worse, then it is maladaptive or dysfunctional.

Adaptive responses

Behaving adaptively also includes the ability to know when your behavior is not working well and to come up with a new way of trying to solve a problem. For example, if you fail your first exam in your mathematics class, you might decide that you need to study differently, find a tutor, or talk to a counselor. These are examples of adaptive responses. Doing nothing, blaming the teacher, and simply "hoping for the best" are examples of maladaptive responses. Becoming so distressed that you cannot think clearly about what to do is also an example of a maladaptive response. In general, behaving adaptively means learning from experience and being flexible in how you deal with life's challenges and problems.

Cultural demands

Whether or not your behavior is adaptive depends on what goals you are trying to accomplish and whether or not your culture approves of those goals. For example, a person who fasts for religious reasons is not displaying maladaptive behavior according to most cultures. On the other hand, a person who is already thin but wants to get even thinner and refuses to eat because they believe that they are overweight is displaying maladaptive behavior. We even have an official term for this condition: anorexia nervosa. Also, most cultures accept or tolerate moderate use of alcohol. But when people drink so much alcohol that they cannot keep a job, we consider their behavior maladaptive or dysfunctional.

Degree of maladaptiveness

As with definitions of normal and abnormal, there is no hard-and-fast line between adaptive and maladaptive or between functional and dysfunctional: The differences are a matter of degree— some people can adapt better to certain situations than others. Most people behave maladaptively sometimes, but it is the extent to which that behavior is damaging to the person's or the society's well-being that matters.

Also, each culture's judgments about which behaviors are adaptive or maladaptive are always based on what that culture believes people should do to have meaningful and fulfilling lives. The judgments always involve the culture's values, its deeply held beliefs about what is right or wrong, what it means to be a good person or a good citizen, and what it means to lead a good life. Again, the problem arises of trying to determine how much deviation from social and cultural norms is too much.

Adaptiveness depends on the standards set by a culture. Since the late 20th century the ideal of female beauty in western societies has been represented by ultraslim supermodels like Jodie Kidd (below). Women who adopt a strict diet to maintain slim figures might be considered adaptive in such cultures but maladaptive in others. Maladaptiveness is also a matter of degree, however. So, if a woman diets to the extent that she damages her health, then her behavior is maladaptive.

ABNORMAL AS DISTRESSED

Perhaps one of the most compelling factors that psychologists consider when assessing people is the degree of distress experienced by a person. Distress can take many forms, including sadness, anxiety, anger, loss of appetite, and irritability. It is important to consider distress as a factor in defining abnormality because feeling depressed or anxious can be a painful or unpleasant experience. Distress is also important because it can interfere with our ability to function effectively in daily life: It can be maladaptive. In many situations, however, distress is normal.

One problem with using distress as a sign of abnormality is that we are still left with two difficult questions:
• How much distress in a given situation should we consider to be too much?
• How long need someone's distress continue before it is termed maladaptive?

For example, how much and for how long should someone grieve after the death of a spouse, child, or parent? If someone is unable to drive a car because their anxiety about traffic is so great,

should we consider their anxiety to be maladaptive or dysfunctional? Does it matter whether they live and work in Los Angeles, where driving one's car is widely considered to be the only efficient way of getting around; or whether they live in New York, where they can rely on much better public transportation and never have to drive?

> *"People do not come to clinics because they have some abstract definition of abnormality. For the most part, they come because their feelings and behavior cause them distress."*
> —*Miller and Morley, 1986*

Another problem with the distress definition is that not all examples of abnormal behavior or mental disorders are accompanied by distress. Adults who sexually abuse children might feel little remorse or distress about their behavior, although the children they abuse undoubtedly do feel distress. People with antisocial personality disorder do not feel remorse for the many times that they lie, cheat, steal, and otherwise use people for their own personal pleasure or profit.

SOCIAL ACCEPTABILITY

Many behaviors are considered normal because they conform to social standards of acceptable or good behavior. Similarly, behaviors that deviate from socially acceptable actions might be considered abnormal. Some behaviors are considered normal and adaptive because they help people get along better and make everyday life more orderly and predictable. Examples include good table manners or waiting your turn in line.

While, on the one hand, conformity is useful, on the other hand, too much conformity or conformity to the wrong beliefs and practices can be maladaptive, not only for the individual but also for

A survivor weeps in the aftermath of the 1980 San Francisco earthquake. Distress is a normal reaction to stressful events. When distress is excessive and prevents day-to-day living, it could be seen as maladaptive.

The Indian social reformer and freedom fighter M. K. Gandhi (1869–1948) challenged the social norms of his time by protesting against British colonial rule with fasting and nonviolent resistance. His unusual methods might be considered maladaptive (since they often involved endangering his well-being), but they resulted in profound historical changes.

society. A person who is constantly worried about whether or not what they do or how they appear is approved of by others is not a psychologically healthy person and is not usually viewed as normal. For example, a person who goes deeply into debt to pay for repeated plastic surgeries because they are trying to reflect society's idea of perfect beauty probably would not be viewed as normal by most people—a little nonconformity can be healthy for us. It can also be healthy for society.

Sometimes people violate social norms because of deeply held beliefs that such norms are wrong. For this reason some violations of social beliefs and practices can be viewed as acts of courage. The acts often prompt long-overdue change. M. K. Gandhi's pacifist resistance to British rule

PSYCHOLOGY & SOCIETY

LEGAL ISSUES REGARDING ABNORMALITY

How we define abnormality can affect whether or not we find someone guilty of an alleged crime and also, if found guilty, how we decide to treat or punish the person.

In 1985 a Japanese-American woman named Fumiko Kimura carried her two children (one aged four years and the other six months) with her into the Pacific Ocean, reportedly intending to drown them and herself. Although both of her children died, Mrs. Kimura lived. She said that she decided to kill herself and her children to save them from being dishonored by her husband's affair with another woman. Kimura's lawyer used a cultural defense, explaining that her Japanese cultural beliefs led her to commit the murders. She served one year in prison and five years on probation.

Sixteen years later, in 2001, a woman named Andrea Pia Yates admitted to drowning her five children in a bathtub (*see* pp. 142–163). Yates had a history of mental illness, and the postnatal (after birth) depression from which she was reportedly suffering possibly worsened her illness. Her attorneys argued that during and perhaps also after the murders she was in a psychotic state (a detachment from reality) and should not be held responsible for her crimes. However, while the jury agreed that she was mentally ill, they held that she knew at the time of the drownings that she was doing wrong and so found her guilty of capital murder.

Both of these cases illustrate the complexity of defining abnormal behavior. If people behave in a way that is in

keeping with their cultural values, even if it means killing someone, should we find them guilty of a crime? If people commit murder while they are unaware of what they are doing, should they be held legally responsible? These are difficult questions that cannot be answered by science because they are concerned with values, not facts.

In some trials, as in the case of Andrea Yates, the accused person's lawyer might plead not guilty by reason of insanity. This essentially means "my client committed the crime, but she is not responsible because she was not of sound mind at the time." The defendant may not have known what they were doing or may have felt compelled to commit the crime, so they could not have formed the intent to kill as required by law.

The terms sanity and insanity are legal terms, not medical, psychiatric, or psychological terms. Sanity and insanity refer to a person's ability to control their behavior or even know what they were doing at the time. A person can be judged to have been legally insane at the time a crime was committed without being diagnosed as having had a formal mental disorder. Similarly, a person can be diagnosed with a mental disorder yet still be judged to have been sane at the time they committed a crime. Establishing clear differences between sanity and insanity is as difficult as establishing clear differences between normal and abnormal psychological functioning.

in India eventually resulted in the creation of an independent nation in 1947. When Rosa Parks refused in 1955 to give up her bus seat to a white passenger in Alabama, she helped begin the Civil Rights movement in the United States. Without such violators of contemporary social norms a society and its culture would remain static and possibly steeped in injustice. Science and art are also advanced by daring people who defy the status quo. Galileo defied the Catholic Church by insisting that the Sun, not Earth, was the center of our solar system. Painters such as Cezanne and Picasso defied conventional ideas of beauty and of what the world looks like to the human eye. They were ridiculed by many at the time. Without them and other unconventional people and their nonconformist ideas the world could be a much poorer place in many ways.

ABNORMAL AS DISORDERED

Do the people we consider psychologically abnormal have some kind of disorder that makes them abnormal? The answer to this question depends on how we define disorder. We can use the term "disorder" simply to refer to a pattern of thinking, feeling, and behaving that is generally maladaptive. In other words, it is

disordered because it disrupts the order in the lives of the person and other people. For example, severe depression disrupts the life of the depressed person. It also disturbs the lives of many other people such as family, friends, and coworkers. For this reason we can say that depression is a mental or psychological disorder.

The DSM definition

The American Psychiatric Association (APA) provides an official definition of "mental disorder" in the DSM as:

> *"a clinically significant behavioral or psychological syndrome or pattern that occurs in an individual and that is associated with present distress, for example, a painful symptom, or disability, that is, impairment in one or more important areas of functioning, or with a significantly increased risk of suffering, death, pain, disability, or an important loss of freedom. In addition, this syndrome or pattern must not be merely an expectable and culturally sanctioned response to a particular event [and] must currently be considered a manifestation of a behavioral, psychological, or biological dysfunction in the individual."*

How Common Are Psychological Disorders?

How many people are abnormal? How many suffer from psychological or mental disorders? One of the most famous studies of mental disorders in the United States was the Epidemiologic Catchment Area Study (ECA). It was conducted over more than 10 years and involved more than 19,000 participants; the results were published in 1991. The researchers used the third edition of the DSM (1980) to determine whether or not a person had a psychological or mental disorder. They found that 32 percent of adults had met the criteria for at least one mental disorder at some point in their lives. They also found that 20 percent could be diagnosed with a disorder at the time of the study.

The scope of the term "mental disorder" has broadened since the DSM was first published in 1952 and since the ECA was conducted more than two decades ago. Since then, more disorders have been added to the DSM (see facing page: Scientific or social?). This means that, in theory, more people could be diagnosed with mental disorders than ever before.

Eventually, if the majority of the population were diagnosed with a mental disorder, then they would make up the norm, and their condition could no longer be considered abnormal. The conditions from which they suffer might well still be considered disorders, though, since deviation from the norm is only one factor to consider.

This definition includes the notions of maladaptiveness and distress but avoids the issues of normal and abnormality—so a disorder may be common yet still be a disorder. It also indicates that we need to consider a person's culture when determining whether or not that person's behavior is abnormal. The DSM also avoids the use of the terms "illness" or "disease." Instead, it talks of "mental disorders," which are those psychological conditions that make people distressed, disabled, and at increased risk of harm, regardless of whether the cause is clearly a biological disease (as in Alzheimer's dementia) or not (as in eating disorders).

The DSM does have its critics, however. Some claim that the APA defines disorders in an unscientific way and then uses the definitions as scientific fact, which is neither helpful nor correct. Definitions of disorders are used to explain the behavior that led to the definition in the first place. For example, if you are feeling depressed, it is because you have depression. What is

Firefighters in action. Some people in occupations involving life-threatening circumstances might be diagnosed with posttraumatic stress disorder. PTSD has only been recognized in the DSM as a mental disorder since 1980.

depression? One symptom is feeling depressed. Depression is simply a label for certain experiences. It does not provide information about how your life or the way you are thinking about your life are contributing to the way you feel.

> "[The DSM] *is not a scientific document…it is a social document."*
> —*Widiger and Trull, 1991*

Scientific or social?

One of the most important features of a culture is the assumptions that most of its members share about what is important in life and what it means to live a good life. The number of pages in the DSM has increased from 86 in 1952 to over 900 in 2000, and the number of mental disorders increased from 106 to 297. As the boundaries of mental disorder have expanded with each DSM revision, many everyday life problems have been pathologized, or turned into disorders, and the sheer number of people with diagnosable mental disorders has continued to grow. For example, many common difficulties are now considered abnormal, such as children's temper tantrums, being drunk, excessive smoking, not desiring or enjoying sex, and learning difficulties. Masochistic personality disorder, caffeine dependence, sexual compulsion, low-intensity orgasm, sibling rivalry, self-defeating personality, jet lag, pathological spending, and impaired sleep-related painful erections were all proposed for inclusion in DSM-IV (2000) as mental disorders. At the turn of the millennium mental health practitioners discussed Internet addiction, road rage, and pathological stock-market trading at scientific meetings; it is possible that some of the activities might end up in a new edition of the DSM.

MODELS OF ABNORMALITY

Abnormal psychologists recognize various models of mental disorder that describe the underlying causes of abnormalities or recommend how to treat them. These models include the medical

KEY POINTS

• The field of abnormal psychology is concerned with mental disorders. Mental disorders are not always easy to diagnose or identify since judgments have to be made about whether or not a person is psychologically abnormal, usually in the absence of hard biological facts—most mental disorders do not have an underlying physical cause that can be tested for.

• Defining a mental disorder always involves defining what is abnormal psychologically. This has many important implications that affect both society and individuals.

• Factors that are considered when defining what is abnormal psychologically include: deviation from the norm, being maladaptive (or dysfunctional), levels of personal distress, and social acceptability, which varies from culture to culture.

• The DSM, published by the American Psychiatric Association, provides a widely accepted guide to defining and describing mental disorders.

• The medical model sees psychological disorders as diseases. Other models of mental disorder include the behavioral, cognitive, and biopsychosocial models. The ICIDH published by WHO (see box p. 18) is based on a biopsychosocial model.

model, the psychoanalytic model, the behavioral model, and the cognitive model. Different psychologists might routinely apply certain models, while others view more than one model as valid. Some psychologists have developed models that integrate all possible causes of mental disorders. Brief summaries of different types of models follow, and they are covered in more detail in Chapters 4 and 5 (see pp. 92–141).

Medical model

The medical model views psychological abnormality as similar to a disease—something inside a person that causes them problems and distress, just as, say, the malarial parasite is something inside people that causes them to become ill with malaria. This model assumes that people with psychological problems have illnesses with specific symptoms, causes, and cures. The model works well

An elderly woman suffering from Alzheimer's disease (left), the most common form of dementia. The brain damage that this disease either causes or is caused by can only be seen at autopsy. So, medical workers make diagnoses based on abnormalites in behavior and mental functioning.

for mental disorders that have a known and testable cause—many dementias (*see* pp. 57–61), for example. These disorders involve deterioration of mental abilities, which can sometimes be measured in the shrinking of brain disease and the loss of brain cells. Alzheimer's disease involves characteristic plaques (*see* p. 58) and nerve tangles in the brain, but it is not known whether they are a cause or consequence of the disease. Researchers working within the medical model have located specific genes that may be responsible for the disease.

Researchers often spend a great deal of time looking for such causes. Not only do they study genetics, but they also consider how the brain works and the role of brain chemicals such as neurotransmitters (*see* Vol. 2, pp. 20–39).

Psychological models of abnormality
Many psychological problems are difficult to diagnose and treat if just the medical model is followed, though. It may not be possible to classify a disorder as present or absent. Take anxiety, for example. Each of

IS IT ABNORMAL TO BE FEMALE?

PSYCHOLOGY & SOCIETY

Many disorders, such as major depressive disorder, agoraphobia, social phobia, eating disorders, and many personality disorders, are diagnosed much more often in women than in men. The ratio of females to males receiving a diagnosis for these disorders varies from 2:1 to 9:1. According to some researchers, the gender differences in rates of diagnosis occur because the definitions of certain disorders are biased against women. They believe that because the DSM is developed mostly by male psychiatrists, it sets diagnostic criteria using the psychological functioning of adult males as the standard for mental health and creates disorders out of normal female psychological functioning.

A controversial female disorder once under consideration for inclusion in the DSM was premenstrual dysphoric disorder—or feelings of sadness or depression before the beginning of monthly menstruation. Many women felt that this disorder was an example of men pointing the finger at women and calling them abnormal.

Critics of the DSM target personality disorders as particularly unfair to women. For example, the definition of dependent personality disorder includes features that reflect an exaggerated female role, such as going to "excessive lengths to obtain nurturance and support from others, to the point of volunteering to do things that are unpleasant" (DSM-IV, p. 668). Yet some argue that traditionally women are taught by society to value social support and to do just about anything for other people. Another criterion, having "difficulty expressing disagreement with others because of fear of loss of support or approval" (DSM-IV, p. 668), is also a typically female problem, since many women are brought up to

believe that asserting their opinions might create a negative impression or lead to rejection by others. Carol Tavris argues that, if, on the other hand, the female role were used as the standard for comparison, men would form self-help groups to learn how to become more nurturing, interdependent, and responsive to others' needs.

To provide an example of how gender bias can influence definitions of psychological disorders, in 1988 the Canadian psychologist Paula Caplan and sociologist Margrit Eichler coined delusional dominating personality disorder, colloquially known as macho personality disorder. This disorder was proposed for inclusion in the DSM, with criteria such as being "unable to identify and express . . . feelings and to know how other people feel" and having a need to "affirm . . . importance by appearing with females who are submissive, conventionally attractive." Other criteria included suffering from delusions, such as "the delusion that women like to suffer and to be ordered around" and "the delusion that physical force is the best method of solving problems."

Another view about the differences in diagnosis with disorders among men and women is that women seek the help of mental health professionals more than men do. Others say, however, that women are taught that it is acceptable to seek help for psychological problems, while men are taught that seeking help is an unacceptable admission of weakness. Also, some argue that women face a host of issues, such as gender discrimination, economic disadvantages, social pressures to be thin, passive, and unassertive, physical and sexual abuse, and rape, much more often than men.

THE ICIDH

The DSM is not the only manual that provides a classification system of mental disorders. The World Health Organization (WHO) has also attempted to create a standard system of classification for health and mental health problems. The system they use to describe people and their problems is called the International Classification of Functioning, Disability, and Health (ICIDH—originally the word "impairment" was used instead of "functioning"). One advantage of a standard classification system is that it gives researchers and mental health professionals from different countries a common framework for conducting research on the causes and treatments of psychological problems. The goal is for everyone to use the same system for describing and assessing clients and patients and for doing research on the effectiveness of treatments.

The WHO was founded in 1948. It was created to unify the various health organizations scattered around the world into a single system, to promote worldwide health and health education. The WHO now has members from 193 countries. Unlike the American Psychiatric Association, the WHO emphasizes health and well-being in addition to disease and difficulties. It defines health as "a state of complete physical, mental, and social well-being and not merely the absence of disease or infirmity."

The WHO's revised classification manual, ICIDH-2, is based on a biopsychosocial model, which means that the authors have attempted to address biological, psychological, and social factors (and their interaction) that lead to illness and wellness. For example, categories in ICIDH-2 include an evaluation of how the person is doing at home, work, school, in the community, with relationships, with regard to their physical health, and many other areas. ICIDH-2 also evaluates positive and negative aspects of the categories it assesses, rather than focusing only on problem areas. Some people have predicted that ICIDH-2, with its thorough classification scheme, will become the new standard worldwide for the defining and classifying of psychological disorders.

The headquarters of the World Health Organization in Geneva, Switzerland. The WHO publishes the ICIDH, an international classification system for mental health.

us feels different amounts of anxiety at different times depending on the situation. It is not that a small group of people feel extreme anxiety all of the time while the rest of us feel no anxiety at all. This is true for almost every psychological problem.

Psychodynamic models of disorder attempt to redress this problem by considering the mental, rather than the physical, origins of problems. Sigmund Freud, himself a qualified physician, believed that mental disorders were largely due to conflicts between different aspects of the personality: the id, ego, and superego (*see* Vol. 1, pp. 52–65).

Some of these conflicts, he suggested, might have remained unresolved since childhood. Freud developed psychoanalysis to treat mental disorders. This model of mental disorder is called the psychoanalytical model; it is one type of psychodynamic model.

While most of Freud's specific theories have fallen out of favor, the psychoanalytic model still has many followers. It has been criticized, however, for the lack of experimental support and scientific rigor and for its simplistic view of life—in its most pure form the model views people as driven by animal instincts.

Other psychological theories of mental disorder include the behaviorial, or learning, model. Based on the work of behaviorists such as B. F. Skinner (*see* Vol. 1, pp. 74–89), this model focuses on fixing the behavioral problem itself rather than on its possible causes, which are the focus of psychodynamic models. Cognitive models of mental disorder focus on the thoughts, processes, and feelings that accompany mental disorders.

Social construction "model"

A particularly challenging model of mental disorder is that proposed by social constructionists. Social constructions are not real things but ideas that societies build over time through numerous interactions among its members. Thinkers who hold this view are known as social constructionists. They say that we create our reality through our attitudes, beliefs, and feelings—which are always changing. For example, our notions of beauty and justice have changed over the past 100 years, as have our ideas of normality and abnormality. Also, different cultures have different definitions of beauty and justice. The terms are not defined by a culture once and for all: They change over time—and sometimes over relatively short periods of time.

Members of a culture define what is normal and abnormal by talking to each other—sharing

This young woman proudly sports tattoos and piercings. Her grandmother might have viewed this as a sign of mental disorder. Today, however, the practice is increasingly common and not considered abnormal.

ideas, engaging in formal and informal debates. This discourse, or exchange of ideas, takes many different forms: informal conversations between friends; formal debates among professionals in scientific publications; newspaper articles; and even television programs and movies. All of us take part in this discourse, and so we all influence the definitions of such terms as "beauty," "justice," and "abnormality." In addition, we are all influenced by these definitions because how our culture defines these terms influences how people in our culture think about each other and behave toward each other. Since normality and abnormality are similarly defined, they should be seen as social constructions rather than scientific facts.

CULTURAL CONSIDERATIONS

The mental disorders in the DSM are defined by North American psychiatrists following western concepts of disorder, normality, and abnormality. The definitions do not always work in other cultures. Certain disorders are even unique to particular cultures. They are called culture-bound disorders. The existence of culture-bound disorders, of which anorexia nervosa is an example, suggests that psychological, social, and other non-physical factors are very important in the onset and origin of mental disorders.

CONNECTIONS

- Mental Disorders : pp. 20–67
- Psychotherapies: pp. 92–117

- Physical Therapies: pp. 118–141
- Emotional Development: Volume 4, pp. 112–129
- Social Development: Volume 4, pp. 130–149
- Relating to Others: Volume 5, pp. 28–49

Mental Disorders

—— A wide spectrum of unusual behaviors seen from different perspectives ——

People have always been affected by mental disorders that have caused them varying degrees of distress. Throughout history the treatment of the disorders has taken many forms— sometimes unusual, sometimes humane. With the growth of modern research clinicians diagnose more mental disorders than ever before, and equally, they are able to prescribe from a greater choice of effective treatments.

Mara never left the house. She sat day in, day out, with the curtains closed and had loud music blaring from her radio to block out any other noise. Her husband came to visit some weekends, but most of the time he wasn't there. He worked away from home. Her days were spent crying and sleeping. She didn't really eat, since she had lost her appetite. Nobody came to visit her during the day, and some days she didn't get out of bed at all, except to get things for her baby. She was anxious and depressed all the time. Was Mara mentally ill? Was she suffering from extreme anxiety or depression? Were these the kinds of behaviors that doctors would describe as "mental disorders"?

When we think about Mara's wider context (the situation in which she lived), her behavior might make more sense. Mara lived in a war-torn country. There was gunfire directly outside her window. The last time she left the house, she was shot in the left leg by a sniper. The previous week Mara's neighbor was raped by a group of men out on a rampage. The neighbor had not been the same since then. This terrified them both. Mara had a baby eight weeks ago, and her husband was not around because he was off fighting.

At first sight Mara's behavior and emotional state might seem different, deviant, and abnormal. But does this mean she had a mental disorder? When we understand more about her background and the time and place in which she was living, we might change our minds. We might even think that her responses were, in fact, very normal reactions to her situation. If Mara's circumstances had been different, she might have been diagnosed with a mental disorder.

HISTORICAL PERSPECTIVE

Throughout history there have been a number of ways of classifying and dealing with mental disorders. Ancient

A refugee sits, depressed, beside her sleeping child. Whether or not people are diagnosed with a mental disorder depends to a large extent on their circumstances.

Greek and Roman philosophers and physicians, for example, described a number of such disorders. They principally were: melancholia (sadness); mania (frenzied activity); delusions (blatantly false beliefs); hysteria (physical ailments with no apparent cause, but thought to be related to the possession of a uterus and, therefore, exclusive to women); and hallucinations (imagined sights and sounds).

Before the 5th century B.C. Greeks generally believed that diseases and mental disorders were caused by gods, spirits, or demons. But then Hippocrates (around 460–357 B.C., sometimes known as the father of medicine) offered other explanations. He was the first to propose that diseases, including what would now be considered mental disorders, are rooted in physical, or natural, causes, rather than being the result of intervention by gods or interference by demons. Hippocrates believed that mental disorders originated from imbalances in four fluids in the body: yellow bile, black bile, blood, and phlegm. For example, he believed that an excess of black bile caused melancholia. To alleviate or cure it, he recommended exercise, a vegetarian diet, and not drinking alcohol.

ILLNESS OR DISORDER?

FOCUS ON

Throughout the literature of abnormal psychology the terms "mental illness" and "mental disorder" are often used interchangeably. The two terms can differ in meaning, however. "Mental illness" assumes, or implies, that there is an underlying physical disease responsible for a person's abnormal behavior. "Mental disorder," however, covers all types of psychological abnormalities, including those with apparent physical causes and those without such causes.

Medieval madness

During the medieval period in Europe, after the fall of the Roman Empire in the west (generally dated A.D. 476), the emphasis on religious belief, and particularly the idea that the world was a battleground between God and the devil, led naturally to beliefs in the supernatural basis of mental disorders: that people showing unusual behaviors were possessed by devils or evil spirits. The cure for mania, for example, would be to expel the demons that possessed the sufferer. Clergymen administering such treatment would chant and pray to exorcise the evil spirits. They might prescribe holy water or potions. They

BEDLAM

PSYCHOLOGY & SOCIETY

The Hospital of St. Mary of Bethlehem—possibly the world's first asylum for the mentally disordered—was originally set up as a priory in London, England, in 1247. It became a hospital for the mentally disordered in 1402 and was given to the City of London by King Henry VIII in 1547. "Bethlehem," soon contracted to "Bethlem," became "bedlam," a generic term for all asylums and popularly used to mean chaos or uproar. The hospital even became a popular tourist attraction, and people from all over Europe would come to stare at the inmates. Today the Bethlehem Royal Hospital still functions as a psychiatric hospital, now relocated in southern England and allied to the renowned Maudsley Hospital, home of the Institute of Psychiatry of the University of London.

A print from William Hogarth's series of paintings "The Rake's Progress" (1735) shows visitors viewing the inmates in Bedlam mental hospital.

might even order the destruction of the body in order to save the soul. One aspect of this was that some people whom we would today consider mentally disordered were at the time thought of as having a link to the supernatural that gave them special gifts or insights.

By the end of the Middle Ages, however, and from the 15th to the 17th centuries other ideas became important. Mental disorders became equated with physical ailments and were not seen as caused by the devil. Some city councils and municipalities set up establishments to care for the physically sick and the mentally ill under the supervision of trained medical authorities. However, across most of Europe treatment was still primitive and barbaric, with just a few institutions offering what we would call adequate care. And despite good intentions, the asylums that were built were often vast institutions, frequently converted hospitals or monasteries, that grew increasingly crowded and eventually overflowed with people. Standards of hygiene were low, and care and conditions were inhumane by modern standards.

Moral treatment
During the 18th century there was, in some countries, a marked improvement in the treatment of the mentally ill. Two leading figures in Europe, Philippe Pinel (1745–1826) in France and William Tuke (1732–1822) in England, initiated massive reforms in the management of asylums. They suggested that asylums should become places of calm where just a few people could lodge in comfort. Guests could come and go, and patients were treated with consideration and care, being offered rest, talk, prayer, and simple work to help them recover. In the United States Benjamin Rush (1745–1813) was a key player in the expansion of this type of treatment: He is sometimes known as the father of American psychiatry. Rush was a leading physician at the Pennsylvania Hospital. He focused all his energies on studying mental disorders

and working with sufferers. He developed a humane approach to treatment and encouraged hospitals to employ only very caring, intelligent, and considerate staff to work with patients. Carers would be encouraged to read to patients, talk with them, and take them on walks. Rush even suggested that doctors give presents to their patients.

In both Europe and North America the treatment of mental disorders became a growing problem during the 19th century, partly because rapid industrialization put large numbers of people into an alienating urban environment. Large asylums built to house the mentally disordered became feared institutions, tucked away from centers of population.

Somatogenic or psychogenic?
From the late 19th to the early 20th centuries there emerged two other views of mental disorders that still

Physician and reformer Benjamin Rush devised this tranquilizing chair (below) to control the flow of blood to the brain. Like many others, he believed mental disturbances were caused by inflammation of the brain. The hood and constraints kept the patient still so as not to disturb the blood flow.

inform our thinking. Emil Kraepelin (1856–1926) revived the idea, first proposed by Hippocrates, that psychological abnormality has physical causes, known as the somatogenic perspective or the medical model. The other is called the psychogenic model or psychogenic perspective. According to this model, psychological problems can actually cause physical ailments. The psychogenic perspective follows in the tradition of the Greek doctor Galen (around A.D. 130–200), who believed that many mental disorders were caused by fear, loss, love, and other emotions. More recent proponents of the psychogenic perspective have been Anton Mesmer (1734–1815), Jean Martin Charcot (1825–1893), Sigmund Freud (1856–1939), and Carl Gustav Jung (1876–1961) (*see* Vol. 1, pp. 52–65).

The medical model

Physicians are trained to identify symptoms: for example, a runny nose, a temperature, and a cough. They then classify these symptoms into certain groupings and give each one a name, the name of the disorder; for example, a cold. With the diagnosis they are able to investigate and treat the symptoms. In the same way, mental symptoms, or abnormal behaviors, are identified, grouped together, classified, and investigated to find effective treatments for them. This approach to diagnosis is typical of the medical model (*see* p. 16).

The first detailed attempt to classify abnormal behavior was undertaken in 1913 by the German psychiatrist Emil Kraepelin. After carefully observing patients in hospital, he suggested that there were 18 types of mental disorder, each with its own characteristic pattern of symptoms (a syndrome). Each syndrome took a particular course, had particular causes, and had a characteristic outcome, just like a cold. Kraepelin's work was highly influential and led to the development of two further classification systems after World War II (1939–1945).

These systems are still in wide use today and are known as the International Standard Classification of Diseases, Injuries, and Causes of Death (ICD) and the *Diagnostic and Statistical Manual* (DSM) (*see* p. 9).

In this chapter the following sections discuss some of the most common and familiar mental disorders classified in the DSM. The next chapter (*see* pp. 68–91) looks at disorders associated with childhood. Treatments are covered in more detail in Chapters 4 and 5 (*see* pp. 92–117, 118–141).

Elementary school students in Mexico take an exam. Any form of test can produce anxiety: It is a normal response in the circumstances and could help people perform better.

ANXIETY DISORDERS

Anxiety disorders are a group of conditions that include fear of confined spaces (claustrophobia), episodes of extreme physical arousal and fear (panic disorder), fear of a particular object (specific phobia) or social situation (social phobia), prolonged experiences of anxiety (generalized anxiety disorder), reexperienced fear after an accident or traumatic event (posttraumatic stress disorder), and fears of contamination that inspire strenuous efforts to achieve near-perfect levels of cleanliness (obsessive-compulsive disorder).

Anxiety is a common emotion that everyone experiences at one time or another. It involves a general feeling of

FOCUS ON

TYPES OF MENTAL DISORDERS

The mental disorders listed in the DSM can be roughly grouped into the following categories, listed here in alphabetical order:

• **Anxiety disorders** (*see* pp. 23–30) involve prolonged and excessive levels of anxiety and include posttraumatic stress disorder, general anxiety disorder, panic disorder, phobias, and obsessive-compulsive disorder.

• **Childhood disorders** (*see* pp. 68–91) are those typically first diagnosed before adolescence. They include learning difficulties, autism, attention deficit disorder with hyperactivity, separation anxiety, and speech disorders.

• **Cognitive disorders** (*see* pp. 57–67) affect a person's ability to process information and, therefore, think, remember, and perceive things. They include dementias, amnesias, and delirium and can often have a physical cause.

• **Dissociative disorders** (*see* box on p. 57) involve temporary changes in consciousness that cannot be attributed to physical causes; they include multiple personality disorder.

• **Eating disorders** (*see* pp. 46–51) involve severe disturbances in diet. The two main forms are anorexia nervosa and bulimia.

• **Factitious disorders** (*see* box on p. 29) are those in which both physical and psychological symptoms are intentionally imitated or deliberately brought on.

• **Impulse-control disorders** (*see* box on p. 53) include kleptomania (irresistible urge to steal) and other disorders in which people fail to control certain impulses. Disorders in other categories, such as paraphilias and substance-related disorders, are also types of impulse-control disorders.

• **Mood disorders** (*see* pp. 39–46) involve significant and emotional disturbances and include depression, seasonal affective disorder, and bipolar 1 disorder.

• **Schizophrenia** (*see* pp. 30–39) and some other disorders are characterized by psychotic symptoms, such as hallucinations, disorganized speech, and disordered behavior.

• **Substance-related disorders** (*see* pp. 51–57) involve the abuse of both legal and illegal drugs.

• **Sexual disorders** and **gender-identity disorders** (*see* box on p. 66) are grouped together by the DSM. Sexual disorders includes paraphilias such as pedophilia and sexual dysfunctions.

• **Sleep disorders** (*see* Vol. 2, pp. 110–139) include sleep-walking, insomnia, and involuntary periods of sleep (narcolepsy).

• **Somatoform disorders** (*see* box on p. 26) are those disorders with physical symptoms but no physical cause; they include conversion disorder (sometimes known as hysteria) and somatization disorder (sometimes known as hypochondria).

• **Personality disorders** (*see* p. 63) include antisocial personality disorder and narcissistic personality disorder.

worry or fear and affects our physical well-being, behavior, and thoughts. It is often a normal response to challenging situations and can act as a motivator or protective mechanism. It might inspire someone to study for a test or exam, or it can alert the body and senses to a possible danger (for example, responding to a loud noise in the middle of the night). Anxiety can help or hinder performance in certain situations. Test anxiety can sometimes help a person perform well, although too much of it reduces the chances of doing well even if the person knows the answers.

> *"The sensation of anxiety is commonly experienced by virtually all humans."*
> —*Kaplan, Sadock, and Grebb, 1994*

Psychologists often make a distinction between two types of anxiety: state and trait. They believe that state anxiety varies according to the situation with which the person is faced. It involves the experience of anxiety at a particular time. Trait anxiety is relatively constant over time and refers to a person's general predisposition, or vulnerability, to anxiety. When anxiety begins to cause significant distress and affects a person's ability to socialize, go to work, or even leave their own home, an anxiety disorder might be diagnosed.

Panic disorder
Panic disorder is a form of anxiety diagnosed when someone experiences sudden and repeated physical discomfort caused by fear. The symptoms include shortness of breath, dizziness, nausea, and anxiety about losing control or going crazy. The person experiences these intense symptoms in short bouts, typically for several minutes at a time. These attacks often lead to the development of anticipatory anxiety, that is, a fear that further attacks will occur.

Panic disorder can be accompanied by agoraphobia, the fear of being alone and helpless in an inescapable situation. The two conditions are often diagnosed together, although they can also occur separately.

Panic disorder tends to occur in early adulthood. It affects women three times more often than men and is estimated to affect approximately 3 percent of the U.S. population. Agoraphobia has been estimated to affect between 1 and 6 percent of the population.

Anxiety disorders are mainly treated by behavior and cognitive therapies, as well as psychoanalytic psychotherapy. A psychiatrist might prescribe medication to help the person cope with the anxiety, but medication will not cure the anxiety.

Specific phobias

A fear develops into a specific phobia when the amount of danger attached to a particular object and the harm it can cause are magnified. Specific phobias include: excessive fear of certain animals; fear of situations such as confined spaces, open spaces, or heights; and fear of choking or vomiting.

When encountering the feared object or situation, the individual experiences an increase in physical anxiety reactions and tries to escape. For example, arachnophobics (people with a fear of spiders) might experience a racing heartbeat, nausea, and extreme terror if they see such a creature close to them. They might react by trying to escape the situation. Reactions like this might also occur when the person is only exposed to images of the object or situation.

Specific phobias have been estimated to affect as many as 10 out of every 100 people. They are the most common mental disorder diagnosed in women and the second most common disorder in men after substance

In the traditional nursery rhyme "Little Miss Muffet" (illustrated below) a spider "frightened Miss Muffet away." Fear of spiders, or arachnophobia, is a common specific phobia. Cognitive behavioral therapy might have helped Miss Muffet.

disorders (*see* p. 51). The age at which someone can develop a specific phobia depends on the type of phobia. People tend to develop phobias related to the natural environment or blood in childhood. Situational phobias, such as fear of flying, heights, and confined spaces, tend to develop sometime during the person's twenties.

Social phobias

People often experience a certain level of anxiety in social settings, but sometimes this fear becomes so great that a social phobia develops. It involves a dread of public rejection or embarrassment. People with such phobias often avoid situations in which they might be the center of attention, such as public speaking, for example. They might fear blushing in front of others, being watched, or choking on food when eating in public places. Often they fear being criticized or humiliated in such situations.

Again, research indicates that woman tend to be more affected by social phobias than men. The typical age at which the disorder sets in is the late teens, although the range can be from 5 to 35 years of age. As many as 3 in every 100 people of the U.S. population are believed to be affected by social phobia.

Generalized anxiety disorder

Generalized anxiety disorder (GAD) is excessive, long-term worry. It is caused by fears of not being able to cope, failure, rejection, or death. The person also experiences physical symptoms, including increased muscle tension, sensitivity, a high breathing rate, and increased arousal levels, such as a racing heartbeat.

GAD is a common disorder. It tends to affect women twice as often as men. Although the age at which a person can be

SOMATOFORM DISORDERS

Somatoform disorders are characterized by physical symptoms that suggest a medical cause but are not fully explained by any medical condition, such as drug use, disease, or another mental disorder. Often, investigation reveals that the causes are psychological, not physical. However, this does not mean that the symptoms are under the person's control, in contrast to factitious disorders (see box p. 29). The two best-known types of somatoform disorders are sometimes called hysteria and hypochondria, though these terms have generally fallen out of favor.

Hypochondria: somatization disorder

Hypochondria (or Briquet's syndrome) is now more likely to be called somatization disorder. Sufferers report feeling pain in many different parts of their body. The condition is relatively common and occurs in about 1 percent of adult women. It is very unusual for men to have this disorder. The onset of this disorder is generally before the age of 30.

Hysteria: conversion disorder

Hysteria, or conversion disorder, involves unexplained physical symptoms that affect voluntary motor functions (control of bodily movements) in a way that suggests the functioning of the nervous system has been affected, though evidence of any damage cannot be found and is probably not present. Symptoms include tics, tremors, "pins and needles," blindness, deafness, and loss of sensation in or paralysis of arms or legs.

Causes and treatments

By definition, there are no obvious physical causes of somatoform disorders. They might be related to unresolved emotional conflicts (see Vol. 1, pp. 52–65), or the behavior may be attention-seeking. Medical professionals try not to encourage the patient's desire to blame physical causes for their symptoms, partly by insuring that physicians and surgeons do not administer excessive diagnostic procedures or surgical remedies in response to the complaints.

---

affected by it varies, people tend not to seek treatment for it until they are in their twenties. GAD is believed to affect between 3 and 8 percent of the U.S.

> *"People with this disorder [GAD] worry constantly about yesterday's mistakes and tomorrow's problems."*
> —Wayne Weiten, 1992

population. Psychologists estimate that more than 50 percent of people with GAD have another disorder, for example, depression or a different anxiety disorder.

Posttraumatic stress disorder

Posttraumatic stress disorder (PTSD) refers to a range of symptoms that people might experience after they have been involved in violent or catastrophic events that have stressed and frightened them. Sufferers have typically lived through wars, been tortured, abused, raped, or assaulted,

been involved in automobile accidents, fires, building disasters, floods, earthquakes, or famines. Symptoms of the condition include repetitive and distressing thoughts about the incident and flashbacks (vivid, distressing images of the events), sleep disturbance, irritability, and a sense of isolation.

The experience that triggered PTSD will have posed a threat to someone's own physical safety or that of others and leaves them feeling fearful and helpless. While PTSD can occur at any age, it appears most in young adults. It can occur at any time between one week and 30 years after the traumatic event. It is most likely to occur in individuals who are single, divorced, or widowed, or in people who are socially withdrawn. War veterans and survivors of disasters often experience PTSD symptoms. Estimates of PTSD in the U.S. population range from 1 to 3 percent, although this figure might be lower than the actual number, since people often do not seek treatment.

Obsessive-compulsive disorder

Obsessive-compulsive disorder (OCD) is a long-term and disabling condition characterized by the experience of persistent thoughts (obsessions) that result in anxiety and repetitive actions. The person feels compelled (forced) to perform the actions (compulsions) over and over to avoid anxiety. Common obsessions include fears of germs, disease, or a disaster. Common compulsions include hand washing, persistent cleaning or grooming, and checking behaviors, such as repetitively turning a door handle to see if it is locked.

OCD affects between 1 and 3 percent of the general U.S. population. It occurs equally in men and women, and typically begins in early adulthood, although it can date from childhood. People often delay seeking treatment because they might fear change or embarrassment. Consequently, the obsessive-compulsive symptoms are likely to be well established by the time treatment begins.

Biological theories

Biological theories of anxiety disorders focus on the effects of chemical and physical changes within the brain. When neurotransmitters (chemical messengers) are released in the brain, they stimulate the autonomic nervous system, causing changes in heart rate, breathing, and muscle tension. People with anxiety disorders might have excessive responses to stimulation of the autonomic nervous system. For example, some people with PTSD have higher levels of the neurotransmitter norepinephrine than the rest of the population, making them more aroused and alert to danger.

> *"Scientists are beginning to unravel the neurochemical bases for anxiety disorders."*
> —*Wayne Weiten, 1992*

Unfortunately, inconsistent research findings often limit the scope of biological theories for the causes of anxiety disorders. Research suggests that although biological changes are a factor in the development and continuance of anxiety disorders, they are not the only factor.

Genetic theories

Many studies of families and twins have shown a genetic component in anxiety disorders—in other words, a tendency for the disorders to be inherited. Approximately

People with obsessive-compulsive disorder cannot stop performing certain actions, such as repeatedly washing their hands (right). Their actions might be in response to some anxieties that they find difficult to deal with.

50 percent of people affected by panic disorder also have a family member with the same condition. Likewise, studies of twins estimate that between 30 and 90 percent of identical twins will develop an anxiety disorder if their twin is similarly affected. The studies have found that nonidentical twins have a higher incidence of anxiety disorders than the general population but less than that of identical twins. This suggests that other factors influence the development of the disorders, such as parenting styles. Research also suggests that certain environmental conditions must be present for a disorder to develop. Scientists, therefore, suggest that people can inherit a vulnerability to developing a particular anxiety disorder, which becomes active when certain environmental conditions arise.

> *"Obsessions increase a person's anxiety, whereas carrying out compulsions reduces a person's anxiety."*
> —*Kaplan, Sadock, and Grebb, 1994*

Behavioral theories

Behaviorists (*see* Vol. 1, pp. 74–89) take the view that some people can acquire anxiety disorders because they associate fear with something that in itself would not provoke anxiety. They then reinforce the fear by associating it with other situations or objects and by making a habit of avoiding the feared object. For example, a child who gets pushed under the water by another child might develop a fear of water. She begins to feel anxious when she is near water, for instance, on boats or over bridges, and she reduces her anxiety by avoiding such situations.

Behavioral theorists propose that anxiety is maintained by operant conditioning. For example, when a person who suffers from obsessive-compulsive disorder keeps repeating certain behaviors, the repetition reduces the original fear because the expected consequences of not performing the actions do not take place. Anxiety levels that rise when the obsessional thoughts or images occur might be reduced if the person carries out a certain action or thinks a particular thought. Thus the compulsive behaviors are reinforced.

Cognitive theories

Behavioral theories, however, fail to account satisfactorily for specific phobias. First, it is not uncommon for people with a specific phobia to be unable to identify the initial traumatic event or conditioning process that led to it. Second, there are many people who might have been exposed to the same traumatic event or association but who do not develop that specific phobia. Cognitive theories of anxiety provide some explanation of the differences.

Cognitive theories explain anxiety disorders in terms of the connection between emotional responses and cognitions (thought processes). Incorrect

An anxious child clings to her father. She might do this in response to something that is truly frightening for her, or she might have "learned" to react in this manner from a previous situation. Even though the original danger might not be present in similar situations, she might associate such situations with the first unpleasant experience.

FACTITIOUS DISORDERS

Both factitious and somatoform disorders (*see* box p. 26) can be characterized by symptoms that have no physical cause. Unlike somatoform disorders, however, which involve no intent, people suffering from a factitious disorder will deliberately and voluntarily try to convince others that they are afflicted with a physical or a psychological ailment. They will intentionally fake symptoms and even inflict harm on themselves to produce the symptoms of a disease or evidence of a supposedly accidental injury. A patient might heat up a thermometer to fake a fever, for example, take drugs to induce vomiting, or throw themselves down a flight of stairs. Around 1 percent of people in consultation with mental health professionals in large hospitals are diagnosed with a factitious disorder, more commonly in women than men.

Despite the intent, such people are in fact suffering from a real psychological disorder. The causes of this disorder are not financial gain (getting extra time off sick, for instance), nor avoiding legal responsibility (to get out of jury duty, for instance), nor excuse-making—such reasons would exempt someone from a diagnosis of a factitious disorder. The motivating factor is the desire to assume the role of a sick person, which brings social rewards in the nature of attention from and improved relationships with other family members, friends, and medical professionals. In some respects this is similar to somatoform disorders, which can also be motivated by the desire to assume the role of a sick person. Again, however, the difference is one of intent. Sufferers of factitious disorders know that they are not sick; sufferers of somatoform disorders do not. As with somatoform disorders, treatment generally involves trying to address the underlying conflicts that have lead to the disorder.

Münchausen's syndrome

The most severe and long-term factitious disorder is commonly referred to as Münchausen's syndrome, after Baron Münchausen (1720–1797). The baron was a German country gentleman and former soldier in the Russian army who was famed for his extraordinarily "tall tales." In inventing their medical histories and symptoms, sufferers of factitious disorders often relate elaborate and fantastic stories that intrigue listeners. In Münchausen's syndrome patients can inflict severe harm on themselves. This form is more common in men than women. Some people suffer from Münchausen's by proxy, in which they inflict harm on others in their immediate care, again to seek attention. Although rare, there have been highly publicized cases of parents inflicting harm on their children as part of this disorder.

In an early case of Münchausen's syndrome by proxy, in 1932 Harriet Paul slashed three of her four children (left) on the throat and wrists as well as herself. She claimed that a strange woman attacked them in their home, but the children told police, "Mama did it."

interpretations of a situation (cognitive errors) are the main factors considered in cognitive theories of anxiety. Psychologist Aaron Beck (*see* pp. 107–108), an important figure in the development of cognitive theory, noted that socially anxious people have a heightened sense of vulnerability in social settings: They are more aware of how they appear to others and are highly sensitive to feedback or criticism. Beck also noted that people who experience panic attacks consistently overestimate the significance of the physical sensations they experience. They interpret a racing heartbeat as a sign of a heart attack or other health problem. Beck suggested that such people's ability to accurately interpret physical sensations is limited.

As the symptoms of anxiety occur, they make a series of misinterpretations and overestimate the threat. This leads to an increase in the physical symptoms being experienced and the likelihood of a panic attack.

Other research investigated the beliefs of people with a specific phobia for snakes. The people were shown a series of slides with images of either "fear-relevant" stimuli (stimuli that aroused fear), such as hissing snakes, or of fear-irrelevant stimuli (stimuli that did not arouse fear), such as flowers. Following each image, the people were presented with a series of different "events": They felt an electric shock (an aversive, or off-putting, event), or heard a tone, or nothing happened to them. At the end of the experiment they were asked to rate the degree of association between the fear-relevant stimi (pictures of snakes) and the three events (shock, sound, no response) that followed. Even though the three events occurred with equal regularity across all the images presented, those who were frightened of snakes thought that most of the electric shocks had been administered when snakes were shown on the screen. They

overemphasized the connection between the fear-relevant image of the snake and the aversive event, the electric shock.

People with other anxiety disorders also overestimate the threat or negative outcome. For example, people with GAD think that they would be unable to cope with threatening events, and those affected by OCD anticipate a harmful event if they do not repeatedly act in a certain way.

SCHIZOPHRENIA

There is much misunderstanding about schizophrenia, what exactly it is, and how it is best treated. "Schizo" is often used as a term of playground abuse, a way to put down people or tell them that that they are crazy. Unfortunately, films, books, and the broadcast news media often portray people diagnosed with schizophrenia as dangerous people with "split personalities" —normal one moment, crazy the next— in the manner of the main character in Robert Louis Stevenson's 1886 novel *The Strange Case of Dr. Jekyll and Mr. Hyde*. In reality schizophrenia is very different from its popular portrayal.

Schizophrenia, as we know it today, has been recognized only for the last 100 years or so. It used to be known as dementia praecox, which literally means "senility of youth." The term "dementia praecox" was coined by Emil Kraepelin, who observed the behavior of many of his mentally ill patients over long periods and put forward the first of his findings in 1898.

A research study showed that peoples' beliefs strongly influence their phobias. People who were frightened of snakes were presented with identical series of events when shown pictures of both snakes and flowers (left and below). They associated more of the painful events with pictures of snakes than occurred.

The main characteristics of the disorder, as he described it, were delusions, hallucinations, negativism, attentional difficulties, stereotyped behaviors, and emotional dysfunction. The problem with Kraepelin's work was that he focused only on defining the symptoms. Even in the eighth edition of his textbook he was busy grouping symptoms of dementia praecox into 36 categories. This was useful to an extent, but it made no attempt to integrate these symptoms or to identify causes and possible treatments.

Swiss psychiatrist Eugene Bleuler (1857–1939) tried to find the core of dementia praecox and to move on from descriptive categorizations. Bleuler disagreed with Kraepelin on two key points. First, he thought that the disorder did not necessarily start in adolescence, and that it could begin much later for some people. Second, he found that the described symptoms did not automatically lead to dementia. That is why he decided to change the name of the disorder to *schizophrenia*, a word of Greek origin that literally means "split mind" or "divided self."

In 1911 Eugene Bleuler (left) explained that he had renamed dementia praecox as schizophrenia: "because . . . the 'splitting' of the different psychic functions is one of its most important characteristics."

An everchanging disorder

How would you know if you met someone diagnosed with schizophrenia? There are wide variations in the behaviors of such people. It is often described as "a single disorder with a number of faces."

In all the three cases illustrated on page 32 the sufferers seem to have regressed (gone back) from a relatively normal level of day-to-day functioning to one in which they are unable to face the outside world with the same degree of normality. Each case history contains an account of external circumstances that might help us understand their situation. However, there are plenty of other people who have similar stories who do not display the symptoms of schizophrenia.

In their efforts to understand schizophrenia and to make diagnosis easier clinicians have tried to group the symptoms of schizophrenia into three broad categories: positive symptoms, negative symptoms, and psychomotor (movement) symptoms. Research shows that men are likely to display more negative symptoms than women, but that both sexes show the same number of positive symptoms.

Symptoms

Among the positive symptoms of schizophrenia are any bizarre behaviors that go beyond what is conventionally regarded as normal behavior. They might include delusions, disorganized thinking and speech, and hallucinations.

Delusions are ideas that some people strongly believe in but have no obvious basis in fact. Some people diagnosed with schizophrenia have a single delusion that dominates their lives; others have a range of different delusions. Delusions of persecution occur when people feel that the whole world is out to get them. In the first case history (*see* box p. 32) Clare shows a few signs of this: She thought that her sister-in-law and people on the street were saying evil things about her. Delusions of reference attach a particular meaning to the behaviors of others. People diagnosed with schizophrenia, like

THREE FACES OF A DISORDER: SCHIZOPHRENIA

Clare

Clare was born in London, England, and was a high achiever at school. She was extremely musical and trained at the prestigious Royal College of Music. She was planning to become a concert pianist and was admired by all her peers and seniors. Clare performed throughout Great Britain and had begun to tour Europe and the United States.

On one of the tours she met her husband, Derk. Derk was besotted with Clare and showed a great interest in all that she did. He was an important financier in Germany. After several years in a passionate but long-distance relationship Derk and Clare decided to get married. They lived in Germany near Derk's family.

Clare kept up the piano in the beginning, but over time she lost contacts and confidence in her ability to perform well. She had no friends in Germany and socialized mainly with Derk's sister. Derk and his sister were very close, and Clare often felt like an outsider when they were together.

The couple had no children, but in their fifth year of marriage they got a dog that Clare adored. The following year the dog became very ill, and Derk and Clare fought over whether or not it should be put to sleep. Derk didn't care for the dog at all, but Clare found it gave her support.

Derk had the dog put to sleep without Clare's consent. At around the same time, Clare started fighting with her sister-in-law and her neighbors on the street. She felt that they were always talking about her, saying evil things. She really believed this. When she watched TV, she started to feel that the characters were reading her mind. She thought they knew what she was thinking and just repeated it. She became frightened of her world and wanted it all to stop. She would end up shouting at the TV, at her sister-in-law, and at her husband. She couldn't stop herself.

John

John is a 19-year-old who went to see his doctor because he couldn't carry on with his studies or any other part of life. John was always a quiet boy. He had only one friend and a very close relationship with his mother. His father died when he was younger; and although he had an older brother, he didn't really see much of him. John had started to feel unable to cope with his studies. He felt that he was incapable of doing anything right, and his mother was always nagging him to get dressed and get things done or shouting at him for doing things wrong.

John began to feel highly anxious about doing anything. He was unable to get out of bed in the morning and could not get dressed. He did not even listen to the radio or watch TV—he just couldn't be bothered. When he did get up, he felt that everyone was always getting at him, and that he could never do anything right, so he just went back to bed. He could do nothing practical for himself. It was his mother who finally managed to get him to see the doctor—she didn't know where else to get help.

Mary

"Have you got some money for the phone? Have you got any money? Where am I? Can you tell me where I am please?" Mary can often be found standing in the hospital grounds asking people questions like these. She has been doing this for the past 10 years and has even become a bit of a friendly face for the staff at the hospital.

Mary has been diagnosed with schizophrenia. She hears voices telling her what to do to herself and others. The doctors have tried to find out about her past, but the records are confused, and they cannot rely on her to provide sufficient details. They think that she was born to a woman who probably suffered from a mental disorder herself.

The story had it that Mary was conceived after a rape, and that her mother never really wanted her. As a child Mary was the main carer in the family from a very young age. She would cook and clean in the house and look after her mother and her younger brother. At school she was unable to control her behavior and stick to the rules, so she was thrown out of one school after another. In those times there was little welfare help, and she had no one to turn to for support.

Apparently, Mary ran away from home at the age of 15 and lived on the streets for 10 years. It is not known what exactly happened to her there, but she probably was involved with drugs and prostitution. She ended up in a hostel for the homeless for a while, but the staff there were unable to contain or care for her properly, nor could they protect her from the other residents, so they called for the hostel doctor to help them out.

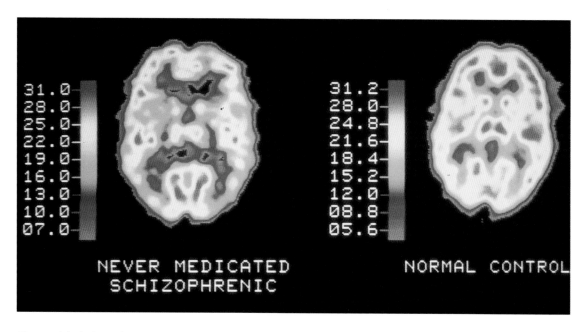

NEVER MEDICATED
SCHIZOPHRENIC

NORMAL CONTROL

Clare, might believe that someone on the TV is referring specifically to them. Delusions of grandeur occur, for example, when people believe themselves to be a famous person that they obviously are not, such as Jesus Christ or Abraham Lincoln, or that they can do impossible things, such as control the weather. Delusions of control occur when people believe that all their actions are governed by external forces, such as radio signals, or imagined beings, for example, aliens from outer space.

Disorganized thinking and speech occur when a person switches illogically from one topic to another. The person might make incoherent links and suffer great confusion, which can make conversation with others impossible. Some people diagnosed with schizophrenia use neologisms (made-up, private words that others cannot understand without explanation), or they use words in ways that make no sense (often called "word salad"). They might also perseverate—repeat words or phrases again and again.

People diagnosed with schizophrenia often report heightened perception. Some are overcome by the sights and sounds around them, so it is impossible for them

to organize them in their mind and to focus on any specific event or thought. Hallucinations are perceptions of objects, people, or events that have no basis in reality. You might, for example, smell smoke when there is nothing burning; you might see something that isn't there or taste sourness when there is nothing in your mouth. All five senses can be involved in hallucinations.

KEY TERMS

• **Schizophrenia**—a cluster of symptoms, or a syndrome, that are grouped into positive, negative, and psychomotor symptoms

• **Positive symptoms**—unusual behavior and thinking, such as delusions, disorganized thinking and speech, and hallucinations

• **Negative symptoms**—lack of adequate behavior, for example, poor speech

• **Psychomotor symptoms**—unusual, involuntary movements, such as grimacing

• **Delusions**—irrational beliefs

• **Hallucinations**—imagined images or sounds

This image of a PET scan shows a horizontal cross section through the brain of a person diagnosed with schizophrenia and that of a normal brain. PET scans (see p.88) are used to diagnose mental disorders because they reflect the function of a part of the body more than its structure. Here red shows areas of high activity, and blue or purple, areas of low activity for both the brains.

the disorder. *Hebephrenic* literally means "youth mind." This form of the disorder is usually diagnosed in childhood or early adolescence. It is thought to last a lifetime, and the symptoms tend to get worse over time. The main characteristics are incoherent language, vivid hallucinations that are often sexual or religious in their content, disorganized delusions, and extreme social withdrawal.

The main characteristic of catatonic schizophrenia is lack of movement. People who have this type of disorder can hold set positions for long periods without moving. They can look like statues. Their limbs grow stiff and might become swollen from lack of movement. Other

> *"If you talk to God, you are praying. If God talks to you, you have schizophrenia."*
> —Thomas Szasz (born 1920)

St. Antony of Padua (about 1193–1231) has a heavenly vision. Many people who have intense spiritual experiences claim to see visions or hear voices. People diagnosed with schizophrenia can also experience visual and auditory hallucinations —they see things or hear voices that other people cannot experience.

Negative symptoms of schizophrenia are those that tend to show an absence of adequate behaviors. One of the main examples is poor speech. Psychomotor symptoms include a lack of control over movement and the development of odd grimaces and mannerisms that are often repetitive and might seem purposeful.

Types of schizophrenia
Schizophrenia is so complicated and variable that it is almost impossible to describe it as a single, unified affliction. In an effort to overcome this problem, psychiatrists have tried to classify the disorder by separating it into different types. The DSM-IV and the ICD (*see* p. 23) describe four different categories of schizophrenia: hebephrenic, catatonic, paranoid, and atypical.

Hebephrenic schizophrenia is widely regarded as the most severe form of

sufferers become agitated and move in wild, uncontrollable, excited ways. Some victims become mute; and although they might be aware of what is being said around them, they are unable to respond.

The strongest characteristic of paranoid schizophrenia is the presence of a highly organized and thought-out delusional belief system. In the examples on page 32 Clare displays this. She firmly believes that people on television are echoing her thoughts. People diagnosed with paranoid schizophrenia often appear to be fully functioning. They take care of themselves, engage in social interactions, and involve themselves in the world, but they remain essentially deluded. They might be either contemptuous of or angered by those who do not share their delusions. Paranoid schizophrenia is perhaps the most homogeneous type of schizophrenia: Two people diagnosed with paranoid schizophrenia will display more of the same symptoms than two people with another form of schizophrenia.

Atypical, schizophrenia is really a catch-all term for forms of the condition that do not fit neatly into any of the above categories.

There are also two further forms of schizophrenia:

● **Schizophreniform psychosis** is similar in symptoms to schizophrenia, but lasts for fewer than six months.

● **Schizotypal disorder** is a category used to describe unusual behavior, thoughts, and feelings that resemble the symptoms of schizophrenia, but without the other, abnormal characteristics.

Schizoaffective disorder is a subclass of schizotypal disorder. It has prominent schizophrenic and affective (mood) characteristics, but the disorder does not warrant a diagnosis of either schizophrenia or mood disorder.

COURSE OF SCHIZOPHRENIA

Schizophrenia usually starts sometime between the late teens and the early thirties. Although the course of the disease varies from one person to another, there generally tend to be three distinct stages.

The condition begins with the prodromal phase, during which sufferers begin to show the first signs of deterioration and are less able than before to carry out their daily tasks. They might even develop strange personal habits, such as collecting trash from garbage cans or not washing themselves.

During the active phase the schizophrenic symptoms become clearer. The active phase is sometimes triggered by a particular event—in the case of Clare it was when her dog was put to sleep.

Finally, in the residual phase there seems to be a return to the prodromal level of functioning. The intensity of the symptoms diminishes a little, but the sufferer might still seem emotionally flat and will fail to take on the basic responsibilities of day-to-day life.

Each of these three phases might last for days or years. It is said that a quarter of all people fully recover from the schizophrenic symptoms, but the

remainder live out their lives with some sort of impairment, loss of functioning, and lasting emotional damage.

Diagnostic difficulties

A psychiatrist sees a young man named John who seems to have no will to do anything and is not caring for himself. John also has strange thoughts, unusual perceptions, and mood swings. He has been like this for almost a year. What diagnosis should the psychiatrist make? It needs to be right so that the appropriate treatment can be prescribed. John could be given a diagnosis of schizophrenia or bipolar 1 disorder (manic depression, *see* pp. 45–46). His symptoms fit both categories according to DSM-IV. People diagnosed with schizophrenia often have mood swings, and people with bipolar 1

People with paranoid schizophrenia appear to function normally, but they have strongly held beliefs about the world that are not rational. For instance, they might think that people on TV can read their thoughts and are plotting against them.

disorder often demonstrate unusual belief systems. Faced with a case like this, the psychiatrist could give a diagnosis of schizoaffective disorder, which covers both sets of symptoms. But many clinicians argue that this is a cop-out. Some suggest that the psychiatrist should choose one diagnosis, prescribe the appropriate medication, and see if it works. If it does, the problem is solved; if not, the other diagnosis should be tried. It might sound a bit hit-and-miss, but it is the way that many psychiatrists have to work because there are no easy answers, and there is much that is still unknown about the nature and causes of schizophrenia. Some people do not go along with any medical explanation of the disorder, preferring to look at the social and environmental context of the patient as a starting point for treatment (*see* pp. 38–39).

As with most other psychological disorders, it is impossible to look at schizophrenia without considering the biological, psychological, and social factors that contribute to its development. Biological research shows that chemical and structural abnormalities are associated with the disorder, although it is not known what role they play. Sociological studies show how a society's expectations can increase the likelihood of schizophrenic symptoms developing. Psychological research makes connections between schizophrenia and internal, family, and environmental circumstances. Which of these hypotheses do we opt for, or is it better to think of schizophrenia as the result of a combination of all these factors? In any case, how can useful treatment be selected?

Medical models

The likelihood that a person will develop schizophrenia is about one in a hundred. If you have one parent diagnosed with schizophrenia, though, your chance of being diagnosed with it increases to one in five. If both your parents are diagnosed with schizophrenia, your chance of being diagnosed increases to one in two or

It can be very difficult for a psychiatrist to diagnose a mental disorder accurately the first time around because many disorders share characteristics. If the treatment that the psychiatrist prescribes after the first diagnosis does not work, another diagnosis and treatment might have to be tried.

three. In light of these findings some researchers have argued that schizophrenia is a genetic (inherited) disorder. Many studies have been carried out on pairs of twins. They have found a higher incidence of schizophrenia in identical twins, who come from the same ovum, than in fraternal twins, who come from different ova. Other studies have found a higher incidence of schizophrenia in adopted children who are placed with parents who are diagnosed with schizophrenia. So it seems that although genetic factors do play an important role, there must still be some environmental factors at work.

One of the ways in which genes can alter behavior is through brain chemistry, so scientists have closely studied biochemical influences in schizophrenia. According to one theory, which is sometimes known as the inborn-error of metabolism hypothesis, some people inherit metabolic problems. Because of

these errors in the functioning of their bodies their bodies break down naturally occurring chemicals into toxic ones that produce schizophrenic symptoms.

The dopamine hypothesis proposes that schizophrenia is caused by overactive synapses. People diagnosed with schizophrenia are thought to have numerous or densely packed receptor sites for the neurotransmitter dopamine (*see* Vol. 2, pp. 20–39). In experiments in which people not diagnosed with schizophrenia were given certain drugs—notably cocaine and amphetamines, which increase dopamine levels—they showed symptoms identical to those of schizophrenia. Similarly, drugs that block the dopamine receptors tend to reduce schizophrenic symptoms. Some scientists, however, criticize the dopamine hypothesis. Other studies have suggested that the positive symptoms of schizophrenia —such as hallucinations and delusions— might have a single cause that is related to dopamine, while negative symptoms— such as social withdrawal—might have some other cause related to brain damage, such as oxygen deprivation at birth.

Another biological theory suggests that schizophrenia might be caused by the brain failing to develop normally. The theory claims that a viral infection during pregnancy might prevent the formation of crucial brain connections. However, the evidence concerning such viral theories is very mixed.

The psychoanalytic view

In contrast to the biological explanations, the psychoanalytic view (*see* Vol. 1, pp. 52–65) suggests that schizophrenia develops when the ego—the part of the psyche that distinguishes between the self and real world—has problems in making these distinctions. Freud proposed that the two key processes involved in schizophrenia were regression to a pre-ego state followed by attempts to reestablish ego control. He believed that schizophrenia resulted from conflict between a person's self-gratifying impulses and the demands of the real world. When the external world

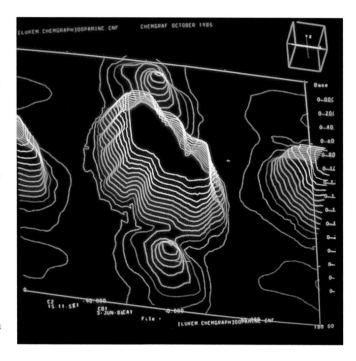

seems harsh or hostile, people diagnosed with schizophrenia regress to an earlier period in their functioning.

According to Freud, neurotic people partially regress and rely on ego defense mechanisms to cope with the real world (*see* p. 95). With people diagnosed with schizophrenia, the regression is thought to be deeper, and they go back in their minds to an even earlier stage in their developmental functioning. Regression really takes them to a place of primary narcissism, similar to that of infants who feel only their own needs. This total regression can lead to delusions of grandeur, among other symptoms. Although many psychoanalysts stand by this theory of schizophrenia, very little research has been carried out to support or undermine it. Most practicing psychoanalysts today tend to include biological as well as psychodynamic factors in their explanations.

The behaviorist view

Behaviorists (*see* Vol. 1, pp. 74–89) generally look to theories of conditioning to explain the symptoms of schizophrenia. They propose that people are taught to

A computer graphic represents the levels of the neurotransmitter dopamine in a human brain. The dopamine hypothesis states that overproduction of dopamine might contribute to schizophrenia.

behave in certain ways by their families, friends, and environmental contacts. Most people are able to attend to social cues, such as smiling and body language. They learn how to do so almost from the minute they are born. Behaviorists suggest that people diagnosed with schizophrenia have not had the opportunity to learn these social norms. Important figures in their lives might not be socially competent, and as a result, the necessary reinforcement is not provided.

Instead of focusing on social cues, some people are thought to pay too much attention to extraneous inputs, such as the noise level in a room or the brightness of a light. Attention to these other cues might be reinforced, and so this behavior is likely to recur. Experiments in which people diagnosed with schizophrenia are offered rewards or reinforcement for socially acceptable conduct have shown that such behaviors can be taught. There is not enough evidence, however, to prove that all such behaviors developed in this way in the first place. The behavioral view is generally regarded as only a part of the whole picture of schizophrenia.

The family view

In the 1940s the psychodynamic theorist Frieda Fromm-Reichmann (1889–1957) said that a mother who is cold, domineering, and pays no attention to her children's needs was the cause of schizophrenia in her children. Such a parent was called schizophrenogenic, someone or something that brings on the symptoms of schizophrenia. This view appealed to many clinicians but not to many mothers, who found it all too blaming. The theory was challenged by a wealth of research that suggested a very different personality style was evident among the mothers of people diagnosed with schizophrenia. This was one of introverted, shy, and withdrawn behavior.

One of the best-known family theories is the double-bind hypothesis put forward by Gregory Bateson (1904–1980) in the

Gregory Bateson was an anthropologist and social scientist who proposed the theory of double bind for people diagnosed with schizophrenia. It implies that they get conflicting signals from those with whom they are trying to communicate and feel trapped because they are deprived of any power over the communication.

1950s. According to the theory, parents repeatedly send contradictory messages that put their children in a double bind. For example, the primary communication in words might be "It's good to see you," but the metacommunication (the tone, gestures, and context) of the message might be the opposite. Because of the contradiction the children cannot be sure what their parents are really telling them. The views and behaviors that such children might adopt to cope with their environment might well be seen as schizophrenic symptoms.

Other family theories focus on the marital skew between parents, and how it affects the development of their children. So far, there is no single family explanation that has universal credence, but research continues, and clinicians working with people diagnosed with schizophrenia generally accept the importance of the role of the family in the development of such disorders.

The sociocultural view

Sociocultural theorists (see Vol. 5, pp. 50–71) are thinkers who say that our social and cultural context defines who we are. Sociocultural theorists believe that the diagnosis of schizophrenia itself contributes to the causes of the disorder. They propose that the label "schizophrenic" is attached by society to people who deviate from cultural norms. This is borne out by reports in the United Kingdom published in 2000 that show that young black men regularly receive a diagnosis of schizophrenia far more than young white men. Sociocultural theory is popular with clinicians who have noticed how a label sticks, and how diagnoses are often made on the basis of inaccurate data.

MOOD DISORDERS
Mood disorders are a group of conditions in which the person experiences significant emotional disturbance. Mood disorders affect how people think about themselves, interact with others, work, and plan their lives. Depression and bipolar 1 disorder are two types of mood disorder that commonly affect people.

Depression
Most people, at some point in their life, experience at least some degree of low mood or depression. It is generally felt as sadness—a normal response to painful circumstances, such as financial losses, the breakup of a relationship, or losing a job. However, sometimes the depressed mood continues for a prolonged period of weeks or months. At this stage a psychiatrist might diagnose a depressive disorder.

Depression is a term used to describe a mood state in which the main symptoms or features include prolonged feelings of sadness or emptiness and lack of interest in previously enjoyed activities. This causes depressed people significant distress, since they lose motivation to participate fully in their lives. Depressed people often have difficulty spending time with other people and might lose contact with friends and family, which could deprive them of essential support. They might even lose their job because of poor work performance or attendance.

Depression can also result from medical conditions or other psychological disorders. For example, people suffering from adrenal and thyroid dysfunction often display depressive symptoms due to their being either very over- or underweight. Similarly agoraphobics might become depressed because their fear of being vulnerable in public places makes it difficult for them to experience taking part in social activities. This prevents them from having essential, healthy contact with other people.

Typical symptoms
The typical emotions experienced during depression include sadness, guilt, and despair. It is also common for a depressed person to experience irritability, agitation, and anxiety. People suffering from

Most people suffering from depression find it difficult to get a good night's sleep. They might keep waking up, or they might find it difficult to sleep all through the night.

The public image of the movie star Marilyn Monroe (1926–1962) was that of a fun-loving woman. But like many well-known people, in her private life she suffered from bouts of depression.

such as slowed movements or lack of movement, to restless activity (psychomotor agitation), such as pacing up and down.

Depression causes a range of changes in physiological, or body, functioning, such as reduced or increased appetite, fatigue or excessive tiredness, and loss of sex drive. Sleep disturbance is also very common and has been estimated to affect more than 90 percent of depressed individuals. Sufferers generally report early morning wakening as the main type of sleep disruption. Depression can also cause shorter periods of sleep and increasingly broken sleep.

> "*Depression plunges people into feelings of hopelessness, dejection, and boundless guilt.*"
> —*Wayne Weiten, 1992*

If a depressed mood lasts for more than two weeks and causes the person significant distress, the possibility of a major depressive episode should be considered. DSM-IV outlines the criteria for a major depressive episode and also for the presence of a single episode of depression and recurrent episodes. For a major depressive disorder to be considered recurrent, a period of two months must separate each depressive episode.

depression can feel less motivated to participate in activities or interests they previously enjoyed. As the depression becomes worse, they might not bother to eat or cook for themselves, stop going to work, or taking care of their appearance. Sometimes depression makes people not want to live, and they might contemplate, attempt, or even commit suicide.

The effects of depression on a person's thinking include indecisiveness, reduced concentration, and decreased speed of thought. People experiencing depression often have negative ideas, including self-criticism (believing they are failures); they feel that others do not understand them or are punishing them (for example, if friends do not call them when they usually would), and they do not look forward to the future.

Depression can also cause changes in the sufferer's psychomotor activity (movements). The changes can range from inactivity (psychomotor retardation),

Prevalence

Depression is a common disorder in the United States. Approximately 10 to 25 percent of women and 5 to 12 percent of men experience a period of major depression in their lifetime. At any one time the estimates of someone experiencing depression are between 5 and 10 percent for women and 2 and 4 percent for men. This means that women are affected by major depression twice as often as men. The average age for the development of depression is 40, with an estimated 50 percent of all patients experiencing major depression between the ages of 20 and 50.

There has been mounting evidence that depression is beginning to affect people at increasingly younger ages. Researchers suggest that this might be due to the growing use of alcohol and drugs and the consequences of substance abuse.

Causes of depression
Interpersonal and social factors that might affect the development of depression include social isolation (few friends or little social support) and either separation from a partner or divorce. Some evidence also suggests that depression occurs more commonly in rural areas than in cities. Although there do not seem to be different rates of depression among different cultural groups, researchers have noted that people from nonwestern cultures tend to be underdiagnosed or given a diagnosis of schizophrenia when seeking help for depressive symptoms.

Biological factors that might influence the development of depression include changes in neurotransmitter levels within the brain. Neurotransmitters carry chemical messages between neurons (nerve cells) and can influence mood and behavior. Each neurotransmitter performs a specific action. As the message arrives at the next neuron, it might stop where it is or be converted into another chemical message and continue traveling through the brain (see Vol. 2, pp. 20–39).

Research into the effects of neurotransmitter levels in depressed people has generally focused on three types of neurotransmitter: serotonin, dopamine, and norepinephrine. These particular neurotransmitters assist in the regulation of emotions, including stress, sleep functions, and appetite. All three are often found at lower levels in depressed people than in nonsufferers.

Much of the research into the changes in neurotransmitter levels in depression has focused on the action of antidepressant medications that assist in the regulation of neurotransmitters in the brain. For example, the medication fluoxetine (trade name, Prozac) is a selective

seratonin reuptake inhibitor (SSRI). This means that the drug alters the levels of serotonin being passed through the brain. Its use has been shown to result in a reduction of depressive symptoms (see pp. 124–25).

It is still not clear what the actual effects of medications are in the treatment of depression. Their ability to alter neurotransmitter levels is generally immediate, although changes in the

> "Biological processes are known to have considerable effect on mood."
> —Davison and Neale, 1994

individual's behavior and mood are often not apparent for a few weeks. Also, it is not known whether changes in neurotransmitter levels cause depression, or whether these changes are the results of a preexistent depression.

SAD
Sometimes people can experience depression at particular times of the year, especially in northern countries and typically in winter. This seasonal pattern to the depression is often called seasonal affective disorder (SAD). People with SAD are often treated with light therapy (exposure to artificial lights that imitate daylight) to lift their depressive episode.

Genetic factors
Researchers who have studied the frequency of depression among family members have estimated that people are between one and a half and three times more likely to develop depression if one of their parents or brothers or sisters has the disorder. Also, twin studies

Depression is often treated with medication, most famously, Prozac. (below). Prozac is the trade name of the drug fluoxetine, a selective serotonin reuptake inhibitor. By preventing reuptake of the neurotransmitter serotonin, it increases levels of the neurotransmitter in the brain and affects the mood of the depressed person.

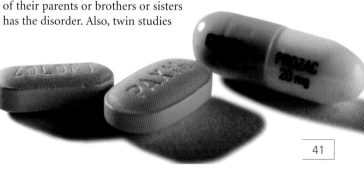

have shown that if one identical twin develops depression, the chances of the other twin developing the disorder can be as high as 75 percent. This provides some evidence of the role of genetics in the development of the disorder.

Most researchers, however, agree that while genetic factors might play a part in the development of depression, there are also other important things to consider. It would seem that a combination of genes might be involved in the development of a vulnerability to depression, which increases a person's chances of developing depression. If people have a vulnerability to depression, it does not mean that they will develop the disorder. Rather, it means that they might develop depression if other factors or situations also occur. Examples include growing up with parents who are overly critical or rejecting, losing friends or jobs, or being placed in stressful or traumatic situations.

Psychological theories

The fact that the rate of depression in identical twins is not 100 percent indicates that other factors influence the possibility of depression developing. They might include medical illnesses, traumatic experiences (such as abuse, war, or accidents), job stress, substance use and abuse, and the adjustment required following serious injury.

Psychological theories of depression consider these factors as important in the development of the disorder. They focus on sufferers' subjective experiences, and how they interpret the events that occur in their lives. The three main theories are psychoanalytic, interpersonal, and cognitive.

Psychoanalytical theories

Sigmund Freud (1856–1939) suggested that depression occurs as a result of anger being turned inward, especially after the loss of a valued family member or friend. This loss can be either real, such as after the end of a relationship,

or imagined, for example, people who feel that they will never be loved again. Freud stated that this internally directed anger leads to self-criticism and blame, and that the aim of the treatment is to release this anger. It has been shown that a consistent feature of major depression can be irritability, often directed toward family members or close friends.

Psychoanalytic explanations of depression such as Freud's have been criticized by other theorists. Depression can affect people who have not suffered the loss of a loved one. Also, Freud's theory that depressed people have internalized anger is generally not supported by dream analysis research. Dream analysis examines the content or themes of dreams. According to Freud, the dreams of depressed people should have themes of anger, violence, or rage. In fact, the dreams of depressed people tend to center on failure and loss.

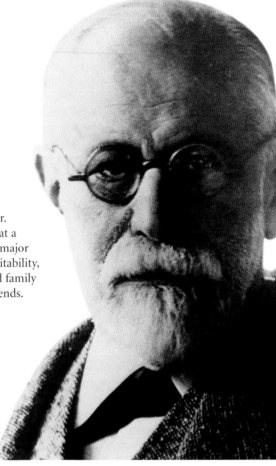

> "The depressed person feels a sense of incompleteness and despair at not receiving the longed-for response."
> —Kaplan, Sadock, and Grebb, 1994

Some of the latest psychoanalytic theories of depression have tried to address these limitations. They propose that depression develops when people

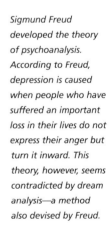

Sigmund Freud developed the theory of psychoanalysis. According to Freud, depression is caused when people who have suffered an important loss in their lives do not express their anger but turn it inward. This theory, however, seems contradicted by dream analysis—a method also devised by Freud.

believe they have not reached their true potential, such as achieving good grades in school or gaining promotion or a pay raise at work. The effects of recognizing and accepting that they have not reached their expected goals affects their ego. The result is a general feeling of helplessness and low self-esteem that leads to depression.

Interpersonal theories

Interpersonal theories about the development of depression suggest that depressed people have poorer social skills than people not experiencing depression. Social skills include the ability to relate to other people, for example, by making appropriate eye contact, being able to communicate clearly, being able to show empathy, and having a positive regard for others. People experiencing depression have also been observed to have poor problem-solving skills and to make poor day-to-day decisions, say, buying an unchecked automobile or spending over their budget. Observations also tend to show that people who experience recurrent depression make poor decisions between depressive episodes.

Additional research has shown that depressed people are more likely to be rejected by their friends or peers. It has been suggested that they have an aversive interpersonal style—they might reject participation in enjoyable activities, talk about their negative experiences, or engage in conflict with others because they are irritable. Such reactions can lead to social isolation as others begin to avoid them.

Cognitive theories

Cognitive theories of depression suggest that depression is caused by the misinterpretations, or errors, people make about themselves, their world, and the future. These errors are often negatively focused. For example, sufferers might see themselves as useless, the world as uncaring, and the future as hopeless, despite being successful in their jobs and having devoted families.

Beck's cognitive triad

Psychiatrist Aaron Beck (*see* pp. 107–108) developed a model of depression through his clinical interactions with patients. He observed that depressed people tend to make specific errors in their thinking: for example, deciding that they are stupid simply because they make one mistake in a test. Beck suggested that depressed people develop specific beliefs with strong negative elements based on these thought errors. A number of factors might lead to

"Depressed people often have sparse social support networks and may even elicit negative reactions from others."
—*Davison and Neale, 1994*

the development of these beliefs, including critical parents or rejection by friends. Beck proposed that these negative beliefs influenced the person's subjective experiences. He also suggested that information that did not fit with these beliefs was ignored or considered irrelevant. A depressed woman, for example, might discount the fact that

"Laugh and the world laughs with you." Depressed people can alienate others. Because of their depression they might prefer not to join in with social activities, and people might reject them because they feel that they cannot enjoy themselves in the company of someone who is depressed.

COGNITIVE ERRORS OR BIASES IN DEPRESSION

Arbitrary inference

Drawing a conclusion from an event or situation when there is lack of evidence to support this conclusion.
Situation: Waiters in a restaurant forget to take your dinner order.
Thought: "They're ignoring me; I'm obviously not worth their time."

Black-and-white (all-or-nothing) thinking

Taking an extreme view of a situation.
Situation: Getting a test back and achieving 70 percent.
Thought: "If I don't get 100 percent, I'm a total failure."

Magnification/minimization

Exaggerating or ignoring a particular aspect of a situation.
Situation: A woman finds out she hasn't been invited to a friend's party.
Thought: "They obviously don't like me anymore. I must be a bad person."

Overgeneralization

A gross generalization based on a single event.
Situation: Being unable to answer a question asked by a teacher.
Thought: "I'm going to fail the rest of the year."

she passed a test and instead focus on a previous test that she did not pass. She might then overgeneralize and assume that she will fail everything. Beck's cognitive triad of depression (below) shows how she views aspects of the situation:

Self: "I'm a failure."

World: "I'm being punished."

Future: "I will never be any good."

There has been some criticism of the theory that depressed individuals make cognitive errors. That is because it has been shown that in some situations depressed people actually make more accurate interpretations of their situation than nondepressed people. For example, depressed people have been able to accurately estimate their likelihood of success, while nondepressed people tend to overestimate their ability to succeed. In a study published in 1979 by Lauren Alloy and Lyn Abramson of the University of Pennsylvania, participants were asked to estimate how much control they had in winning some money when they pressed one of two buttons. In fact, the experimenters controlled the outcome of when the money was won. Alloy and Abramson

found that the depressed people were more accurate in their estimates of control in this situation.

Helplessness theories

As with cognitive theories, helplessness theories of depression explore the specific thoughts of an individual when depressed. The concept of learned helplessness was demonstrated in experiments conducted by Martin Seligman (born 1942). Seligman observed that animals that received repeated electric shocks from which they could not escape became passive and eventually stopped trying to avoid the shocks. Seligman likened this reaction to the development of depression in people. That is, sufferers believe or find that they have little control over their lives and become passive. As an example, in experiments on people who were presented with inescapable noises or shocks, researchers found the participants did not try to escape the noises or shocks in later trials.

Learned helplessness theories have included the concept of attribution. This refers to people's explanation of a particular event and their response to it. For example, depressed people might attribute failure to themselves when faced with a situation they have difficulty controlling, such as a difficult science test.

Bipolar 1 disorder

Another type of mood disorder that features depression is known as bipolar 1 disorder. It was previously known as manic depression because it is characterized by periods of both depression and mania (excitement). It was first described as manic depression by Emil Kraepelin in 1899. The typical emotions experienced during a manic episode include elation, euphoria, irritability, and impatience. The sufferer typically becomes very sociable. Mania often increases a person's level of motivation. This might include beginning or completing house renovations, work projects, or the development of ideas or inventions. Impulsive behavior is very common—for example, the person might go on spending sprees, book vacations, or invest money speculatively.

> *"Self-esteem skyrockets as the person bubbles over with optimism, energy, and extravagant plans."*
> *—Wayne Weiten, 1992*

The cognitive aspects of mania include racing thoughts and flights of ideas. Sufferers have difficulty keeping to one line of thought and randomly and quickly talk about a range of topics. It is often characterized by excessive levels of activity (hyperactivity) and less sleep than usual. Appetite tends to fluctuate, and sufferers may have an increased sex drive.

Mania usually gives sufferers increased self-confidence or a belief that they have special talents or abilities. Sometimes sufferers develop delusional beliefs, thinking, for example, that they have superhuman strength or that they are members of a royal family.

Diagnosis of bipolar 1 disorder

The DSM-IV provides specific criteria for a manic episode, which include a period of elevated mood and symptoms of mania for at least a one-week period. Bipolar 1 disorder is diagnosed when a person has experienced a manic episode followed by a period of major depression. The DSM-IV also specifies further criteria for a single manic episode, recurrent episodes, and the severity of the mania and depression.

The average age at which bipolar 1 disorder sets in is approximately 30, with some cases occurring in children as young as 5 and in adults as old as 60. The disorder occurs equally among men and women, and is thought to affect 1 percent of the U.S. population.

During a manic episode a person with bipolar disorder might indulge in impractical impulse behavior, such as going on an unaffordable shopping spree.

Research has found higher rates of this disorder in people who are dependent on alcohol and those who are divorced or not in a relationship. People who did not graduate from college also tend to be at higher risk, although there are significant exceptions—most famously, Kay Redfield Jamison, professor of psychiatry at Johns Hopkins University School of Medicine, Baltimore, who is also a noted authority on the disorder.

Causes of bipolar 1 disorder

Psychiatrists think that certain neurotransmitters are involved in the development of bipolar 1 disorder. They have found norepinephrine to be low in depressed people and high in people experiencing a manic episode. Fluctuating levels of this chemical messenger might cause the cycle between depression and mania. They have also found that fluctuations in serotonin alter levels of other neurotransmitters in the brain, with one consequence possibly being that this triggers the start of a manic or depressive episode.

Bipolar 1 disorder has been found to have a strong genetic basis—it runs in families. Research indicates that the children of sufferers are between 8 and 18 times more likely to develop the disorder. Twin studies have also shown a genetic link. Other theorists suggest that bipolar 1 disorder is a defense mechanism against stressful life events.

EATING DISORDERS

Eating disorders are sometimes symptoms of a physical ailment, but they might also be external manifestations of mental disorder. The social causes of mental disorders, the interchange between people and society, and the influence that culture has on our perceptions of reality are probably most clearly demonstrated in the mental disorders anorexia nervosa and bulimia nervosa.

A large number of newspapers and magazines feature glamorous celebrities who devised a special diet and shed pounds to become new, healthy, more confident people. Many psychological and social theorists believe that the influx of media images of thin women, many directed at the young, is a prime cause of the massive increase in eating disorders in the western world.

Although there are several different types of eating disorder, psychiatrists and psychologists generally tend to divide them into two broad categories: anorexia nervosa and bulimia nervosa. In reality it is quite difficult to differentiate between the two since there is a lot of overlap in the behavioral characteristics and psychological processes of each. Indeed, many theorists suggest that people's eating

Diana, Princess of Wales (1961–1997), was considered one of the most beautiful and glamorous women in the world. Yet she confessed that unhappiness about her marriage led to an eating disorder.

habits and their perception of their own body image lie on a continuum—along a scale that extends from extremely distorted eating habits and an unrealistic body image at one end to no psychological or behavioral distortions at all at the other. Everyone stands somewhere within this range. You might know people who think they are fat and sometimes starve themselves, or who are on permanent diets. This does not necessarily mean that they have an eating disorder, but it does show how anorexia and bulimia might be extreme versions of common occurrences.

Anorexia nervosa

Anorexia nervosa literally means "nervous loss of appetite." Yet people with anorexia do not lose their appetites but are often hungry and preoccupied with food. They want to eat but seem to be starving themselves. Anorexics might even love to cook for others. They might read recipe books, prepare meals, shop for food, and even work in restaurants, but they always avoid eating any calorie-rich foods themselves. They usually have a distorted body image and think they are fat when, in fact, they are wasting away. Many anorexic people try to hide their bodies in oversized clothes.

Diagnosis of anorexia nervosa

People are diagnosed as anorexic if they weigh less than 85 percent of the expected weight for their age and height in normal circumstances. They might look extremely thin and feeble because of their significant weight loss, and they often have other health problems, including low blood pressure, constipation, dehydration, and low body temperature.

Prevalence of anorexia nervosa

Anorexia nervosa occurs mainly in women. For every male sufferer there are 15 females who have the disorder. However, there is evidence that the number of men with eating disorders is rapidly increasing. Anorexia usually starts at between 14 and 16 years, although two researchers from Great Ormond Street Children's Hospital in London, England, have reported cases of anorexia in children as young as eight years old. Meanwhile, U.S. studies estimate that about 1 in 250 U.S. females experiences the disorder. In the U.K. the figure is higher, with estimates ranging from 1 in 100 to 4 in 100. It is estimated that between 5 and 15 percent of people with anorexia die from it or from related disorders.

Bulimia nervosa

Bulimia nervosa is characterized by sporadic episodes of compulsive binge eating. People with bulimia rapidly eat lots of carbohydrate-rich foods in a seemingly uncontrolled way. They eat more than just a load of cookies—they could eat a whole pizza, a whole tub of ice cream, several giant packs of potato chips, a whole creamy dessert, a whole quiche, or lots of fizzy or milky drinks. Bulimics do not stop to taste the food, but just shovel it in. They usually choose foods that are soft and easy to eat. The binge usually ends with stomach pains or some kind of purging—either self-induced vomiting or defecating as a result of taking laxatives. Some people begin their binges by eating a colored marker food so they will be able to tell when they have thrown up all the food they took in. Although many people describe themselves as binge eaters, it is the severity and frequency of the binge eating in bulimia that makes it such a severe disorder. In mild cases a person might binge two or three times a week. In more extreme cases it might occur 30 times a week.

The process of bingeing and purging can have all sorts of side effects on the rest of the body. Bulimia sufferers often have puffy cheeks, a bit like those of a chipmunk. That is because vomiting swells the parotid glands in the lower jaw. Their tooth enamel can often decay because of the acid that they bring up when vomiting. You might also notice little calluses on the backs of their hands, caused by the rubbing against the upper teeth while sticking their fingers down their throats to make themselves sick. Bulimia sufferers also have problems with their digestive tract, dehydration, and nutritional balances, and anxiety, depression, and sleep disturbance.

As in most psychology, there is no single theory that can explain why people experience anorexia and bulimia. There are many biological, psychodynamic, family, and sociocultural theories that, when combined, can provide some understanding of what is happening. The theories can lay the foundation for the types of treatment a person might receive, but as yet there is no scientific explanation of why people suffer from eating disorders.

People who suffer from bulimia first indulge in carbohydrate-rich foods, such as burgers, and then force themselves to throw up in order to lose the calories.

Biological theories

Some theorists have suggested that anorexia is caused by damage to various parts of the hypothalamus, the part of the brain that helps balance, monitors bodily functions, and controls the endocrine system via the pituitary gland. The endocrine system consists of glands such as the hypothalamus, the pituitary, and the adrenal glands. Glands communicate with each other through chemicals called hormones.

In an effort to understand the development and maintenance of eating disorders, researchers have come up with the concept of the "weight set point." In experiments with laboratory rats they located two different areas in the hypothalamus that control eating. The lateral hypothalamus (LH) produces hunger when it is activated. Even when a laboratory rat has recently been fed, it will still eat if the LH is stimulated. The ventromedial hypothalamus (VMH) reduces hunger when it is activated. When the VMH is destroyed, the laboratory rat will not stop eating and grows obese.

The theory proposes that the various parts of the hypothalamus all work together to create something like a weight thermostat—a weight set point—that predisposes people to stay at their natural body weight. When the set point falls below a certain level, parts of the hypothalamus are activated to produce hunger, encourage eating, and make the body weight return to the set point. These parts in the hypothalamus would also decrease the metabolic rate if a person is expending too much energy. If people exceed their set point, then another point in the hypothalamus is activated that reduces hunger and therefore reduces eating and restores the weight balance. The set point is thought to be determined by a person's genetic makeup, early eating practices, and the body's need to maintain equilibrium.

The problem with these biological theories is that it is unclear whether brain dysfunction and changes in the neurotransmitters are causes or effects of the eating disorder—the fact that they appear at the same time could be no more than a coincidence.

Some people have wondered whether genetics plays a part in the development of eating disorders. Over the years there have been a series of studies of twins that have tried to determine whether anorexia and bulimia are caused by nature or nurture (see Vol. 1, pp. 22–29). But with much debate and controversy regarding the research, the conclusion seems to be that if genetic factors are involved, the part that they play must be very small.

According to some theorists, the distorted perception that anorexics have of their bodies might be connected to a blood-flow deficiency in the anterior temporal lobes of the brain. The anterior temporal lobes interpret vision; and if there is less blood flowing there, it might explain why anorexics see themselves as fat when they are thin. It seems unlikely that this alone could cause anorexia—there must be other triggers that lead to the development of the disorder.

> "Taught from infancy that beauty is a woman's scepter, the mind shapes itself to the body, and roaming around its gilt cage, only seeks to adorn its prison."
> —Mary Wollestonecraft, 1792

Cultural factors

Many theorists believe that pressures in western societies are mainly responsible for the origin and maintenance of eating disorders. Between 1995 and 1997 Paul Garfinkel and David Garner examined the look of Miss America contestants and *Playboy* centerfold models over a 27-year period and found that the average bust, waist, and hip size of the women featured in the magazine decreased significantly over this period. They also looked at

articles in various women's periodicals from 1959 to 1970 and found that in the 1960s there was an average of 16 articles a year on dieting. By the 1970s that figure had increased to an average of 23 a year.

Society's emphasis on appearance has historically exerted much greater pressure on women than on men. Some sociological theorists believe that this double standard of attractiveness has made women overly interested in their appearance, dieting, and body image. The idea is supported by trends in advertising that have presented, and even to some extent defined, a desirable male physical form that has led men to become more concerned than before about their own eating habits. The increasing preoccupation of the media and leisure world with male attractiveness seems to correlate to an increase in the number of men who now appear at clinics with eating disorders.

Family theories
The family functions like a minisociety and can often be the starting point for the development of eating disorders. Research shows that about half of the families of people with eating disorders have a history of making a big issue of thinness, food, and body image. From early childhood food can be a powerful tool for communication between parents and children.

Systems theorists are scientists and thinkers who see relationships between all sorts of systems, big or small, physical or abstract, scientific or social. Psychologists who subscribe to systems theory take the view that a family will come to set its own level of homeostasis, or balance. They suggest that the presence of someone with an eating disorder in the family is really only an expression of some preexisting family disturbance.

The family therapist Salvador Minuchin is a leading systems theorist who has suggested that an enmeshed family pattern often leads to the development of an eating disorder in one of the children. Enmeshment occurs when parent and child are overly involved in each other's lives. On the one hand, enmeshment can create affectionate, close, and loyal relationships. On the other hand, it can prevent a child or young adult from growing up and becoming independent.

Adolescence can be a real crisis point for enmeshed parents and children since the young are trying to establish themselves in the grown-up world and are searching for identity. It can disrupt the balance of the family. The parents might no longer feel

Men also feel pressure to live up to the idealized images of physical beauty: Increasingly, young men suffer from eating disorders.

49

needed, the roles need to change, and as the family seeks to regain its balance, the child is moved to take on a sick role. If the family functions to look after the sick child, the pain of growing up and many other potential conflicts are avoided. In such instances family therapy can be used to help the family face the underlying tensions and shift the eating pattern.

Anorexia is prevalent in middle-class female children from families with high aspirations whose parents have a professional background. It is also more common in those who go on to higher education than in those who leave school at the earliest opportunity. Anorexia sufferers are often A-grade students who strive for perfection in all they do—including the way they look. The pressure on these young women to succeed might just be too great, and it sends them into a spiral of anorexia or bulimia and anxiety or depression.

Other possible causes

Cognitive-behavioral and psychodynamic theories are derived from the increasingly popular idea that eating disorders are linked with dieting behavior—it is a bit like a stimulus response mechanism. Anorexics might be striving for perfection and so go on diets to achieve their ideal weight. When they reach this goal, they might well receive admiration from those around them, and this further reinforces their dieting behavior—and so it goes on in a vicious circle. Reward for not eating might come in the form of attention from family and friends; there might also be approval—the anorexic looks like an athlete or a supermodel and gets admired for it. For bulimia sufferers the reinforcement might come from bingeing and purging, which reduce their anxious thoughts.

Psychiatrist Hilde Bruch (1904–1984) was particularly influential in cognitive

---

TREATING EATING DISORDERS

FOCUS ON

The treatment of an eating disorder depends on the model followed by the mental health worker and, ideally, the degree of success of the treatment as measured by research and outcome studies of previous, similar cases.

Biological treatments

The results of studies show that biological treatment (that is, medication) on its own results in a 33 percent drop-out rate, as compared to only 5 percent drop-outs in people who undergo cognitive therapy.

Family treatments

- Treatment includes biweekly or monthly family meetings.
- Sometimes friends of the client and other people can also attend the meetings.
- The therapist encourages the family to explore its beliefs and behaviors about the disorder and other related family issues.
- Therapists work in pairs or teams.
- The family is encouraged to do homework tasks.
- The specific nature of the intervention is based on the therapists' working hypotheses.

Cognitive-behavioral treatments

- Weekly to biweekly therapy with cognitive therapist.
- The therapy focuses on interaction between thoughts, feelings, and eating behaviors.
- Behaviors that create and maintain thinness are negatively reinforced (reduced) by the removal of anxiety.
- The client and therapist explore society's perception of physical attractiveness.
- They also examine the client's beliefs about body image.
- An educational component of the therapy consists of assessing dietary and physical possibilities, the client's monitoring negative automatic thoughts, keeping food diaries, and completing rating scales.

Psychoanalytic treatments

- Weekly to five-times-a-week individual therapy.
- The therapy seeks to make conscious the unconscious motivation of disordered behaviors.
- It uses the relationship between the therapist and the client to explore important relationships in the client's early life, for example, the one that they had with their parents.

and psychodynamic understandings of anorexia and bulimia. She argued that disturbed mother–child interactions lead to ego deficiencies in the child (poor sense of autonomy and control), and this causes severe perceptual and other cognitive disturbances. According to the theory, parents fail to respond to their children effectively. For instance, a child cries, and rather than trying to understand what the crying is about—the child might be tired, hungry, or scared—the parent will give food for comfort. According to Bruch, children treated this way fail to develop a cohesive self. They grow up confused and not sure of when they are hungry or when they are tired. As they grow to be adolescents, they need to develop an increased sense of autonomy yet become stuck because they are unable to be independent and judge their own sense of self.

Many addictive substances are legal, including nicotine (which occurs in tobacco), caffeine (found in tea and coffee), and alcohol. Others are illegal, such as the marijuana joint this young boy is smoking. People might be diagnosed with substance abuse disorder only if their habit interferes with their normal functioning.

SUBSTANCE ABUSE AND ADDICTION

People have always used substances to alter states of consciousness. There are many substances available, either legally or illegally, that people take to enhance enjoyment, to escape stress, or as a social activity. The substances can be stimulants or sedatives and include alcohol, cannabis, nicotine, caffeine, heroin, and cocaine.

Substance abuse refers to the regular use of a substance that causes problems in a person's day-to-day functioning. It is considered a mental disorder because it affects a person's mood, thoughts, and behavior. For example, being drunk while at work might adversely affect their ability to concentrate on their job. Consequently, they might endanger themselves or others.

Addiction

There are also certain activities, such as gambling, in which people take part for stimulation. The uncontrollable or excessive use of substances and the participation in such activities are sometimes called addictions. Alcohol, drugs, and gambling all affect the way a

person feels, sees the world, and behaves. For example, alcohol can make people feel happy, sad, or angry. Sometimes prolonged or excessive use of substances or addiction to gambling begins to interfere with people's lives. They might neglect personal hygiene, forget or ignore important family chores or occasions, or make repeated mistakes at work. As might be expected, there are significant consequences for them, their family and friends, and the wider community.

Substance dependency is sometimes referred to as addiction. It is a repetitive action, such as drinking alcohol or smoking cannabis, which then affects some people's lives. Dependency is usually indicated when the substance becomes the central factor in their thoughts, emotions, and actions. For example, they spend time trying to get alcohol, are drunk most of the time, or regularly suffer the aftereffects of drinking excessively, such as headaches, vomiting, or personal injury. They are usually unsuccessful in their attempts to stop substance abuse on their own.

College students get together at a bar. Most societies use alcohol for social purposes because it helps people relax. When it becomes addictive, it might cause problems. Most instances of alcohol abuse occur in people under the age of 45.

A distinction is sometimes made between physical dependency on a substance—cravings for the nicotine in cigarettes, for example (*see* pp. 55–56)—and psychological dependency—using a substance because it forms part of one's social habits, for example, smoking while drinking. Dependency on a substance is often indicated when tolerance and withdrawal effects are present.

Tolerance is the need for increasing quantities of a substance in order to achieve the same effects as were felt before. For example, a person who initially needed three alcoholic drinks to feel a sense of enjoyment might later require five or six drinks to experience the same amount of pleasure. Withdrawal symptoms include the negative physical and psychological effects that occur when a particular substance is stopped suddenly. Common withdrawal symptoms after stopping alcohol or drug abuse include rapid heartbeat, shakiness, and anxiety.

Prevalence

The highest levels of substance abuse are reported for people under the age of 45. This is thought to be mainly because of the social activities in which under-45s participate, such as going to bars and clubs, and the greater availability of substances in such places. Research indicates that approximately 15 percent of 18- to 24-year-olds in the United States have a substance abuse problem. The rates drop as the age of the person increases,

> *"Our society encourages some types of drug use more than others, but all drugs have side effects and carry risks."*
> —*Wayne Weiten, 1992*

with only about 1 percent of people over the age of 65 believed to have substance abuse problems.

Researchers have identified several risk factors for the development of substance abuse problems. Substance abuse is generally higher in men than in women and is more common in unemployed people and among medical professionals with ready access to drugs. Similarly, research has found that bartenders have higher levels of alcoholism than the general population. People who live in cities are more likely to abuse substances than those who live in rural areas. Again, it might be due to the greater availability of substances in more densely populated urban areas.

Research also shows higher rates of alcoholism, nicotine use, and other forms of substance abuse in identical twins than in nonidentical twins. This indicates a possibility that substance abuse can be passed through families. Children of alcoholics also tend to have higher rates of excessive alcohol consumption in later life, even when they have been adopted by nondrinking parents. Therefore, researchers generally agree that genetics plays a part in the development of substance abuse problems; however, they also agree that other factors are involved.

Development

Research has identified some environmental factors in the development of alcohol abuse, including the widespread availability of alcohol. Also, exposure to some substances might lead to higher rates of use and abuse, and peer pressure is frequently a factor in the development and continuation of substance abuse. Cigarettes and alcohol are the substances that people most commonly start to use through pressure from their social group. Media exposure might play a role in promoting substance use, such as billboards on streets and at sports matches and advertisements on TV.

Studies identify family factors as critical in the development of substance abuse. A person is four times more likely to develop a substance abuse problem if a family member has a similar type of dependency than if no family members have a history of addiction. Children and adolescents are more likely to abuse substances if their parents use drugs or indicate to their children that they accept drug use. Other factors, such as inconsistent discipline from parents or having a family member with a criminal history, might also increase the risk of developing addiction.

IMPULSE-CONTROL DISORDERS

These disorders involve a failure to resist impulses to perform an act that is harmful to the individual or to others. The person feels tense before committing the act and relief or gratification after the act. Substance-related disorders and paraphilias (see box p. 24) are types of impulse-control disorders, and impulse control (or lack of) can be a feature of other mental disorders such as schizophrenia and mood disorders. The DSM devotes a separate chapter to impulse-control disorders not elsewhere classified, and they include:

● Intermittent explosive disorder, which involves the inability to control aggressive impulses. People with this disorder may commit serious assaults or destroy property.
● Pyromania, which is the irresistible urge to set fires, generally for pleasure or relief but not financial gain.
● Trichotillomania, or the repeated pulling out of one's own hair that results in noticeable hair loss.

Kleptomania

The repeated failure to resist the urge to steal is the main symptom of kleptomania. The items stolen are rarely needed for any financial reason or for personal use. The stealing is not committed in anger or in response to a hallucination, and the kleptomaniac might even throw or give away the stolen items.

A young girl shoplifts a pair of sunglasses while looking anxious. Although kleptomania is commonly known and often used as a defense in court, it is a rare disorder that only occurs in less than 5 percent of people convicted of shoplifting. The percentage of people in the wider population who have the disorder is not known.

Psychological theories

Alcohol and drugs alter a person's physical and emotional experiences. In some cases they provide people with pleasure, and in others they help people avoid negative or stressful experiences. For these reasons it has been suggested that the effects of substances reinforce their use. For example, alcohol often reduces inhibitions and anxiety by depressing the central nervous system. Alternatively, drugs such as cannabis generally promote pleasurable feelings. Therefore, it has been suggested that these substances reinforce addiction because they succeed in reducing stress.

Psychologists often suggest that certain personality traits lead to the development of substance abuse; however, no consistent personality traits have yet been identified. The lack of regard for social rules or other people that is sometimes observed in substance abusers or addicts is now regarded as a symptom of the abuse rather than a factor in its development.

Alcoholism

Alcohol is the potentially addictive substance that is most frequently used. People have long drunk wine, beer, and spirits at celebrations, with food, and at social gatherings. Alcohol contains the drug ethanol, which passes directly into the bloodstream when consumed and alters the person's mental and physical functioning (*see* box above).

Alcohol abuse, or alcoholism, is the excessive or prolonged use of alcohol, which then causes disruption to the person's life. It is estimated that between 10 and 15 percent of all Americans will be affected by alcohol abuse or dependency at some time in their lives. Alcoholism has significant personal and social costs. Alcoholics typically lose contact with their family and friends, and can develop major financial problems (say, because of the cost of the alcohol or forgetting to pay bills), medical problems, and sometimes legal problems, such as drunk-driving convictions. A significant proportion of traffic accidents are caused by alcohol intoxication.

EFFECTS OF ALCOHOL

FOCUS ON

Immediate effects	Long-term effects
Loss of inhibitions	Loss of appetite
Slowed reactions	Vitamin deficiencies
Slurred speech	Frequent infections
General loss of coordination	Skin problems
Dizziness	Loss of memory
Aggression	Liver damage
Vomiting	Brain damage
Loss of consciousness	Depression

Korsakoff's syndrome

Excessive and prolonged use of alcohol might result in Korsakoff's syndrome, a chronic condition characterized by a significant disturbance of short-term memory. It is caused by thiamine (vitamin B1) deficiency, generally as a result of a long period of poor nutritional intake due to bad eating habits caused by alcoholism. Korsakoff's syndrome is reversible in approximately 20 percent of cases. For treatment the patient orally takes thiamine for between 3 and 12 months.

Drugs

Cannabis comes from the hemp plant (*Cannabis sativa*). It is also known as marijuana, hash, hemp, grass, and pot. Cannabis can be smoked, chewed, or eaten and is used to create feelings of relaxation and pleasure. It has also long

ADDICTIVE DRUGS

FOCUS ON

- **Hallucinogens**: alter perception; include LSD (lysergic acid diethylamide) and magic mushrooms (psilocybin).
- **Depressants**: suppress brain activity; include alcohol, barbiturates, benzodiazepines, and cannabis.
- **Stimulants**: speed up brain activity and give energy; include amphetamines, cocaine, and caffeine.
- **Opiates**: painkillers; include morphine and methadone.
- **Solvents**: provide a temporary "high"; include gasoline, shoe polish, glue, and correction fluid.

been used to relieve pain and alleviate depression. Cannabis was used in the Middle East nearly 1,600 years ago to ease the pain of childbirth and speed up birth. Negative effects of regular cannabis use include poor memory, reduced powers of concentration, increased risk of lung cancer, loss of energy, and poor motivation. Heavy use can result in anxiety, paranoia, and hallucinations.

Stimulants

Stimulants include cocaine and amphetamines. They are often used to increase arousal levels, confidence, and enjoyment. Stimulants are commonly used by people wanting to lose weight because they reduce or suppress appetite. Negative effects of regular use include confusion, agitation, paranoia, physical disturbances such as dizziness, and sleep disruption. Tolerance for stimulants develops quickly, and the person requires increasingly larger doses to reproduce the desired effects.

Club drugs

Many young people use drugs at clubs, bars, and all-night dance parties known as raves or trances. The drugs are mainly stimulants or hallucinogenics and include LSD ("acid"), MDMA ("ecstasy" or "E"), GHB, GBL, ketamine ("special-K"), fentanyl, rohypnol, amphetamines, and methamphetamine.

Sedatives

Sedatives include opium and heroin. They are generally used to reduce arousal levels and pain.

Negative effects of regular use include poor coordination, confusion, and sleepiness. Sedatives are highly addictive, and withdrawal often results in significant negative effects, including vomiting, sleep disturbance, muscle cramps, and pain.

Tobacco and gambling

Nicotine is the addictive substance in tobacco. Around 22 percent of Americans smoke cigarettes daily. Cigarette smoking helps reduces stress or anxiety. Negative effects of regular use include increased risk of heart disease and cancer. Withdrawal effects include depression, disturbed sleep, anxiety, anger, and restlessness.

Problem gambling, or pathological gambling, is an addiction that makes the victim unable, or unwilling, to resist the temptation to wager goods or money on the outcome of a race, the throw of dice, the fall of playing cards, or stock-market prices. Such behavior has significant personal and social costs.

Gambling can become an addiction for some people. Problem gambling can disrupt people's lives. It is likely to bring financial and social problems into the lives of those who are addicted as well as those close to them.

A person might develop substance abuse, such as excessive smoking of cigarettes, due to environmental factors that include peer and media pressure. Another environmental factor is the easy availability of the substance.

Sometimes people take medications to help them in the withdrawal process. If they have abused substances that suppress the central nervous system, such as alcohol and opium, the medication will help them cope with significant side effects. Substance abusers and gamblers often also have significant levels of depression or anxiety and might, therefore, need medication to help reduce the severity of these symptoms.

Therapy

Psychotherapeutic approaches use a variety of techniques to help people stop their addictive behavior. These techniques often rely on the development of insight or increasing addicts' awareness of the destructive effects of their addiction, for example, the health risks of smoking or the loss of family support because of violent behavior after drinking alcohol. It is also important to address addicts' motives for participating in these activities. For instance, are they using alcohol to reduce tension or stimulants to assist weight loss? Because the person should show commitment to the treatment, the therapist also needs to find out how much the person is resolved to stop participating in these behaviors.

Support groups are one of the main resources that assist people to stop addictive behavior. Alcoholics Anonymous (AA) convenes regular gatherings in which people confront their alcoholism through peer pressure from other group members. Group members typically are at different stages of breaking their addiction, so new recruits can learn successful strategies for stopping from earlier recruits. Support is also given outside the meetings. The AA model of group support is also used to treat other substance abuse problems and gambling.

The treatment of choice for substance abuse and gambling is a combination of the above options. Addicts need to be educated, given medication if necessary, and psychotherapy (individual and group) to help them break their addictions. The aim is to help people cope with

In the United States approximately 1 to 3 percent of the general population are problem gamblers. Gambling might develop through exposure to this type of activity as a teenager or poor guidance from parents regarding budgeting or saving. Specific behaviors that gamblers might show include irritability if unable to gamble, illegal activities to finance gambling, and lying to family about gambling behavior. Negative effects of regular gambling include increasing social isolation and financial and legal problems.

A police officer conducts a sobriety test on a driver to see if he is affected by alcohol. One of the effects of alcohol is poor physical coordination and slow responses.

Treating addiction

A major part of any treatment is providing people with educational material about the effects of addictions. Educational material can inform addicts of the potential risks they face because of their behavior, of strategies to prevent continued addiction, and about how to cope with withdrawal effects. It is also important that addicts should be able to develop alternative methods of enjoyment or pleasure to break their addictions.

DISSOCIATIVE DISORDERS

At times most people "dissociate" (or "separate") from their immediate surroundings or life; perhaps they daydream during a boring train journey to work or get lost in a book or movie. In some cultures people deliberately dissociate from reality; for instance, during a religious ceremony a South American healer may enter a trancelike state. These are perfectly normal events and do not signify a mental disorder. For some people, however, dissociation from reality can become a problem.

According to DSM, dissociative disorders occur when one or more mental processes are split off, or dissociated from, the rest of the mind. Symptoms include sudden, temporary changes in the person's consciousness, sense of identity, or motor behavior (physical control). There may be an apparent loss of memory beyond natural forgetfulness and then no memory of the episode during which the person disassociated. In the disorder dissociative amnesia a person cannot recall important personal information, usually of a traumatic or stressful nature. In dissociative fugue disorder a person will wander away from home or work and will be unable to recall their past. Some people even assume a new identity.

Multiple personality disorder

Renamed dissociative identity disorder in 1994, multiple personality disorder is a rare but extreme type of dissociative disorder. People with this disorder develop one or more personal identities, of which they seem to be unaware. Each identity, or "alter," might have its own personal history, personality, behavior traits, and so on. The number of personalities ranges from two to more than 100. Most people with this disorder have fewer than 10, though.

Causes and treatments

By definition, dissociative disorders have psychological not physical causes; dissociations caused by diseases or substances, such as drugs or alcohol, are excluded. Most researchers see these disorders as a way of repressing painful memories, emotional conflicts, and avoiding stress. People with these disorders have often suffered severe physical or sexual abuse as a child.

Treatment generally involves counseling in an attempt to help the person deal with the events that triggered the disorder. People with severe levels of dissociation may need hospitalization while they undergo therapy.

---

withdrawal symptoms and to start rebuilding their lives by learning new ways of coping with stressful situations.

DEMENTIA

As we get older, certain changes begin to take place in our bodies. We might move more slowly than we once did, take longer to heal, or develop wrinkles or gray hair. Mental or cognitive changes also take place. Cognitive functions such as general intelligence, memory, and the speed at which information is processed all begin to decline from the age of 60. Sometimes the rate of decline is rapid, causing significant problems for both sufferers and their families. This fast deterioration could be the result of dementia.

Dementia is a term that generally refers to an inability to learn new information or to remember past events. It often results in a loss of reasoning ability or judgment

and a general deterioration of intellectual abilities. People affected by dementia eventually become unable to perform their normal social and occupational roles. For example, they might forget the names of family members or friends; they might begin an activity such as cooking a meal and forget they have left the water running or the gas on; or they might forget routine tasks at work.

There are many types of dementia, which differ according to their underlying cause; however, all dementias typically have several characteristics in common. Loss of memory is the most common symptom. This deficit typically begins in a mild form, for instance, forgetting where the car keys were put, but gets progressively worse with time. In its later stages dementia can cause people to forget information about themselves, their location, or the time and date.

Development

People affected by dementia show poor attention and concentration. For example, they might have difficulty reading or writing, watching television, or paying attention to a conversation. Language difficulties with dementia typically include aphasia (problems of comprehension and expression). As the disease progresses, sufferers lose the ability to recognize their impairments. The insight they might have had at the start of dementia—for example, awareness of when they did not remember something—begins to disappear. Sufferers become unaware that they have memory difficulties or why they might require care.

Dementia sufferers can develop changes in personality—they might become withdrawn, hostile, or lose concern for others. Some people affected with dementia are also affected by delusions, which could take the form of paranoia.

Prevalence

Estimates of the prevalence of dementia vary widely, but it appears that generally about 5 percent of people above the age of 65 will have or will develop severe dementia. This figure rises to around 20 percent for people over the age of 80. Dementia typically occurs between the 50th and 60th year of life. Age of onset and the degree and speed of cognitive deterioration differ between the different dementia types. It is important to note that some dementias can also be reversible. That is, the cognitive decline that occurs can be stopped, and cognitive functions restored if the causes of the dementia are identified and treated.

> *"With the growing proportions of elderly persons in most industrialized countries, an escalating number of demented persons must be anticipated."*
> —*Muriel Lezak, 1995*

Alzheimer's disease

Dementia of the Alzheimer's type (DAT) was first described in 1907 by the German physician Alois Alzheimer (1864–1915). It can be formally diagnosed as Alzheimer's only after death, when an examination of the brain reveals loss of nerve cells and atrophy (wasting away or shrinkage of brain tissue). Senile plaques (areas of nerve cell loss and waxy deposits termed amyloids) are found throughout the brain of someone affected by DAT. They are typically located near areas

A doctor looks on as an elderly patient does a test to check the progress of Alzheimer's disease. Up to a third of people over the age of 85 are affected by Alzheimer's.

of the brain known to control memory and higher cognitive processes, such as self-awareness, problem solving, and reasoning abilities.

Of all people affected by dementia, approximately 50 percent have DAT. This percentage increases to approximately 70 for those above the age of 85. DAT is progressive, degenerative, irreversible, and inevitably fatal. Although DAT can develop at any age, it typically sets in between 65 and 70 years of age. The average number of years people live following a suggested diagnosis of DAT is typically between 5 and 10 years, although new research indicates that the survival rate for DAT is dropping. Estimates now put the average number of years from diagnosis to death at approximately 3.3 years.

Causes of DAT

The causes of DAT are still unknown, but scientists propose a number of theories. Twin and family studies have found some evidence pointing toward the possibility of dementia occurring through families. Some researchers suggest there are two types of Alzheimer's disease: familial, which is believed to be relatively rare (1 case in 10), and sporadic, which is thought to be responsible for between 60 and 95 percent of cases. Familial Alzheimer's is believed to be genetically based and therefore passed down through families. It occurs more commonly in people who develop dementia before the age of 60. In these people a strong genetic link has been found. Sporadic Alzheimer's has a late onset and does not have a strong genetic basis.

Research tends to show that certain neurotransmitters occur in higher or lower levels than normal during dementia. For example, acetylcholine is underactive in people affected by DAT. Acetylcholine contributes to the effective functioning of movement, attention, arousal, and memory functions. Scientists have noted that medications that block acetylcholine pathways produce symptoms similar to those found in people affected by DAT.

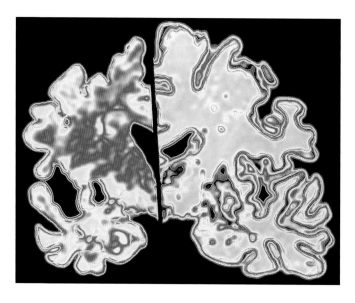

A computer graphic compares the vertical cross section of a brain of someone with Alzheimer's disease (left) with that of a normal person (right). The Alzheimer's brain is considerably smaller because it has lost nerve cells. It also shows deeper folds in the surface.

They think, therefore, that changes in levels of this chemical messenger might be involved in the development or continuation of the disease.

Research has linked environmental toxins to the development of DAT. They include aluminum, cigarette smoke, and organic solvents. In animal research aluminum has been found to cause the same senile plaques that occur in people affected by DAT. Autopsies on some DAT sufferers have revealed that their brains contain high levels of aluminum. Other research has found a high rate of DAT in people with a history of head injuries.

Treatment

No treatment for DAT has yet been identified. Research has investigated the effects of increasing levels of the neurotransmitter acetylcholine. Some studies have found positive effects on short-term memory, but the long-term benefits, if any, are still unclear. Psychosocial and psychological approaches to treating DAT are aimed primarily at management of the symptoms and emotional support for patients and their families. Studies show that education about the symptoms and progress of the disorder reduces the emotional effect on both the patient and carers.

STAGES OF DAT

Stage 1

No evidence of cognitive decline (loss of memory, slower speed of thought). This stage is identified in hindsight, since it involves no impairment.

Stage 2
Forgetfulness

Onset of very mild symptoms, including lapses in memory, such as forgetting things and not recognizing familiar faces. The changes are apparent to those affected and their families but do not compromise sufferers' independent functioning.

Stage 3
Early confusional

Mild cognitive decline. This is evident in a decrease in work performance, reduced ability to concentrate, and increasing memory difficulties, such as not retaining information recently read and difficulty recalling names.

Stage 4
Late confusional

Development of moderate cognitive decline in which the person has difficulty recalling recent events, organizing and understanding simple accounts, and remembering personal information. Some emotional changes also become evident here, including feeling low in spirits and social withdrawal.

Stage 5
Early dementia

Increasing cognitive decline and inability to function independently in personal and social roles. Memory deficits of moderate severity, with sufferers unable to recall well-learned information, such as friends' names and telephone numbers. However, they are still able to look after themselves and can carry out tasks such as personal grooming and toileting.

Stage 6
Middle dementia

During this stage sufferers develop significant and severe cognitive deficits. They often have poor awareness of themselves and their environment, are unable to tell the date or time, and forget the names of family members. They might no longer recognize that they have memory problems. They might require assistance with personal care routines and undergo emotional changes, displaying anxiety and angry outbursts. They might also experience delusions and hallucinations.

Stage 7
Late dementia

At this stage DAT sufferers have lost most higher cognitive functions. They are often unable to talk or walk and require assistance for all activities and personal care.

Other dementias

Dementia of the Alzheimer's type and vascular dementias make up around 75 percent of all dementia cases. The word "vascular" refers to the system of blood vessels. The term "vascular dementias" often refers to dementias caused by cerebrovascular disease (blood disease in the brain), such as a stroke. It generally occurs when blood vessels in the brain become blocked or damaged, causing a lack of oxygen and nutrients in these areas. The onset of vascular dementia is usually sudden. Typical indicators of this type of dementia include emotional ups and downs, inappropriate behavior, and changes in cognitive functioning, such as increased memory difficulties.

Scientists often make a distinction between cortical and subcortical dementia. Subcortical dementias are degenerative disorders affecting the basal ganglia, the thalamus, and deep white matter— parts of the brain that are located under the cortex (the upper layer of the brain) and are involved with movement.

Other dementias tend to produce different symptoms from those of Alzheimer's disease (a cortical dementia), including the development of depression and numerous movement difficulties. Subcortical dementias include both Parkinson's disease and Huntington's chorea.

Parkinson's disease is characterized by motor (movement) problems, including resting tremor (shaking hand when at rest), muscular stiffness, and difficulty starting a particular movement, such as picking up a cup. Scientists estimate that 20–30 percent of people with Parkinson's disease suffer from dementia. The condition primarily affects memory and executive functions, such as problem solving, judgment, and reasoning.

Huntington's chorea is characterized by significant motor abnormalities, such as writhing, dancelike movements. The dementia that occurs with this disease generally results in slowed physical movement. Patients tend not to lose their memory until later stages of the disease. When memory difficulties do occur, they are similar to those that occur in Alzheimer's disease.

Pick's disease
Pick's disease is an extremely rare form of dementia similar to Alzheimer's that results from gradual damage to the frontal lobes of the brain. This damage is caused by loss of nerve cells and the development of Pick's bodies (a type of degraded protein). Pick's disease sets in usually after the age of 50. The disorder is estimated to make up around 2 percent of all people affected by dementia and approximately 0.1 percent of the population.

Frontal lobe dementia
Frontal lobe dementia was recognized as a form of dementia only in the late 1990s. It is similar to Pick's disease, being caused by the deterioration of frontal lobe functioning. The primary difference is that there are no Pick's bodies in the brain of the person affected by the disease. This type of dementia tends to occur after the age of 40 and is believed to make up around 5 percent of irreversible dementias.

HIV-related dementia
The human immunodeficiency virus (HIV) often leads to the onset of dementia. Around 15 percent of people infected by HIV are estimated to develop dementia. In people with acquired immune deficiency syndrome (AIDS) the rate increases to roughly 75 percent.

Pseudodementia
Pseudodementia is a term used to describe the characteristics of dementia in someone who is depressed. Scientists believe that 10 percent of dementias are due to depression. It is, therefore, important for doctors to differentiate between the two disorders. This can usually be achieved by studying the history of difficulties encountered by the patient. For example, a depressed person will often have a sudden onset of symptoms, do well in memory tests, and display negative thoughts or guilt. This is not the normal pattern observed in people suffering from dementia.

DELIRIUM
Delirium is a disorder that causes disruption in consciousness, or awareness, and cognitive deterioration, such as reduced attention and defective memory. The word "delirium" comes from the Latin *delirare*, meaning "to go off track." The disorder is not a disease as such, but a

The boxing legend Muhammad Ali suffers from Parkinson's disease. The characteristic tremors of a person suffering from the disease are caused by the loss of nerve cells in the part of the brain that controls muscle movement.

syndrome, characterized by a set of symptoms. Delirious people change in mood, behavior, and worldview. They might also become agitated and try to hit out at other people or objects because they might think they are being harmed by them.

Delirium is common and can be caused by a range of medical illnesses and medications. It frequently occurs in those recovering from operations, especially, it has been found, hip operations. It is a treatable syndrome that is usually cured once the causes have been identified.

Delirium usually develops suddenly, within hours or days, and symptoms might vary throughout the course of a day. They might become worse at certain times and could often disappear completely for part of the day. Clinicians have noted that the symptoms of delirium often become more severe during the night. That is because, when artificial lighting is switched on, it casts shadows and can cause visual disturbances and confusion.

Symptoms

People affected by delirium might lose orientation, that is, they will not recall where they are or the time or date. Their short-term memory might be affected, and they will not be able to make simple judgments correctly, such as when to cross a busy street. Their language abilities might also be affected, so they might not understand instructions or be able to communicate clearly. They typically have severe problems when trying to write.

Sufferers from delirium might become hyperactive, meaning that they have an increased level of alertness and arousal. They might also complain of nausea, a racing heartbeat, and excessive sweating. They might be restless, highly talkative, and easily distracted by either internal stimuli, for example, visual disturbances such as hallucinations, or external stimuli, for example, the noise of a hospital ward.

On the other hand, delirium can cause some people to become hypoactive, or have reduced levels of alertness.

Hypoactive people often behave as though they are depressed: They tend to lack energy and look tired and dazed, and are often unable to follow conversations.

Delirium can also cause cycles of mood changes. For example, sufferers might feel anger or frustration at one moment, extreme fear or confusion the next. People with delirium might become paranoid, convincing themselves that nurses are trying to harm them when they are trying to give them medication. They can also experience hallucinations (seeing or hearing things that are not real). Hallucinations are estimated to occur in approximately 50 percent of patients with delirium. Hallucinations tend to occur at night as the light changes, and often the person might become terrified or agitated.

People suffering from delirium might sleep during the day and become active during the night. "Sundowning" is the term used to refer to a significant increase in the symptoms of delirium as the person is about to go to bed. It might be due to the changes in natural light as night falls.

A person with delirium might be affected by artificial light. The symptoms tend to worsen at night, and patients might lose their bearings.

PERSONALITY DISORDERS

There is a group of mental disorders that is listed in a separate category in the DSM from the other disorders discussed in this chapter. The DSM calls them personality disorders and groups them into three clusters.

Odd/eccentric cluster

• **Paranoid personality disorder**: People diagnosed with this disorder are constantly preoccupied by extreme doubts about the loyalty or trustworthiness of others. They could also firmly believe that hidden messages are being sent out to them by objects, like the TV, or even by animals.
• **Schizoid personality disorder**: People diagnosed with this disorder are frequently also diagnosed with paranoid personality disorder. They appear dull and lifeless, and do not show an interest in anything.
• **Schizotypal personality disorder**: People who receive this diagnosis usually have excessive social anxiety and social problems. They might have odd beliefs, such as that they are telepathic or can predict the future. They often talk to themselves or do not care for themselves properly.

Dramatic/erratic cluster

• **Borderline personality disorder**: People with this diagnosis would have unstable moods and relationships. They might be highly argumentative, sarcastic, and irritable, and they might be unpredictable and display much impulsive behavior. Some clinicians see the disorder as a "catchall" for people who are erratic and odd but whose behavior does not neatly fit into any other diagnostic category.
• **Histrionic personality disorder**: This label is given to people who are diagnosed as overly dramatic or attention seeking. They might be self-centered or overly concerned with their appearance.
• **Narcissistic personality disorder**: This disorder takes its name from Narcissus, the character in Greek mythology who fell in love with his own reflection. It describes people who require constant attention and adoration, and seem to adore themselves, too.
• **Antisocial personality disorder and psychopathy**: These two terms are often used interchangeably even though there are important differences between them. People diagnosed with antisocial personality disorder consistently break laws and thrive on being aggressive and reckless. People diagnosed as psychopathic are less concerned with behaving in an antisocial manner, but because they show a lack of emotion, they might end up behaving like that. They might find it impossible to think about how others might feel, to learn from mistakes, or to feel love or hate.

Avoidant/fearful cluster

• **Avoidant personality disorder**: People diagnosed with this disorder are highly sensitive, shy, and vulnerable to criticism, rejection, or disapproval. They are reluctant to engage in social interaction or any relationship unless they know that they are going to be accepted and liked.
• **Dependent personality disorder**: People diagnosed with this disorder also lack self-confidence, but to the extent that they cannot rely on themselves in any way. They might be very passive and allow others to decide how they live their lives. They fear losing people's approval and might agree with others even when they feel that others are wrong.
• **Obsessive-compulsive personality disorder**: This is very different from obsessive-compulsive disorder (*see* p. 27). It describes people preoccupied with rules, details, and schedules. They are perfectionists who spend so much time getting details right that they miss deadlines.

Origins, diagnosis, and treatment

Clinicians use different theories to explain the origins and development of each of these disorders. Some argue that personality disorders are inherited, while others suggest that the environment in which we grow up is responsible for our personality traits. Clinicians also differ on diagnosis. For example, when a highly unpredictable, exuberant patient walks into a psychiatrist's room, one psychiatrist might diagnose him as having antisocial personality disorder and psychopathy, while another might say that he has borderline personality disorder. This is because the diagnostic methods used, such as questionnaires, are not very reliable. However, better methods are being devised that might show more of a clear pattern for diagnosis—even across different cultures.

Treatment, too, will vary depending on the view the clinician holds regarding the origins of personality disorders and will also depend on services available. In the case of psychopathy, however, it is thought that because people who have this diagnosis feel no emotion, it is impossible to treat them with any kind of talking therapy. The other disorders are mainly treated with a combination of drug and talking therapies (*see* pp. 92–117; 118–141).

Drug withdrawal Delirium can develop following the withdrawal of alcohol or certain medications, especially those that assist sleep. It is often characterized by motor tremors, such as trembling hands. A severe form, known as delirium tremens (also known as the DTs), might develop following alcohol withdrawal. It is a dangerous and often fatal form of delirium and has been estimated to cause death in 20 percent of people if the cause is not identified and treated.

Infections Urinary tract infections, bacterial meningitis, influenza, and acquired immune deficiency syndrome (AIDS) are commonly associated with increased risk of developing delirium.

Physical illness Diseases of the liver, kidney, lungs, or heart can lead to delirium. Medical problems such as congestive heart failure and pneumonia are also common risk factors.

Other causes Delirium can also occur following allergic reactions to food, heat stroke (excessive exposure to the sun and high temperatures), electrocution, and malnutrition.

Causes

Delirium can develop as a result of a single factor but it is usually thought to arise as a result of a combination of factors. The main causes include:

Brain injury Delirium may occur after sustaining a concussion (hard blow to the brain) or more severe head injury.

Anticholinergic toxicity Scientists think that the neurotransmitter acetylcholine (a chemical messenger in the brain) is involved in bringing on or maintaining delirium because levels of the neurotransmitter activity have been found to be low in people with delirium.

Drug taking Alcohol, poisons, drugs, and some psychiatric medications can cause delirium when taken in certain quantities. Lithium, a medication often used to treat bipolar 1 disorder (manic depression) (see pp. 45–46), can also cause delirium. Older people can suffer from delirium if certain medications exceed the safe, recommended dose.

Withdrawal of alcohol after prolonged heavy use can lead to significant behavioral problems. For example, people might try to physically harm themselves or others. Delirium tremens, caused by the withdrawal, often causes people to experience hallucinations, such as seeing and feeling spiders crawling over the skin, and delusions, for example, paranoia that others are trying to harm them.

Prevalence

Delirium affects 0.4 to 1.1 percent of the general population, with people above the age of 55 at greater risk. Higher rates of delirium occur in hospitals. From 10 to 40 percent of hospital inpatients are estimated to have experienced delirium during their hospital stay, and following an operation, the chances of experiencing the syndrome also increase. This is due to the stress of surgery, postoperative pain, the medication given after the surgery, and the development of infections. Approximately 20 percent of patients who have suffered severe burns experience delirium at some point during their hospital recovery.

Treatment

Delirium can cause significant problems if not treated early. The risk of accident or injury increases because the patient has poor awareness and has difficulty in making safe decisions.

Prevention is naturally the treatment of choice for delirium. In hospitals staff thoroughly assess patients to identify what medication they might be taking and anything to which they might be allergic. Staff also try to be aware of any infection and the consequences of medical procedures. It is also important to find out whether the patient is dependent on alcohol or sedative medications.

Out of a hospital setting people suffering a dementing disorder might experience episodes of delirium. Their family or carers need to be able to recognize the signs and symptoms so they are not missed or misinterpreted as a stage in their dementia. Often, changing the physical surroundings of someone who is experiencing delirium can help reduce the symptoms. Hospitals can be noisy, so it helps to keep the patient in a quiet room, to provide orientation material—clocks, calendars, and information about the person's location, such as room number and the name of the hospital—and adequate night lighting to reduce the chances of hallucinations. Familiar faces of family and friends can provide the patient with consistency and reassurance. Physical support is also necessary to make sure that patients are kept safe, such as bed rails to prevent them from falling out of bed.

Medication

Once a doctor identifies the cause of delirium in a person, the symptoms can be treated quickly. Patients might be put on medication that will treat their disorder or assist their withdrawal from alcohol or drug dependency. Alternatively, if the delirium is caused by prescribed medication that has reached toxic levels, it will be reduced or stopped altogether. The patient should fully recover in one to four weeks after the symptoms first develop. In the elderly recovery can take longer.

If the patient is experiencing delirium tremens, doctors usually prescribe benzodiazepines. Benzodiazepines produce the same effects as alcohol.

The medications are then slowly withdrawn in ever-decreasing doses to reduce the likelihood of delirious symptoms.

Delirium versus dementia

Treatments for delirium also take into account any other disorders that might be producing changes in the person's awareness or cognitive abilities. As we get older, our chances of developing both delirium and dementia increase, so it is important to know how the two conditions differ.

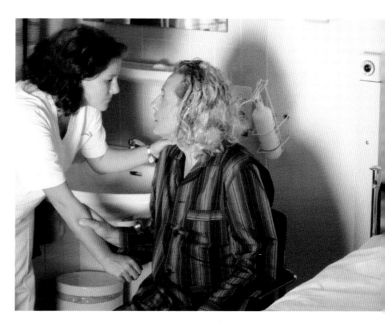

Both delirium and dementia cause disturbances of the person's cognitive functioning, such as attention, memory, and problem solving, but the key difference is that dementia sufferers experience the symptoms all the time, while delirious patients might have periods of poor attention and memory and periods during which these functions are working normally.

A further difference is that people affected by dementia are generally able to engage in a conversation and maintain their attention. In contrast, delirious people have significant difficulty in maintaining attention and are often unable to communicate effectively with

Delirium causes confusion, and patients with the disorder need order and reassurance to help them recover. A calm, organized environment also helps. Delirium is usually a temporary disorder and is treatable once the cause is identified.

SEXUAL DISORDERS AND GENDER-IDENTITY DISORDERS

Sexual disorders affect a person's sexual behavior, practices, and at times the physical functioning of sex organs. Gender-identity disorders affect how people feel about their gender (see Vol. 4, pp 112–129). It can be very difficult to diagnose a sexual or gender-identity disorder; their classifications and their criteria for diagnosis are hotly debated by professionals. This is because both types of disorders are extreme presentations of what many people experience as a normal part of their life. It falls to clinicians to decide at what point these behaviors can be thought of as abnormal and hence symptomatic of a mental disorder. If you like getting dressed up as a member of the opposite sex, or cross-dressing, for example, it does not mean that you have a gender-identity disorder. These disorders are only diagnosed when people's behaviors are causing them distress or are preventing them from functioning.

Gender-identity disorders

The main gender-identity disorder is transsexualism, or simply gender-identity disorder. A person with this disorder feels long-term discomfort with their gender (whether male or female), referred to as gender dysphoria. They might feel disgusted by their sexual organs and strongly believe that they are "supposed to be," or really are, a member of the opposite sex. Symptoms can include cross-dressing, though it alone is not enough for a diagnosis.

A person might be preoccupied with removing the traits of their physical sex, such as facial hair in a man or high voice in a woman. This desire might involve surgery, hormone therapy, or other medical procedures. There is a high risk of suicide and depression as people struggle with their sense of identity and dissatisfaction.

Treatment generally involves counseling, but at times, gender reassignment is recommended, involving both surgery and hormone therapy. With the development of successful surgical techniques and hormone therapy, several thousand transsexuals, male and female, have undergone a permanent sex change.

Sexual dysfunctions

Sexual disorders fall into two main categories: sexual dysfunctions and paraphilias. Sexual dysfunctions include:
● Disorders of desire, such as complete lack of desire (sexual desire disorder) or a great dislike and avoidance of sex (sexual aversion disorder).
● Disorders of arousal, which can make sex difficult or impossible, and disorders of sexual pain, both of which must have no physical causes to be diagnosed.

All sexual dysfunctions must cause distress to be diagnosed. Clinicians take into account a person's age, background, and personal history when assessing whether or not they have a sexual disorder.

Paraphilias

Paraphilias involve intense and recurring sexual urges that involve unusual objects, activities, or situations. Many otherwise normal people have unusual desires and will rarely refer themselves to a clinician unless they are in distress, or their desires have caused conflict with others. Some of the paraphilias involve illegal behaviors, as in the case of pedophilia, which may not distress the child abuser but does distress the child. Some people would argue that if pedophiles feel no distress themselves, then they are simply criminals rather than mentally disordered.

Singer and actor Ru Paul (left) applying lipstick. Transvestites are relatively common around the world, and only in a minority is cross-dressing a sign of a gender-identity disorder. Many, like Ru Paul, are happy with their gender identity, and appearing as a member of the opposite sex can be a positive, or adaptive, thing for them to do.

others. Also, cognitive disturbances in dementia usually take months or years to develop. In contrast, delirium is a rapidly developing syndrome that sets in within hours or days.

Delirious patients can sometimes seem depressed, with periods of little activity. These symptoms appear relatively suddenly, however, and generally pass—unlike in depressed people.

Delirium versus depression
We should also distinguish between delirium and depression. One way in which delirium can affect people is by producing a hypoactive phase in which they appear slow, fatigued, and downcast, rather as if they were depressed.

The difference between delirium and depression is the timing of when the symptoms begin to appear. People usually do not rapidly develop depression, in a matter of hours or days, as in delirium. Also, unlike delirium, depression does not tend to change the person's level of alertness or show fluctuations in symptoms, such as high and low levels of arousal or impaired orientation.

KEY POINTS

- Anxiety disorders take many forms:
- People with panic disorder show physical symptoms when faced with a stressful situation.
- People with specific phobias are excessively afraid of particular things or situations.
- People with social phobias fear social situations, such as gatherings.
- People with generalized anxiety disorder are constantly anxious.
- People with posttraumatic stress disorder suffer anxiety long after a violent event.
- People with obsessive-compulsive disorder feel anxious unless they repeatedly perform certain actions.
- Schizophrenia is a complex disorder whose symptoms can include delusions, hallucinations, disorganized thought and speech, and unusual body movements.
- Schizophrenia can be explained biologically, psychodynamically, behaviorally, or socioculturally.
- Mood disorders include depression and bipolar 1 disorder.
- Most people feel depressed at some time. If the mood persists, it might be diagnosed as a disorder.
- People with bipolar 1 disorder suffer from depression and manic episodes, which highly energize them.
- Eating disorders include anorexia nervosa and bulimia nervosa.
- Substance abuse and addiction include alcoholism, drug dependence, and gambling.
- Dementia includes disorders caused by brain deterioration.
- Delirium is usually temporary. It involves confusion and memory loss.

CONNECTIONS

- What Is Abnormality?: pp. 6–19
- Psychotherapies: pp. 92–117
- Physical Therapies: pp. 118–141
- Psychoanalysis: Volume 1, pp. 52–65
- Behaviorism: Volume 1, pp. 74–89
- Biology of the Brain: Volume 2, pp. 20–39

Abnormalities in Development

Learning disabilities and other childhood developmental disorders

It is likely that you are able to read this book yourself and that you are able to complete assignments at school and chat to your friends about them. All of this is a result of learning and socialization experiences, which develop our knowledge and skills and teach us how to interact with other people. Often, though, life is not so straightforward. Many children grow up with psychological difficulties that affect their everyday functioning and their ability to learn.

Certain mental disorders are usually first diagnosed in infancy, childhood, or adolescence. They are often known as abnormalities in development, and they can be further grouped as learning difficulties or emotional and behavioral disorders. Learning difficulties include disorders such as dyslexia and autism, which involve disturbances in cognition (mental processes related to thinking), language and speech, and academic and motor skills. In emotional and behavioral disorders, such as attention deficit disorder, cognition or academic skills are not affected. However, there is often an overlap: Learning disabilities might involve associated emotional problems, such as depression or frustration, while emotional and behavioral problems often interfere with learning.

What are learning difficulties?

There have always been children who have had problems with learning. Historically, such children were diagnosed as idiots and thought to be untreatable (*see* box p. 79). It was only in the 20th century that learning difficulties became a specialized field of study. In 1963 a number of parents and educators of children with learning problems held a meeting in Chicago. At that time there was no agreed term used to describe such children, so the meeting agreed on the term "learning disabilities," and the Learning Disabilities Association was formed. Today the term "learning

difficulties" is often used where there is no actual intellectual disability to avoid the stigma of being called "disabled." Children with learning difficulties have the potential to learn more, but have certain psychological problems that restrict them doing so, while children with an intellectual disability have a permanently restricted learning potential.

There is no universally agreed definition of learning difficulties because there is such great variation in characteristics from person to person. In fact, the NJCLD (National Joint Committee on Learning Disabilities, 1994) includes in its own definition of learning difficulties the fact that characteristics vary. It also states that:
• Learning difficulties might involve weak language, reading, writing, and math abilities, as well as weak cognitive abilities.

A child with learning difficulties receives one-to-one supervision from a special teacher. Children with learning difficulties require more intensive and often more specialized training than regular pupils of the same age.

FOCUS ON

DEVELOPMENTAL DISORDERS

The *Diagnostic and Statistical Manual* (DSM) lists several disorders first diagnosed in infancy, childhood, or adolescence. They can be roughly grouped as:

Mental retardation: includes mild mental retardation (IQ 50–55 to 70); moderate mental retardation (IQ 35–40 to 50–55); severe mental retardation (IQ 20–25 to 35–40); profound mental retardation (IQ less than 20–25).

Learning disorders: include dyslexia, reading disorder, and mathematics disorder.

Motor skills disorders: include late development of crawling or walking, clumsiness, or poor handwriting.

Communication disorders: include problems using language appropriately; stuttering.

Pervasive developmental disorders: include autism.

Attention-deficit and disruptive behavior disorders: include ADHD; conduct disorder; disruptive behavior disorder.

Feeding and eating disorders: include pica (eating nonfood items, such as dirt or chalk); rumination (bringing up food and rechewing it).

Tic disorders: include disorders that involve quick and irregular repetitions of movement or words or both, such as Tourette's disorder.

Elimination disorders: include inability to urinate or defecate (pass motion) in appropriate places.

Other disorders of infancy, childhood, or adolescence: include separation anxiety disorder (excessive anxiety when separated from home or parents); sterotypic movement disorder involves body rocking, head banging, picking at skin.

The term "learning difficulties" covers a wide range of problems, and it is not surprising that there are a number of conditions that it includes. Some of these problems, such as autism, dyslexia, and ADHD (attention deficit hyperactivity disorder), are recognized by characteristic features or symptoms. Mental health practitioners use manuals such as the *Diagnostic and Statistical Manual* (DSM) (*see* p. 9), which lists learning difficulties under developmental disorders and provides defining features (*see* box left).

Developmental disorders are also classed as either specific or pervasive developmental disorders. The term "specific developmental disorder" is used where development in one skill area is affected. Dyslexia is a specific developmental disorder, since it affects one skill area: reading and writing. The term "pervasive developmental disorder" is used where the disorder affects more than one skill area. Autism is a pervasive development disorder, since it affects a wide range of skills.

Other definitions Confusingly, learning difficulties mean different things in different countries. In some countries, such as the United Kingdom, "learning difficulties" refers to an intellectual disability identified by a low IQ and includes disorders such as Down's syndrome. Conditions including autism, dyslexia, and ADHD are considered developmental disorders but not learning difficulties. The main difference in definitions is that in the United States children with learning difficulties are viewed as being capable of achieving the same as the average child of their age.

• The difficulty must be due to personal factors rather than external influences.
• It is generally biologically based.
• Learning difficulties often occur along with other problems such as social or emotional disorders.

It is important to separate learning difficulties from variations in intellectual ability that can be seen in every classroom. To identify learning difficulties, psychologists measure the difference between the potential ability and the actual achievement of the child. Potential is measured with IQ, or intelligence quotient, tests and other tests of ability. A learning difficulty might be diagnosed if there is a significant gap between potential and achievement.

What causes learning difficulties?
The causes of learning difficulties are unclear. While psychologists generally agree that the causes are often biological, they do not agree about the exact causes. For example, for a single condition different researchers might argue that the cause is genetic (inherited), due to brain structure, brain chemicals, diet, or even a combination of many causes. Because of this, treatment is usually not related

PLACES OF EDUCATION

General education class

Children with learning difficulties are taught in regular classes alongside children who are not learning disabled. They might receive extra attention from the regular class teacher, and a special teacher might provide extra, unusual education some of the time. The children might also spend some of their time receiving special education outside the regular class.

Resource room

This is a room where students with learning difficulties receive special education. They will generally also spend some of their time in the regular classroom.

Separate class

Learning-disabled students sometimes spend the majority of their school time being taught in special learning-difficulty classes.

Separate school

There are schools especially designed for teaching children with learning difficulties. Staff are trained to provide special education.

Children with autism playing at a special school. One of the aims of special education is to enable children with learning difficulties to integrate.

Residential facility

These are places where children receive special education and also live 24 hours a day. They might stay in the facility seven days a week or live there Monday through Friday and return home on the weekends.

Home or hospital

Sometimes children with learning difficulties receive special education at home or in a hospital. That is often because they have a medical condition as well as a learning difficulty.

to the causes. Learning difficulties are most often treated by special education or behavior therapy, both of which usually involve working with an educational psychologist. An exception is ADHD, which is often also treated with medication.

Education

An important concern with learning difficulties is where the child should be educated or treated (*see* box above). There are a number of factors to be considered, and the decision will depend on how severe the learning difficulties are. Children with severe learning difficulties will usually need more intensive, one-to-one teaching by special teachers. It is unlikely that they will be able to be educated in a regular school. Children with milder difficulties are more likely to benefit from being in a regular classroom and might only need a little extra help.

There are a number of methods that have been developed to teach children with learning disabilities, and which of these is used will depend on the child's condition. The behavioral problems often related to learning difficulties will also play a part in the decision about where to educate the child. Disruptive or aggressive children are more likely to be educated outside a regular classroom. How families cope at home is also a factor, especially when it has to be decided whether or not to place children in residential facilities.

The more restrictive a learning environment is, the more limited are the opportunities for the child with learning difficulties to be educated normally. Important aims should be to educate the child in the least restrictive environment possible and to move the child into even less restrictive environments when possible. For example, when educating children in a residential facility, the aim should be for the child eventually to move to a nonresidential school. The overall aim is for children's learning difficulties and behavior to improve to the point where they can be placed in a general education class. This is known as mainstreaming.

AUTISM

In 1943 the Austrian-born child psychiatrist Leo Kanner (1894–1981) studied 11 children at the Johns Hopkins Institute in Baltimore. Interestingly, all their behavior had similar characteristics. The characteristics he described included a sense of "aloneness," little or no use of speech, a dislike of loud noises, obsessively long periods of play with objects, and a dislike of changes in their surroundings. In the early twentieth century the term "autism" was used to describe a type of schizophrenia, but Kanner used it to describe the condition we now recognize as autism. The word "autism" comes from the Greek *autos,* meaning "self," and -ism, meaning "state." The term autism reflects the withdrawn state of a person with the condition.

Autism is classed as a pervasive developmental disorder, since it affects many areas of a person's life. Because it

Children with autism often appear completely absorbed in their own world. Here a child with autism seems withdrawn even from his toys as he plays.

MAIN FEATURES OF AUTISM

People with autism might have all or just a few of the diagnostic characteristics (summarized here from the DSM). Autism is referred to as a spectrum disorder because the severity of the disorder varies from person to person. A mild form of autism, in which language is usually not greatly affected, is called Asperger's syndrome. Autism affects three main areas of development:

Impaired social interaction, including:
• lack of nonverbal behaviors such as eye contact, facial expression, and gestures;
• lack of social relationships with friends;
• lack of pleasure in other peoples' happiness; and
• general lack of social and emotional interaction.

Impaired communication, including:
• delayed or total lack of development of spoken language;
• even if language develops, an inability to start or carry on a conversation;
• use of repetitive or "odd" language; and
• lack of make-believe or social play.

Distinctive behavior patterns include:
• obsessive concentration on particular activities (such as counting objects);
• obsessive following of routines and rituals;
• repetitive body movements, including hand flapping or finger twisting; and
• persistent interest in parts of objects.

involves multiple symptoms, autism is often considered to be a group of disorders rather than a single disorder. The DSM separates the symptoms of autism into three areas: those of social interaction, communication, and behavior (*see* box above).

Social interaction

Some people with autism do not speak at all. Others have the basic skill, can name objects and actions, but are unable to describe emotions or ask questions. People with autism, therefore, often have difficulty in interacting normally with other people. They often appear absorbed in their own world, not even seeming to notice that others are present. This interest in objects rather than people can be seen at a very young age. Some children with autism do not mind if other people try to interact with them, while others find it completely distressing. People with autism often are unable to grasp gestures, tone of voice, or facial expression.

People with autism find conversation difficult and often behave oddly, avoiding eye contact. They might not speak at all, speak too little, or speak all of the time, without listening to the other person— they do not recognize that in conversation

A child with autism looks away from her companions. One of the indicators of the disorder is that the person does not like to make eye contact.

people take turns in speaking. They might, also, make inappropriate comments, not realizing, for example, that it is better not to draw attention to someone's less attractive characteristics. Psychologists think that this is because people with autism do not have the ability to use the normal social rules of most conversation.

A common feature of the speech of people with autism is echolalia, which means repetition. It might be the repetition of a question before it is answered, or it might be the repeated, often unnecessary use of favorite words and phrases.

Psychologists including Henry Wellman, Inge Bretherton, and Marjorie Beeghly have suggested that we understand our world with something called the theory of mind. It is the ability to perceive oneself and others as entities in the world around us as well as to perceive what is going on around us, including recognizing that other people have feelings. There is a theory that people with autism are unable to analyze their own thoughts and are unable to recognize that other people have different thoughts than they do. This helps explain the that difficulty people with autism have in recognizing meaning and emotion in speech, as well as some of their other deficits in social interaction.

Obsessive behavior

People with autism often have obsessive behavior, repeating various actions excessively or displaying a persistent preoccupation with an object, idea, or feeling. Sometimes these are obsessive movements, such as body rocking, hand flapping, or blinking. Often it is an obsessive interest in certain objects— a child with autism might play with a particular toy for hours on end, look at colored lights, run faucets constantly, or insist on watching the same movie or listening to the same song over and over.

A child with autism might be obsessed with certain foods and might only eat one or a few types of food. This can cause health problems if, for example, a child will eat only cereal. Another type of obsession involves routine. For example, in the 1988 movie *Rain Man* (*see* box p. 78) Raymond, the main character, who had autism, always ate spaghetti on Mondays and would not allow chairs to be moved. A child with autism might even find a variation in the route to school extremely distressing. In our

everyday lives things are always changing, so this insistence on sameness can be problematic for others.

Other behavioral problems

There are also behavioral problems associated with autism that are not included in the DSM. Eating, drinking, and sleeping patterns are often disrupted. People with autism will sometimes have a temper tantrum or be aggressive toward themselves or others if, for example, their routine is changed, or somebody tries to interact with them. This is often because they panic in these situations, and because they do not understand society's rules about disruptive behavior. Children with autism frequently do not have self-care skills and toilet training. People with autism might also seem to be anxious, moody, or frustrated.

Autism is usually apparent in a child before the age of three and affects approximately 5 in every 10,000 of the population. Three times as many boys as girls have autism. One theory is that this is because of genetic differences between the sexes, which increase the likelihood of autism in males. Autism is also associated with cognitive deficits or low intelligence, with about 80 percent of sufferers scoring lower than 70 on IQ tests (the average score is between 85 and 115). It is a complicated

A child with autism gazes intently at colored lights. Autistic people often display obsessive behavior, such as having a ceaseless interest in certain objects or images.

issue, however: People with autism score best on the parts of the tests measuring visual–spatial skills (such as drawing, painting, and sorting), math, and memory. In fact, people with autism often have very good memories. They score lower in parts of the tests measuring language, abstract thinking, and logic.

> *"Sometimes when I really need to speak and I just cannot, the frustration is terrible."*
> *— Therese Jolliffe, 1992*

Possible contributing factors

Kanner thought that autism was caused by poor parenting, but research has shown that this is not so. Most psychologists now believe that the causes are biological, but there are still disagreements over exactly how autism is caused.

Genetic factors Studies of twins have shown that there might be a genetic influence on autism. Researchers have found that if one twin has autism, it is more likely that the other also will have autism if they are identical rather than nonidentical twins. They also claim that the brothers or sisters of someone with autism have a 50 times greater chance of having autism themselves than others in the general population. Other genetic researchers claim that autism is associated with "fragile-X syndrome," an abnormality in the X chromosome. Chromosomes carry all of our genes, and a complete set (46 in humans) is found in the nucleus of every cell in the body. Symptoms of fragile-X syndrome can be very similar to those of autism. As with autism, it affects more males than females. This is because males only have one copy of the X chromosome, so if a section of the chromosome is faulty, there is no chance that a working copy occurs on the companion chromosome. Scientists still do not agree about this, though, and estimates of the number of people with autism with fragile-X syndrome vary from 5 percent to 25 percent.

Birth complications There is evidence of a relationship between pregnancy and birth complications and autism. For example, in 1977 Susan Folstein and Michael Rutter found that if one of a pair of twins had autism, it was most likely to be the one that had experienced most problems during pregnancy or birth. Researchers have suggested medication, rubella, or viral infections during pregnancy or difficult labor as factors in autism, although links have not yet been proven to everyone's satisfaction. However, although there seems to be some association between birth complications and autism, the exact effects of the complications are still not clear.

Neurology There have been many scientific studies that have looked for a link between brain abnormalities and autism. Various techniques used to study the brain have provided conflicting evidence. For example, some studies measuring brain activity with electroencephalograms (EEGs) have

A child with autism caught spinning continuously. Repeated movements are another form of obsessive behavior in people with autism.

detected abnormal activity in 20 percent of cases, while others put the figure at 80 percent. Some scientists suggest that the findings are associated with a part of the brain called the reticular activating system, which controls arousal and attention.

A few postmortem brain examinations (examinations of dead bodies) have also suggested an association between abnormalities in the cerebellum and autism. The cerebellum is the large, projecting rear part of the brain that is concerned with the coordination of muscles—controling movement, balance, and posture—and the maintenance of the body's equilibrium. A number of studies of CT (computed tomography) scans, which use X-rays, have also identified unusual features in the cerebellums of autistic people, as have some MRI (magnetic resonance imaging) studies. However, both CT and MRI data have also suggested abnormalities in various other parts of autistic people's brains, so there does not appear to be conclusive evidence.

Because brain abnormalities in people with autism are not common and appear to vary, so features of the brain associated with autism are difficult to identify and a neurological cause for the disorder remains uncertain. Abnormalities could coexist along with the disorder, without necessarily being its cause.

Mother and child work together to build a jigsaw puzzle. Her praise, when he succeeds, encourages him and serves as a reinforcer for his behavior. Applied behavior analysis (ABA) treats children with autism with similar social reinforcers. Behavior analysts train parents and other family members to use ABA techniques, both in courses and during home visits.

Effects of diet Since the 1990s researchers in Norway and England have collected evidence that certain foods might make autistic symptoms worse or even trigger autism. They claim that sensitivity to the proteins gluten and casein are responsible for this. Gluten occurs in wheat, rye, oats, and barley; and casein occurs in milk and other dairy products.

The theory is that people with autism are not able to break down these foods properly. This leads to an excess of chemicals (peptides) that build up in the central nervous system and affect behavior, moods, and cognitive ability. Some parents of children with autism have reported that removing gluten from the diet can reduce autistic symptoms, but as yet there have been no large-scale studies to support this. Since these changes in diet can also have other effects on a child's health, it is generally advisable to seek medical advice before changing the diet.

TREATMENT FOR AUTISM

Autism is a lifelong condition that cannot be cured. However, this does not mean that autism cannot be treated. Research into the causes of autism supports the belief that it has biological roots, but there are a large number of theories, and it is still not clear exactly what the cause is. It is even possible that there is more than one cause. However, the current treatments for autism are mainly educational and behavioral, and can be effective regardless of the cause.

Applied behavior analysis

Applied behavior analysis (ABA) is based on the experimental work of B. F. Skinner from the 1930s onward, which resulted in behavioral learning theory (*see* Vol. 1, pp. 74–89). It focuses on relationships between behavior and events in the environment. The events might occur before or after the behavior. An event that happens before the behavior is called an antecedent event. It is usually something that triggers behavior, such as

A therapist uses shaping to teach a child with autism. The method involves learning through small, systematic steps. He is trying to relate the names of colors in the lower row with the pictures in the upper row.

an unexpected event setting off a tantrum or a request from a parent to sit down leading to a child sitting down. Consequent events happen after the behavior and are generally known as reinforcers or punishers. A reinforcer increases behavior, while a punisher decreases it. Common examples of reinforcers include food, toys, or praise.

Rather than approaching autism as a disease to be treated, behavior analysts focus on behavioral excesses and deficits. A behavioral excess is something a person does too often; examples in autism are throwing tantrums or causing self-injury. A behavioral deficit is something a person does too rarely, such as social interaction or speech. ABA aims to change behavior so that these excesses and deficits are reduced or even removed completely. The therapist works one-to-one with the

child, since ABA procedures are tailored to the need of the individual. The therapy is known as an intervention.

The first step with the ABA approach is to identify the behavior to be changed, which is termed "target behavior." It has to be precisely defined, because it is important that the behavior can be measured and recorded. The next step is to measure a "baseline." This involves recording the behavior before the intervention begins. This is so that a before-and-after picture can be built up showing whether the intervention has been successful. How the behavior is measured depends on what it is. For example, language might be measured in terms of the number of words spoken each hour, eye contact might be measured in terms of length of time per hour, and academic skills in terms of the percentage of questions answered correctly.

The next step is to look for relationships between the target behavior and events in the environment and then change the environment to change the behavior. For example, it is often found that tantrums are reinforced by social attention. In this case the change in the environment that might reduce tantrums would be to avoid giving attention during a tantrum. Removing reinforcement is called extinction. It is also important to give attention when no tantrum is happening, which teaches the child to behave calmly.

Shaping

A common method of teaching new skills to a child with autism is called shaping. It involves teaching a skill in small steps. For example, in teaching speech to a child who has never spoken, the therapist initially reinforces every sound. When the child is making sounds regularly, the therapist will only then begin to reinforce syllables (or parts of words). When this has been thoroughly learned, the therapist will only reinforce complete words. The therapist gradually increases the complexity of speech required for reinforcement to gradually build up the learning of meaningful language.

Therapists also use antecedent events in teaching skills. An example of this is teaching a child to name colors. In the presence of a red object the therapist might say, "That is colored red. Say red." The antecedents are the colored object and the therapist's instruction. If the child responds correctly, the behavior will then be reinforced.

Probably the most famous psychologist to use these methods is Ivar Lovaas, who began applying behavior analysis to autism in the 1960s at the University of California, Los Angeles (UCLA). In the 1990s he and his colleagues reported the results of an experiment carried out with 19 children with autism. They reported that after application of behavior therapy for 40 hours per week for two years, 47 percent of the children were functioning normally. They also found that the effects were permanent, since six years later all but one of the children were unchanged.

Applied behavior analysis has often been found to be effective in changing the behavior of people with autism and in teaching them new skills. Researchers have found that the earlier in a child's life treatment begins, the more likely it is to be successful. It also requires intensive one-to-one contact with the therapist over a long period of time. For this reason, since the late 1990s programs have been set up to train parents to be therapists for their own children. In this way children with autism are more likely to receive the maximum possible amount of treatment.

The TEACCH program
TEACCH stands for Treatment and Education of Autistic and related Communication handicapped CHildren. The program was founded in 1972 in North Carolina by Eric Schopler. Its main aims are to teach communication and understanding of social meaning. The key elements of a TEACCH program are classroom structure and organization.

Schedules bring order to the life of a child with autism. Here, the children's schedules are neatly strung down the sides of their own separate bookcases. They are made up of words and images so that the child can easily recognize them.

Classroom structure and schedules
It is important to organize the classroom in a way that will help the student with autism learn. The setup should not be changed, because people with autism do not like change. Distractions are kept to a minimum, which can be done by covering windows, for example. Different tasks are assigned to different areas of the classroom, with the relevant materials for these tasks kept conveniently nearby. For example, one end of a classroom might be used for art, with art materials kept there, while the other end of the classroom is used for reading, with books kept there. This helps the child with autism understand what tasks should be done where.

Schedules help make the school day more predictable and reduce the stress that unexpected events can cause. Usually there is a schedule for the whole class that breaks the day up into sessions, while each child has their own schedule telling them what they should be doing in each session. If the student is unable to read, teachers can use pictures of activities, along with pictures of the materials the student needs to collect. A picture of a paint box could signal an art session, for example. The schedule also includes breaks. At the end of each activity the teacher provides a reinforcer, such as money, praise, a snack, or a favorite activity, before moving on to the next activity. This motivates the student to work right through a session. The amount and type of reinforcement needed will vary from student to student.

Prompts

The teacher can use a number of different prompts to help students begin and carry out tasks. Spoken instructions and pointing can help students' understanding. Physical prompts such as guiding a student's hands to help them learn a skill are useful.

Promoting communication

There are a number of ways in which the TEACCH program promotes communication between the student with autism and other people. The setting up of joint activities that the student enjoys and that involve learning skills encourages the student to communicate. Another

PSYCHOLOGY & SOCIETY

INSPIRATIONS FOR *RAIN MAN*

In the 1988 movie *Rain Man* Dustin Hoffman plays an autistic savant. To prepare for the movie, he spent time with a number of savants, including Joseph Sullivan and Kim Peek, and partly based his character on them.

Joseph Sullivan has great mental arithmetical skill: He can multiply two three-figure numbers very quickly without writing them down. He is also skilled at memorizing numbers and can read and memorize encyclopedias. He can recall the license plates of passing automobiles he saw several years earlier. Sullivan also has a number of rituals, such as eating cheeseballs with a toothpick, a mannerism that Hoffman used in the movie.

Kim Peek is also mathematically gifted, but his main skills are in reading and memory. Before he was two years old, he could memorize any book read to him. He was able to read when he was three and has read and memorized more than 7,500 books. He reads each book only once.

Peek is not behaviorally autistic—he has a warm and affectionate nature. Known as Kimputer, he is a walking encyclopedia on several subjects, including literature, zip and telephone area codes, sports statistics, history, highway routes, and classical music—he can identify pieces of music and knows the date they were composed and the place and date of the composer's birth and death.

Dustin Hoffman (far left) with Tom Cruise in the movie Rain Man, *in which he played the role of Raymond Babbitt, an autistic savant (see p. 79).*

The Wild Boy of Aveyron

In 1800 Jean-Marc-Gaspard Itard, chief medical officer of the Institute for the Deaf and Dumb in Paris, France, was introduced to a young boy, aged about 13, who had been found living in the forest in Aveyron in southern France. Nobody knew his name, so he was called the Wild Boy of Aveyron. He did not speak, avoided contact with people, rocked back and forth, and took little notice of his surroundings. From descriptions of his behavior many psychologists now think that he had autism. He was diagnosed with congenital inborn idiocy and declared untreatable. Itard disagreed; he named the boy Victor and set about educating him. Although Victor learned very little speech—he could only say *lait* (milk) and *O Dieu!* (Oh God!)—Itard taught him to read and write, and the boy's understanding and emotions developed.

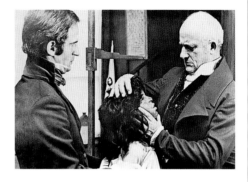

In this still from the 1969 French movie L'Enfant sauvage, *Victor, the "wild child" of the title, is examined by a doctor.*

---

method is to create a break in the student's routine. People with autism like routine, so the breaks provide an incentive for them to communicate that they want the routine reestablished.

SAVANT SYNDROME

The term "savant syndrome" refers to people with developmental disabilities

> *"I may be the star, but you are the heavens."*
> —*Dustin Hoffman to Kim Peek, 1987*

who are skilled in one or more areas. Most people associate savant syndrome with autism, but only about half of savants have autism, with the other half exhibiting various other disabilities. The level of skill varies. Often it is noticeable because the person has profound developmental disabilities but possesses one particular skill that is normal. There is a minority, though, who are classified as prodigious savants. In such cases the level of skill is far beyond that which could be expected from someone in the general

population. Prodigious savants have brought a lot of publicity to autism, but they are very rare, with probably fewer than a hundred in the whole world. They exhibit various skills, such as memory, math, music, and art. Sometimes the skills are so extreme, and present without having been learned, that they are hard to believe.

In his 1985 book *The Man Who Mistook His Wife for a Hat*, a collection of anecdotes about people with various kinds of brain damage or disorders, Oliver Sacks describes savant twins John and Michael. They were variously diagnosed as having autism, being psychotic, or retarded, but had a number of unusual skills. They were "calendar calculators": If you gave them any date from the last or the next 40,000 years, they would very quickly say on which day of the week it would fall. It was claimed that they used an arithmetical method to do this, but it was found that they had IQs of 60 and could not add or subtract, let alone use the multiplication or division they would have needed if it were a math trick. They could also memorize numbers hundreds of digits long and could recite the events of any day of their lives from their fourth year onward. Sacks thought that they could "see" numbers. For example, he once saw them look at a fallen box of matches and immediately say "111" and "37, 37, 37." There were in fact 111 matches, and 111 is three times 37. They also played a game in which they exchanged prime numbers up to 12 digits long—as yet no one knows how they did this, because they did not have multiplication or division skills. They took great pleasure in their joint activities with numbers. However, in an attempt to aid their treatment, they were separated. Once they were parted, they seemed to lose their savant skills.

Leslie Lemke (born 1952) has brain damage, mental disability, cerebral palsy, and is blind. When he was about 14 years old, it was discovered that he has a remarkable musical talent: He seemed to play perfectly parts of Tchaikovsky's *Piano Concerto No. 1* that he had heard in a TV movie earlier in the day. Lemke had never played the piano before. Incredibly, he is able to reproduce any piece of music in this way, and he began to play publicly, and then on TV programs. He has played concerts internationally and also composed his own pieces. He has never had a music lesson in his life.

DYSLEXIA

In 1896 W. Pringle Morgan, an English doctor, wrote that Percy, aged 14, "has always been a bright and intelligent boy, quick at games, and in no way inferior to others of his age. His great difficulty has been—and is now—his inability to learn to read." Morgan called this condition "word blindness." These days it is called dyslexia.

The term "dyslexia" usually refers to problems in reading. It involves difficulty in recognizing words and interpreting written or printed information. People with dyslexia might also have difficulties in reading other symbols, such as written music. The reading of numerals can also be affected, causing problems with arithmetic. This is termed dyscalculia. If people with dyslexia are able to read at all, they generally read slowly and hesitantly. They often read inaccurately, identifying words incorrectly.

People with dyslexia often have difficulty writing as well. The trouble is usually associated with reading problems, but might occur on its own. The technical term for this is dysgraphia. It involves difficulty in forming words and writing in a straight line. People

A dyslexic child working on a writing exercise copies a correctly spelled sentence. In the first attempt she has displaced letters in some words. Her second attempt is more successful.

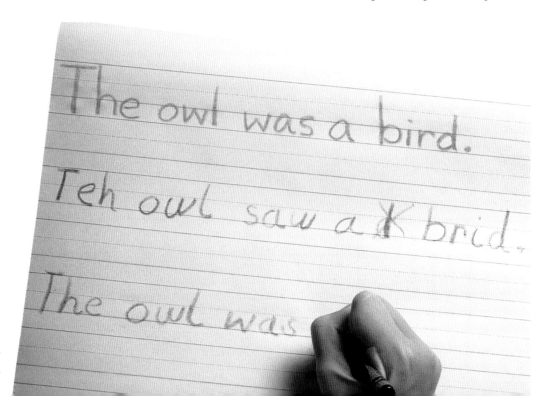

with dyslexia often spell words in an unusual manner: They might write the letters in the wrong order, for instance. Certain letters are often confused, such as "m" with "w" or "p" with "d."

Prevalence

Estimates suggest that about 10 percent of the population are dyslexic to some degree, with about 4 percent being severely dyslexic. Dyslexia is a condition that is present from birth. Without special education the problems associated with it will continue

> "Naturally enough, parents are often puzzled why their child is doing badly at school when he seems bright enough in every other way."
> — Bevé Hornsby, 1984

Several famous people have dyslexia, including the singer and movie star Cher. Although nearly one in ten of the population has the disorder, some go on to achieve great success in a wide variety of fields.

throughout a person's life and make everyday tasks very difficult: Imagine not being able to read a menu in a restaurant, direction signs in an unfamiliar building, or an instruction manual, or to fill in an application form or write a letter.

Other problems are also associated with dyslexia, such as a confused sense of space and difficulty in following directions, a poor sense of time, bad organization, and bad short-term memory of things such as the days of the week. People with dyslexia are generally of average or above average intelligence, though, and are often skilled in things like problem solving, model making, electronics, or art.

Dyslexia can lead to emotional problems such as distress, frustration, and a fear of reading and writing. This is especially true if the dyslexia has not been recognized, and the person does not understand what is wrong. Some people suggest that this frustration can lead to crime.

About 2–6 percent of children are diagnosed with dyslexia, but many go through school and into adulthood with the condition unrecognized. It is sometimes

not diagnosed until the age of 30, 40, or older and might possibly never be diagnosed in some people. Teachers can mistake dyslexia for lack of intelligence or laziness, although awareness of the condition has increased in recent years. It is often misinterpreted in this way because academic achievement is so closely linked with reading and writing. Also, people with dyslexia often develop strategies to avoid reading and writing and hide their problem, which can make it harder to notice. Problems with reading make it much more difficult to pass exams; so, unless the problem is recognized and dyslexic people given support, their employment prospects can be affected.

Dyslexia is a complex condition: Severity of the disorder and characteristics vary from person to person.

Phonology

Phonology is concerned with the individual elements from which words are constructed. Even short words are made up of a number of smaller units or sounds, called phonemes. For example, the word "dog" is made up of three phonemes: "duh," "oh," and "guh." When we speak, we automatically, and very quickly, put these units together to make words. When we read, we perceive marks on a page (letters) with our eyes and brain, and mentally convert them into phonemes before they come together as words. The phonological model suggests that dyslexia involves a problem in converting written letters into phonemes, making it difficult for the reader to recognize words. Many researchers have found that a lack of ability to break words down into phonemes coincides with dyslexia. The problem is not that dyslexics cannot understand words: Most dyslexics understand spoken words very well; they simply cannot recognize the written word.

Genetics

There are three types of studies that suggest that dyslexia can be inherited: family studies, twin studies, and linkage studies.

A number of studies have found that dyslexia tends to run in families. In 1986 in Sweden Ingvar Lundberg and Lars-Goeran Nilsson compared reading skills within families over generations. They found that poor reading runs in families and so can be inherited. This does not prove a genetic influence, though, since characteristics can pass through families because of environmental influences: Children could pick up both skills and disabilities from parents.

Twin studies have found that twins can be similarly affected by dyslexia and associated conditions. One way of assessing whether this is because of a genetic influence is by comparing identical and nonidentical twins. Identical twins have exactly the same genes, while nonidentical twins have different sets of genes. If both members of a pair of identical twins have reading problems more often than both members of a pair of nonidentical twins, we can assume that the difference is because of a genetic influence. In 1985 Sadie Decker and Bruce Bender carried out just such a study. Of the twins they studied, they found that 85 percent of the

identical pairs were both dyslexic, while 55 percent of the nonidentical pairs were both dyslexic. This seems to show that there is some genetic influence, although critics argue that because of the small numbers involved in twin studies, we should be cautious about the results.

Linkage studies involve identifying gene defects that are passed from one generation to the next and linking this with behavioral characteristics that are inherited. Researchers in the 1990s believed that they had found links between specific chromosomes and dyslexia. Researchers linked chromosomes 1 and 6 with faulty phonological processing, and chromosome 15 with problems with word recognition.

Brain structure and dyslexia

One area of the brain that has been linked with dyslexia is the planum temporale. There are two plana temporale, one in each hemisphere, and they are located in

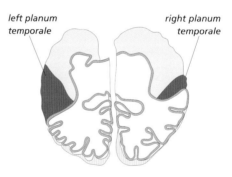

left planum temporale

right planum temporale

Brain of normal person

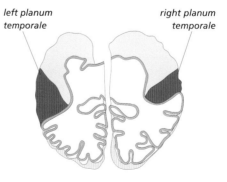

left planum temporale

right planum temporale

Brain of person with dyslexia

The left planum temporale (red) in the brain of a normal person (above) is larger than that on the right, hand side (also red). In a dyslexic person's brain (below) both are the same size. It is not known what the function of the plana temporale is because it is difficult to test them, since they are buried deep within the brain. The left planum temporale, however, is situated near the language cortex. (In both these diagrams the cross section shows both plana temporale partially covered by other brain structures.)

areas that deal with language. For most people the one on the left side is larger than the one on the right. However, when Dr. Albert Galaburda of Harvard University carried out postmortem examinations, he found that in dyslexics this area is often the same size on both sides. The left-hand side is the same size as normal, but the right-hand side is larger than usual, making the two sides symmetrical. This has also been found in MRI studies, so the relationship between symmetrical plana temporale and dyslexia seems clear. We do not know how this affects reading, but the fact that one of the plana temporale is in the area of the brain associated with language links with the phonological model outlined above.

Postmortem examinations have also found that small wartlike clusters of brain cells, called ectopias, are also common in dyslexics. It is likely that they appear before birth, when the brain is still developing. Studies with mice have shown that ectopias are associated with difficulty in learning new tasks.

Research has also found that there are differences in the thalamus, an area of the brain that is part of our sensory system (*see* diagram, p. 87). In dyslexics, the cells in the thalamus that deal with visual information are smaller than usual. This can affect eye movements, spatial skills, and visual attention. The cells in the part of the thalamus dealing with sound information are also smaller, and this might be linked to the phonological problems associated with dyslexia.

TEACHING METHODS

The overall aim of treating dyslexia is to increase the fluency of reading and writing. Because it seems that faulty phonological processing underlies dyslexia, most, but not all, teaching uses a phonetic approach, which concentrates on sounds. The main problem in dyslexia is relating sounds to letters and groups of letters, so the general aim of special teaching applied to dyslexia is to establish these connections.

Examples of Alpha and Omega cards that teach the dyslexic student to read and write in simple steps. One side of a card shows a picture, while the reverse shows the first letter of the word.

The Alpha to Omega method

Alpha to Omega is a popular and effective method for treating dyslexia developed in the early 1970s by Bevé Hornsby and Frula Shear of London University in the United Kingdom. It is a program that involves structured step-by-step teaching, gradually building up from simple reading skills to complex skills.

The first step is to teach associations between single letters and sounds. Students are shown a card with a letter on one side and a picture on the other. The teacher shows the picture and names it "apple," for example, then turns over the card and reads the letter "A." The students repeat these sounds and also copy the letters and read them out loud. This continues until they have learned all of the letters and can read them by themselves, and can write them when the teacher dictates them.

When the students have learned single letters, the process is repeated with phonemes (sounds) made up of more than one letter, such as "th" and "sh." There are 44 phonemes in the English language, and the students are taught all the letters and groups of letters that represent them.

Students also need to learn that letters might be pronounced differently depending on the word they are in, so they learn how to construct words from phonemes. Also, the way letters are pronounced in different words is based on phonetic rules, and all of them have to be gradually learned. An example of this is the different "a" sound in the words "bat" and "car."

As students learn phonemes and rules, they apply the skills to sentence construction. First, the teacher says a sentence, which students repeat. Then the teacher slowly says the sentence again, while the students write it down. They then read aloud what they have written. Finally, the teacher helps them correct any reading and writing errors. It is important that these sentences only include phonemes and rules that the students have used so far. It is also important that the sentence is understandable, relevant, and interesting to the students. As their skills improve, they can learn more complex sentences.

The Fernald method

The Fernald method was introduced in the 1940s by Grace Fernald of UCLA and is still used today. It is most often used in cases in which phonetic methods have been unsuccessful. Unlike the phonological methods that break words into parts, the Fernald method teaches students to read whole words. It involves the use of vision, sound, movement, and touch. One of its techniques is tracing. The students choose which word they want to learn, and the teacher writes it down in large letters. The teacher reads it, and the students repeat it. The students then trace over the written word with their finger, pronouncing it as they go. Sometimes the letters are cut out of materials with an interesting texture, such as sandpaper. Helen Keller (1880–1968), who was blind and deaf, was taught to write with the Fernald method. It has been shown to be successful in teaching many dyslexics (*see* box right).

Computer-aided learning

There are a number of computer programs that help teach reading. In one such method students can choose from a number of texts that the teacher can load onto a program, along with pictures to illustrate the meaning of the text. Whenever the students come across a word they cannot identify, they can highlight the word on

A change in background color can help a person with dyslexia read. People with dyslexia can place a colored see-through sheet over the text to help them read better.

the screen, and the computer pronounces it. In this way students can guide their own learning and seek help whenever they feel they need it. The program also stores a list of the words highlighted, so the teacher can monitor the students' progress.

Colored overlays, lenses, and lamps

Researchers have found that for some people who have dyslexia, printed text seems to move around on the page. Scientists have discovered that colored transparent plastic overlays placed over the page can reduce this problem and improve reading. Colored lenses in glasses

SUCCESS STORY

CASE STUDY

When he was a child in the 1950s, Jack D. Barchas's ambition was to be a doctor and researcher. At school, though, he had problems with reading and spelling. In second grade his teacher told his father that he was retarded. His father disagreed and took him to see Dr. Grace Fernald.

At first Dr. Fernald tutored Jack in her home. After a while he enrolled in the small class in which her program was run. Here there was a student-teacher for every two pupils, with Dr. Fernald in charge of the class. The program worked so well for Jack that he is now Professor Jack D. Barchas, chair of psychiatry at New York Hospital Cornell Medical Center. Previous to that he was dean of neuroscience and research at UCLA. He is one of many successes, and nearly 50 years later the Grace Fernald School at UCLA is still helping young people with dyslexia overcome their difficulties.

or colored lamps shining on the page can also help, especially for writing.

TREATING DYSGRAPHIA

Dysgraphia is the term that describes the handwriting problems often associated with dyslexia. As with dyslexia, students can learn many strategies to overcome dysgraphia. Most involve repeated practice aimed at increasing the quality, accuracy, and speed of writing. Some of these strategies are copying and tracing words and filling in missing letters in words to improve spelling. It is, of course, important that the students have already learned to read the words they are learning to spell, so what they are writing has meaning to them.

One such strategy is the "look, cover, write, check" method introduced in the 1960s. Students first study a written word, then they cover it and attempt to write it. Finally, they uncover the example, compare it with what they have written, and describe any differences. In this way they recognize their errors and learn to write and spell more accurately.

ADHD

Attention deficit hyperactivity disorder (ADHD) is the most common reason for children to be referred to psychiatrists and psychologists. It is estimated that between 4 and 6 percent of people in the United States have ADHD, and doctors are increasingly diagnosing more with the disorder. About three-quarters of people with the disorder are male. About half of those diagnosed with ADHD in childhood still have the symptoms when they become adults. The DSM lists three main types of symptom typical of someone with ADHD: inattention, hyperactivity, and impulsivity (*see* box right). The symptoms are types of behavior that very many children display at one time or another. For a diagnosis of ADHD six of the symptoms should be present for at least six months and should be considered to be inappropriate for a child of that age.

MAIN FEATURES OF ADHD

FOCUS ON

Inattention
- does not pay attention to details or makes careless mistakes
- has difficulty paying attention to tasks and activities
- does not seem to listen when spoken to
- does not follow instructions and fails to complete tasks
- has difficulty organizing tasks and activities
- avoids tasks that require concentration
- often loses things
- is easily distracted
- is often forgetful

Hyperactivity
- often fidgets or squirms in seat
- often leaves seat when sitting is expected
- often runs around or climbs excessively in inappropriate situations
- has difficulty playing or carrying out activities quietly
- often seems very energetic
- often talks excessively

Impulsivity
- often shouts out answers before questions have been completed
- often has difficulty waiting turn
- often interrupts conversations or games

(Summarized from the DSM)

Inattention

Children with ADHD find it difficult to concentrate for long periods of time. If the teacher sets a task, after a short time the child will stop paying attention and begin to show more interest in other activities not related to the task. The problem of inattention worsens with repetitive, "boring" tasks and is usually worse in the afternoon and evening than it is in the morning. Because children with ADHD also find it difficult to listen for any length of time, they find it difficult to learn.

Inattention also applies to activities outside school. ADHD children finish their meals after everybody else because they do not concentrate on eating, they find it difficult to have long conversations, and they often change from one activity to another. Inattention does not apply to all

A child diagnosed with ADHD might prove disruptive in the classroom. They will find it difficult to sit still and pay attention to the task set by the teacher.

less than other children, going to bed late and getting up early. The hyperactivity of children with ADHD is very frustrating and tiring for their parents and teachers.

Impulsivity

ADHD children are often impulsive. This is considered by many as being the most important symptom in diagnosing the condition. Children with ADHD seem to act without thinking. They shout out answers in class before being asked and even before the teacher has finished asking the question. They interrupt conversations, are not good at taking turns, and might be aggressive to other people. Because ADHD children do not plan their actions, they appear to be disorganized and make mistakes. They are not good at following rules because they do not think about them before they act. Their impulsivity can be dangerous since they often have poor road-safety skills and take part in dangerous activities without thinking of the risks. The impatience of children with ADHD can lead to frustration when they do not quickly get what they want.

Associated problems

The symptoms of ADHD can affect a person's life in many ways. Psychologists think that children with ADHD have difficulty in learning because they are easily distracted and have trouble concentrating. Because of this, they might miss part of what the teacher is talking about, not read all of the information they are required to, and not complete assignments. They then fall behind in their schoolwork and find it very difficult to catch up. Children with ADHD often have very untidy handwriting because they tend to rush everything they do. ADHD can have an extreme effect on academic performance, with children with ADHD being far more likely than their peers to drop out of school early and less likely to go on to a college education. Although children with ADHD very often are behind their peers in terms

activities, though. Children with ADHD will often have a few favorite activities, such as video games or TV programs, on which they concentrate even more than other children do.

Hyperactivity

ADHD children are very active. They find it difficult to sit still and often fidget and wriggle in their seat at school. They frequently have difficulty staying in their seat for more than a few minutes and will get up and move around the classroom.

Because of this, children with ADHD spend less time on their academic work than other children, and their behavior disrupts the classroom. This problem is more noticeable at school, where children are expected to sit still for long periods of time, but might also cause problems at home. ADHD children can run around a lot, climb on things, make a lot of noise, and disrupt the activities of other members of the family. They often sleep of academic achievement, psychologists think that ADHD children are probably of normal intelligence. It is difficult to measure the IQ of these children, however, because they have great trouble in concentrating on the tests.

ADHD also affects people's social lives. Children with ADHD find it difficult to make friends. That is because they are unable to concentrate and become easily bored during conversations and will often butt in. They are also poor at taking turns in games. Also, their hyperactive and impulsive behavior sometimes makes other children avoid them. Children with ADHD are often labeled as badly behaved, so parents of other children

> *"The child becomes the victim twice over—first of their disorder and second because of misappropriated social disapproval which erodes the child's self esteem."*
> — *Cooper and Ideus, 1996*

might not want their children to mix with them. Children with ADHD, however, are eager to make friends and mix with other children, but because of their behavior they have problems in doing so and often become lonely.

Poor academic performance and difficulty in making friends can lead to people with ADHD having low self-esteem and other emotional problems. They might become frustrated and aggressive, often losing their temper easily. This might be so severe that there is a diagnosis of conduct disorder, which involves aggressive, destructive behavior. Some children might even become delinquent, carrying out criminal acts. It is thought that this is a result of feelings that they are being excluded from society and punished for behavior they cannot control. There might also be major symptoms of depression and anxiety.

Attention deficit disorder

Not all children with problems of attention and impulsivity are hyperactive. The term ADD (attention deficit disorder) without hyperactivity is used to describe these children. While they experience very many of the same problems as children with full ADHD, such as learning difficulties and difficulties in making friends, they are more often not diagnosed. That is because hyperactivity is one of the more noticeable symptoms of the condition. Without hyperactivity ADD children are often labeled as day-dreamers or lazy. While children with full ADHD are often wrongly labeled as "bad children," they are more likely to be correctly diagnosed because of the hyperactive element of their condition.

Possible causes

There are many theories as to what might cause ADHD, and it is possible that there are a number of causes. Most researchers think that the main factors that lead to the development of ADHD are biological.

Neurological factors MRI studies have found differences in several parts of the brains of ADHD children. The corpus callosum, which connects the left-hand and right-hand halves of the brain, is smaller

The limbic system in the brain is involved in how we express our mood and instincts. Its main parts are the thalamus and the corpus striatum (green), which consists of the caudate nucleus and the lentiform (comma-shaped) nucleus. The caudate nucleus is smaller in people diagnosed with ADHD.

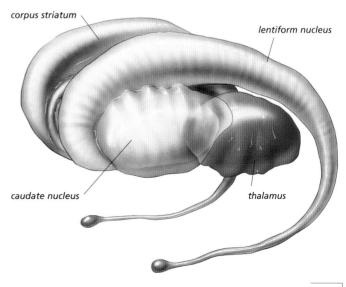

corpus striatum

lentiform nucleus

caudate nucleus

thalamus

than usual in some children with ADHD. This could explain some aspects of ADHD because the corpus callosum is the pathway through which information from the two halves of the brain is integrated. Another region that scientists have studied is the caudate nucleus, which is also smaller in children with ADHD. The functions of the caudate nucleus include self-control and attention. It is part of the limbic system, which is located in the forebrain and controls memory and emotions.

Research has also suggested that brain activity, rather than brain structure, might be connected to ADHD. The research uses PET (positron emission tomography) scans and CT (computed tomography) scans. They measure brain activity by detecting blood flow and the amount of glucose (sugar) that neurons (nerve cells) consume. Results have suggested that the brains of children with ADHD function slightly differently than those of children who do not have the condition. It seems that there is less activity than normal in frontal areas of the brain, areas that help control activity, attention, and emotion.

Another neurological factor that might have an effect is chemical activity. There is evidence that people with ADHD have lower levels of certain neurotransmitters (the chemicals that carry messages around the brain) than normal. A lack of the neurotransmitters that are involved with self-control and attention would help explain the symptoms of ADHD. The three main neurotransmitters thought to be affected are serotonin, dopamine, and noradrenaline. In fact, some studies have found that children with ADHD have fewer of the waste products of noradrenaline in their urine than normal.

Genetic factors The main evidence for a genetic influence on ADHD comes from twin studies. ADHD affects between approximately 4 percent and 6 percent of the population. However, if one twin has ADHD, there is about a 30 percent chance that the other twin will also have the disorder. For identical twins, the

Some observers think that the comedian and movie star Robin Williams has ADHD. He is well known for his rapid-fire speech and impulsive movements—traits that he has put to highly effective comic use in his career.

probability rises to more than 75 percent. Since the late 1990s studies have been conducted attempting to identify a specific gene that can be associated with ADHD. One gene that might be linked to ADHD is called the DRD4 repeater gene. This gene is also linked to the behavior of seeking novelty, which could account for the restlessness and lack of concentration in ADHD children. Other genes being studied are those associated with the dopamine system, which produces important neurotransmitters in the brain.

TREATING ADHD
ADHD is treatable, and there are a number of treatment methods, which are often used together. The methods fall into three main types.

Medical treatments
In the 1930s scientists unexpectedly discovered that amphetamine drugs can reduce hyperactivity and aggression and increase concentration and attention.

This has led to psychiatrists using stimulant drugs to treat ADHD. The most commonly used drug is called Ritalin, which doctors prescribe to about 4 million children in the United States. It is taken in tablet form, and the dose should be carefully controlled and supervised. Ritalin begins to have an effect about a half-hour after it is taken and lasts for between three and five hours. This means that it is generally taken three or four times a day. It works by increasing the amount of dopamine in the brain, which then reduces ADHD symptoms.

The use of drugs to treat ADHD is controversial, however. Because the disorder is difficult to define, many people think that children are being drugged when they just need different types of help. Although doctors think Ritalin, when used properly, is safe and not addictive, there are some possible side effects: Sleep patterns might be disturbed and appetite reduced, and some children become tense or twitchy.

While medication is generally effective in reducing the symptoms of ADHD, it is often used with other treatments. That is because even though symptoms have lessened, ADHD children are often behind other children of their age both academically and socially. They need help to catch up and might even have to "learn how to learn." Techniques for doing this might also be effective by themselves, without medication.

Educational techniques

There are many educational techniques that can help a child with ADHD learn. Teaching should be structured, but flexible enough to be appropriate for the particular needs of the student (*see* box below).

Psychological approaches

There are a number of psychological methods that can be used to treat ADHD. Behavior therapy can be used to deal with the behavior of the child, while psychotherapy concentrates on feelings.

Behavior therapy, as outlined for autism (see pp. 75–76), can be useful in treating ADHD. Behavioral techniques are often used in the classroom. The techniques can

---

TEACHING APPROACHES WITH ADHD CHILDREN

- The child should be seated near the teacher so that the teacher can easily give individual attention to the child.

- The child should be seated away from distractions.

- Tasks should be broken down into small steps—it is easier to concentrate on a small task than a large one. For example, the teacher should assign math problems five at a time instead of, say, 50 at a time.

- The teacher should vary tasks to keep the day interesting.

- The teacher should be careful about setting time limits—a child with ADHD generally takes longer to complete tasks than other children.

- Pupils with ADHD often need to be encouraged to work slowly and carefully, since they tend to rush things.

- When the child pays attention for a while, the teacher should praise the child.

- The teacher should reward improvements, even if the child needs to make more progress. This will help improve the self-confidence of the child. The teacher should praise what has been done, rather than draw attention to what has not been done.

- The teacher should focus on the child's strengths as well as weaknesses.

- The teacher should encourage the child to make lists to help self-organization skills.

- If the child seems to make no effort to work with the teacher, the teacher should deal with the behavior firmly, but not harshly or judgmentally.

A child with ADHD might benefit from psychotherapy—as might the parents. Talking to a therapist might help them deal with the emotional side of the disorder and help them understand how to deal with it.

also be used by parents. Positive behavior should be noticed and rewarded. It should also be recognized that disruptive or argumentative behavior can be accidentally rewarded by attention; it is often better to ignore such behavior. Doing this removes the positive consequence that the behavior has been getting. Punishment is generally ineffective in dealing with ADHD behavior, although "time out" can be effective. Time out involves removing disruptive children from the situation and requiring them to spend a period in a situation in which there is no available reaction to the behaviour. It may involve asking them to stand outside the classroom for five minutes, for example.

Children with ADHD often feel anxious, inadequate, frustrated, and hopeless. If treatments such as medication or behavior therapy can improve their behavior, that can help them feel better about themselves. Psychotherapy is an additional treatment that tackles the emotional side of ADHD. It involves the children talking with a trained therapist about their behavior and their feelings. A greater understanding of themselves can help them develop a more positive outlook and tackle their problems.

HELP FOR FAMILIES

Developmental disabilities directly affect not only the child concerned, they also affect the whole family. The behavior of the child is often extreme and disrupts the routine of the home, and parents might find it difficult to cope. Parents often need to spend a lot of time dealing with the child, which can be very stressful, and nonlearning-disabled brothers and sisters might be jealous or resentful. Often people blame parents for a child's problems, which can lead to feelings of guilt. The parents might doubt their own parenting skills and feel helpless and inadequate if their child's condition does not improve despite their efforts to solve the problem. There are a number of ways in which parents and other family members can be helped.

One of the most important things for parents is that they feel involved in their child's treatment. The level of involvement might vary. Parents might simply be told of the treatment their child is receiving in the classroom or clinic and be advised on how to interact with their child at home to ensure consistency in their life. This can make things easier both for the teacher or therapist and for the family. Alternatively, parents might receive professional training so that they can provide extra therapy for the child at home.

Parents often find support groups very useful. Here they come together to share their experiences of living with a child with developmental difficulties. The group can help them feel that they are not alone. They can share information and advice on how to cope with and help their children.

Finally, family counseling can be very helpful. Parents often feel guilty, angry, confused, or even resentful of their child. Counseling can help parents (and other family members) cope with their feelings and approach family life in a positive way. While developmentally disabled children can be disruptive or demanding of time, given a positive outlook and the necessary support, such children can bring as much joy and happiness to a family as any child.

KEY POINTS

• Developmental disorders include learning difficulties and emotional and behavioral disorders.

• Learning difficulties are generally biologically based.

• Autism is a learning difficulty. People with autism do not interact well with other people. Autism cannot be cured, but it can be treated. Some people with autism have exceptional abilities.

• Dyslexia is also a learning difficulty. People with dyslexia find it difficult to recognize words. They can be taught to read by various methods.

• ADHD is an emotional and behavioral disorder. People with ADHD have poor attention. It is treated with therapy and medication.

Parents of children with developmental difficulties need help, too. Support groups bring together people with similar problems. By sharing their concerns, the parents can learn from each other and gain confidence. They could even start or support a campaign to get authorities to provide better help and support for their children.

CONNECTIONS

• What Is Abnormality?: pp. 6–19
• Biology of the Brain: Volume 2, pp. 20–39

• Attention and Information Processing: Volume 3, pp. 24–43
• Stages of Development: Volume 4, pp. 58–77
• Development of Problem Solving: Volume 4, pp. 94–111

Psychotherapies

"All real living is meeting."

Martin Buber

Sigmund Freud pioneered psychotherapy—or the "talking cure"—with his theory of psychoanalysis. But the idea of talking to someone to relieve anxiety or distress is not a new one: It is an age-old tradition practiced across many countries to help people who are confused about their lives and circumstances. Nowadays many different psychotherapies are used to treat a wide range of mental disorders.

The word "psychotherapy" refers to the treatment of mental disorders by psychological rather than biological or physical means. Any treatment that does not use drugs or other physical methods could be called psychotherapy. The most important element is talking. It is the ideas behind the therapy, the way that it is applied, and the nature of the relationships that develop between the client and the therapist that differentiate between types of psychotherapy.

In the late 19th century Sigmund Freud's particular form of talking—psychoanalysis—heralded the beginning of psychotherapy as we know it; but psychotherapy and religious belief have the same roots. A definition of psychotherapy as a spiritual "cure of the soul" (*psyche* meaning "soul," *therapy* meaning "cure") establishes it as a profession that used to be the work of a priest. Some people say psychotherapy should be called the "listening cure," since psychotherapists listen and, most importantly, recognize—without judgment—the clients and their problems. Nowadays, however, therapy is more directive and conversational, with therapist and client often actively engaging in problem-solving tasks.

Aims of psychotherapy

Psychotherapy involves techniques intended to help people with emotional disturbances coexist more peaceably with themselves and others. Psychotherapy is predominantly suitable for those with so-called neurotic problems (with which sufferers are aware of the problem) as opposed to psychotic problems (with which sufferers seem to have lost touch with reality). However, psychotic disorders might be alleviated by psychotherapy when combined with drugs. In general, there is no reason why medication and psychotherapy should not be used together.

The opposite of the talking cure could be seen as the silent treatment: Isolating prisoners (solitary confinement) or ignoring friends (ostracizing) remains a form of punishment, and the experience of isolation is usually central to depression. Silence or disengagement on the part of a client might be symptoms of a mental disorder.

A large proportion of patients visiting doctors' offices come with problems

A Buddhist healer in Ladakh, northern India, sucks out spiritual poisons from a woman's forehead with a bamboo tube. Many illnesses have their source in psychological problems, and such rituals can have a powerful effect on a believer. Psychotherapy—which some people consider a spiritual cure—can similarly help alleviate mental problems.

considered best treated by psychological, rather than physical, means. There might be a number of reasons for this, among them the breaking up of the nuclear family, lack of religious involvement, and the breakdown of community living and values. Unfortunately, many people do not—or think they do not—have any close family or good friends to turn to for help. Loneliness and isolation can be difficult to escape. Psychotherapy aims to alleviate distress through providing a healthy relationship with another person. Since the 1990s demand for the talking cures of psychotherapy and counseling has increased: Some people even call them "the new religion."

Clinicians mainly recommend psychotherapy for depression, anxiety, panic disorder, posttraumatic stress disorder (PTSD), eating disorders, obsessive-compulsive disorder, personality disorders (see pp. 20–67), and some somatic (bodily) complaints, such as chronic pain or chronic fatigue.

Psychotherapy is provided by mental-health professionals from a range of mental-health disciplines, including psychiatrists, clinical and counseling psychologists, psychotherapists, art and drama therapists, and counselors.

Types of psychotherapy

Psychotherapies reflect the many different approaches, or perspectives, that historically people have used to study psychology. Each of these perspectives offers a contrasting explanation of why people act as they do. Broadly speaking, the approaches are psychoanalytic, behavioral, cognitive, phenomenological (see Vol. 1, pp. 66–73), and neurobiological (see pp. 118–141). This chapter deals with the first four approaches.

Numerous types of therapy have developed since Freud, based on the above perspectives, or schools of thought. They include Freudian psychoanalysis and related therapies (the psychodynamic approach); behavior therapy (the behavioral approach); cognitive and cognitive behavioral therapy (the cognitive approach); and other types of therapy, in particular, humanistic therapy, based on the phenomenological approach.

PSYCHOANALYSIS

Psychoanalysis was the first psychodynamic theory. The term "psychodynamic" describes the root causes of behavior and the forces within the personality that motivate it. It comes from the Greek *psyche,* meaning "soul," and *dynamic,* meaning "movement." The psychodynamic model sees mental disorders as stemming from an imbalance between the id, ego, and superego, the three principal components of the personality proposed by Sigmund Freud (1856–1939) (see Vol. 1, pp. 52–65 and 104–117).

Freud and those who worked closely with him developed psychoanalysis, the first formal method of psychotherapy. Notably, Freud did not see boundless happiness as part of the human condition. Rather, he aimed to turn neuroses into "everyday unhappiness." For example, instead of becoming depressed, the person could feel and tolerate ordinary sadness.

The unconscious

The basic assumption of Freud's theory is that much of our behavior stems from processes that are unconscious.

Talking cures include psychotherapies based on various psychological schools of thought that developed mainly in the 20th century. They are based on a confiding and nonjudgmental relationship between the client and therapist.

Emotionally painful feelings, memories, and wishes can become repressed, that is, diverted to the unconscious. Thoughts and impulses diverted to the unconscious can reach consciousness in disguised ways, through dreams, irrational behavior, mannerisms, and slips of the tongue.

The purpose of psychoanalysis is to bring out repressed fears and motives from the unconscious into the person's consciousness so they can be dealt with in a more rational and realistic way. When people understand what is motivating them, they can deal more effectively with their problem.

Freud assumed a connection (association) between aspects of behavior, for example, stopping talking, and repressed material. His interpretation of dreams was also based on associations. The persons or objects in the dreams were not necessarily important: Associations made about them were more important in arriving at crucial conclusions. The technique formed the basis of psychoanalysis, since Freud believed that it gave clients the means to bring into consciousness previously unconscious material.

Psychoanalysis typically involves about six sessions per week over several years. During its course the analysand (the term for the client) might be vulnerable and helpless for long periods. This is thought to occur when the analysand's old defenses are broken down, but the ego is still not strong enough to cope with the conflict.

Anxiety and defenses

Freud believed that most mental disorders are the result of unconscious conflicts between the aggressive and sexual impulses of the id and the constraints imposed by the ego and superego. These conflicts, repressed since childhood, prevent the person from coping in adulthood in a mature way. If the ego is too weak to cope with the demands of either the id or superego, it defends itself by repressing them into the unconscious.

The desires of the id are powerful forces that must be expressed in some way. People with an urge to do something for

Taking part in vigorous, highly competitive sport, such as a game of squash, can be a way of diverting the impulses of the id— the primitive, unruly forces that according to Freud form part of personality.

which they will be punished are likely to become anxious. The greater the restraint on expression of impulses by parents and society, the greater the conflict will be between the three parts of the personality.

Prohibiting expression of id impulses, however, is not an answer: One way of reducing anxiety is to express the impulse in a disguised form; for example, the impulse for aggression might be alleviated through sports or dictatorial behavior at work. The other way is to repress the impulse and push it out of consciousness into the unconscious.

Both ways are seen as defensive procedures, or defense mechanisms, to avoid painful anxiety. However, defense mechanisms are never totally successful, and residual tension spills out into everyday life. This tension might be seen in nervousness or restlessness, a price that Freud believed we pay for being civilized.

We all use defense mechanisms to deal with stressful situations. Basically, defense mechanisms are unconscious processes that protect us against anxiety by distorting reality in some way. They

change the way we see things. All defense mechanisms involve an element of self-deception. However, defense mechanisms are only considered to be a symptom of ill health when they are the dominant mode of responding to a given problem.

Freudian defense mechanisms

There are eight basic defense mechanisms through which the ego unconsciously controls behavior.

Repression Freud proposed that an exceedingly unpleasant or otherwise painful event might be so disturbing or troublesome if held in the conscious mind's memory bank that it would be pressed down into the unconscious, or repressed. Once repressed, although it had the advantage of no longer troubling the person, it also had disadvantages for a healthy psychological life. For example, the advantage of repressing a marital problem by hiding it and pretending that it did not exist could be that the problem did not worry the people concerned on a day-to-day basis. However, if they could bear to face it in the real world, they would also have a better chance of ultimately solving it. Also, the effect of repression could lead to symptoms such as impotence. Following this line of reasoning, Freud argued that if the unwisely repressed material could be dredged up and people forced to confront the crisis rather than deny it, then full recovery should follow.

Rationalization If we act impulsively or because of motives we feel guilty about, we find a rational reason for this. We opt for the good reason rather than the true reason and so make a number of excuses. The classic example used is the fox in Aesop's fable who could not reach the grapes he wanted and therefore rationalized that he no longer wanted them because they were "too sour."

Reaction formation refers to how we can conceal a true feeling or motive with a strong expression of the opposite one. For example, a mother who feels guilty about not wanting her child might become overindulgent and overprotective to prove to herself that she really is a good mother.

Projection All of us have undesirable traits that we do not acknowledge. When we avoid acknowledging them by assigning them to another in exaggerated amounts, the process is known as projection. For example, if we have a tendency to be critical, but would dislike ourselves if we acknowledged this, we convince ourselves that people around us are critical or unkind. If we then treat them harshly, our behavior is then rationalized as being due to their fault and not ours. Similarly, if we assure ourselves that everyone is always cheating on exams, our own cheating from time to time does not seem so bad. This defense mechanism is said to be used a great deal in western culture.

Intellectualization is an attempt to gain detachment—and so lessen psychological pain—from a stressful situation by dealing with it in abstract, intellectual terms. People, such as soldiers in battle, going through a distressful or frightening event may try to control their fear and nerves by intellectualizing their feelings. Intellectualization becomes a problem, however, when it becomes so much part of some people's lives that they cut themselves off from all emotional experience.

Denial prevents us from admitting to reality. When an external reality is too unpleasant to face, a person might deny that it exists. Because we cannot tolerate the pain that acknowledging reality would produce, we resort to the defense mechanism of denial. It might be seen when a diagnosis of serious illness is given or when a person disregards a whole series of clues suggesting that their partner is having an affair.

Sublimation Another process by which tension is released is sublimation. For example, during the anal

In Aesop's fable, when the fox could not reach the grapes, he decided he did not want them—because they were sour. According to Freudian theory, we use such rationalization as a defense mechanism when we cannot accept the true reasons for our actions.

stage (2–4 years) the child's impulse might be to handle or smear feces. However, such a drive might be sublimated, or expressed in another manner, through creative activity such as artistic play or mud-pie making.

Sublimation is important not only because it allows us to express socially forbidden drives, but also because many such sublimations form part of what we consider civilized life: art, for example. However, if sublimations are repressed by a defense mechanism, they will continue to seek an outlet. The defense mechanism will have to be used constantly to contain the sublimation. When used in this way, it is thought that defense mechanisms—especially those of repression and denial—are unsuccessful.

For example, fear that the ego cannot contain the impulsive id might lead to yet more anxiety, such as phobic anxiety, or a fear fixed on a specific object, or generalized anxiety disorder (GAD), in which no specific object or situation is linked to a general sense of fear (see pp. 20–67).

Displacement Through displacement a motive that cannot be gratified in one

> *"Sometimes I wonder how all those who do not write, compose, or paint can manage to escape the madness, the melancholia, the panic, and fear which is inherent in the human condition."*
> —Graham Greene, 1981

form—perhaps because of restrictions laid down by society—is directed into a new channel. According to Freud, displacement was the best way of handling aggressive and sexual impulses. For example, hostile impulses might be expressed in physical-contact sports. This defense is unlikely to remove the frustrated impulses altogether, but it will lessen the tension. Another example is mothering, being mothered, or seeking companionship, which might partially satisfy unmet sexual needs.

Attitudes during analysis

According to Freud, during analysis the analysand shows certain attitudes that the analyst can use as the basis of the analysis. They include:

Resistance Freud developed the concept of resistance to address blocks in therapy on the part of the client. During free association the client must speak freely about anything that comes to mind, without inhibition. Freud not only observed carefully what his clients said, but also when they faltered or stopped talking altogether. When clients remained silent, they were thought to be resisting the recall of certain thoughts and feelings. Freud believed that

KEY TERMS

- **Denial**—not admitting to reality.
- **Displacement**—transferring an impulse from one form of expression into another.
- **Fixation**—retaining childhood psychosexual attitudes.
- **Intellectualization**—dealing with a stressful situation in abstract terms, to avoid pain.
- **Projection**—denying one's own unpleasant attitudes by attributing them to others.
- **Rationalization**—an attempt to deny guilt by opting for a good rather than true reason.
- **Reaction formulation**—denying a true feeling by displaying the opposite.
- **Repression**—burying unpleasant memories in the unconscious.
- **Resistance**—the client's mental blocks during psychoanalysis.
- **Sublimation**—expressing forbidden impulses through socially acceptable methods.
- **Transference**—the attitude a client develops toward the analyst.

certain successive psychosexual stages of childhood. If children fail to develop appropriately at any of these stages, they will tend to show behavior associated with—or be fixated at—that stage, even when adult. The degree to which the childhood behavior or childhood patterns are transferred to adulthood depends on the amount of libido (sexual energy) that was used in trying to overcome the conflict at the time.

Freud's successors

Since Freud's time numerous forms of psychotherapy have been developed based on psychoanalysis, but not all are described as psychodynamic.

While all Freud's successors acknowledged the effect of past experience on present problems, those who came after Freud gave greater recognition to factors other than biological drives in shaping human behavior. For example, Alfred Adler (1870–1937), Erich Fromm (1900–1980), and Carl Roger (1902–1988) emphasized the importance of social and cultural factors, while Carl Jung (1875–1961), who originally worked very closely with Freud, emphasized spiritual and religious factors (*see* Vol. 1, pp. 52–65).

Others placed more emphasis on the ego in directing behavior and solving problems and less emphasis on the role of unconscious drives. These followers of Freud are called ego analysts and are sometimes referred to as the second generation of psychoanalysts (*see* Vol. 1, pp. 52–65). They include Melanie Klein (1882–1960), with her object relations theory; Anna Freud (1895–1982), with child psychoanalysis; and Erik Erikson (1902–1994), with his theory of psychosexual development. They suggested that people were more rational in their planning and decisions than Freud had proposed, and emphasized the effect of early relationships on mental health.

Broadly speaking, psychodynamic therapists take developmental (childhood) and unconscious conflicts into account when treating clients, and other therapies

resistance results from the person's unconscious control over sensitive areas, and that these areas are precisely the ones that the therapist should explore.

Transference During analysis the client's attitude toward the analyst is considered to be an important part of treatment. Sooner or later clients develop a strong attitude toward the analyst. The attitude might be positive and friendly or negative and hostile. Clients express attitudes that they feel toward people who are (or were) important in their life—usually parents or primary caretakers. Often these reactions are considered not to reflect what is taking place in therapy; rather, a repetition of the original feeling is dredged up from the past but transferred during therapy onto the analyst. This tendency for clients to make the psychoanalyst the object of emotional responses is called transference. Analysts use these feelings to explain to clients the origins of their concerns or fears.

Fixation Freud maintained that the id, ego, and superego first appear during

In the 1977 movie Annie Hall Woody Allen (above) says of the psychiatrist he's been seeing for 15 years: "I'm going to give him one more year, and then I'm going to Lourdes." Classical psychoanalysis involves nearly daily sessions over a period of several years. Other psychodynamic therapies based on psychoanalysis often take less time.

The German-born psychoanalyst Erich Fromm began as a follower of Freud but broke away from Freud's teachings because he thought people's personalities were shaped by society as well as biological drives. In turn, he used psychoanalytic thinking to explain the nature of modern society.

emphasize the here-and-now of a problem. For psychoanalysis and other psychodynamic therapies to be successful, it is particularly important that the client has an interest in self-exploration and can tolerate frustration in relationships.

Psychodynamic therapists generally use a number of Freud's basics, such as the 50-minute session, in simple and uncluttered treatment rooms that let client and therapist work undistracted. However, the therapist is less of a "blank screen" and will often engage in discussion on current problems. Therapy can be more directive, with less emphasis on completely going through childhood experiences and more attention on current problems.

Psychoanalytic psychotherapy is most closely linked to classical Freudian analysis in that it is based on the assumption that mental disorders stem from unconscious conflicts and fears. But it differs from classical psychoanalysis in several ways. For example, the classical methods of psychoanalysis have been modified: Therapy is briefer and less intense; sessions are not necessarily conducted every day but usually twice a week. Although some psychoanalysts still adhere rigidly to

Freud's techniques, most have modified the three basic principles: repression, the unconscious, and infantile sexuality.

Limitations of Freud's work

Although Freud's work has had an enormous effect on psychology in terms of both personality and therapy, it is not without its shortcomings:

• Psychoanalysis is difficult to study scientifically, since many of its concepts, such as the unconscious, repression, sublimation, or transference, are difficult to define and measure. It is not a scientific theory and therefore cannot be proved wrong.

• Most psychoanalysts who practiced and modified Freud's theories were not trained in scientific research methods. Therefore, little scientific measurement of psychoanalysis has been conducted, although research has been under way since the 1980s. However, it has been argued that a good theory requires a long period of hypothesis generation (putting forward of ideas) as well as testing.

• The case studies historically used to support psychoanalysis have been carefully selected and therefore might be biased. Also, if psychoanalysis fails, it is often seen as the fault of the client. In addition, where insight has been achieved or accepted by the client but no behavioral changes are made, the insight is considered only to be intellectual (in itself, another Freudian defense mechanism).

• Psychoanalysis is a closed system: Someone who raises questions about its validity can be described as suffering from resistance, since the critic is said not to recognize the therapy's value.

• Psychoanalysis is best suited to highly motivated people with good verbal skills.

• Freud placed heavy emphasis on childhood sexuality and on the instinctive biological impulses of people; he failed to take into account that people are products of the society in which they live.

• Freud's data were biased toward the clients that he saw—mainly middle-class Jewish women during the late 19th

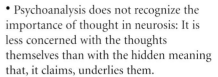

century, when sexual standards were very strict, and much of his clients' conflict centered on guilt regarding sexual desires. Today, sexual standards are less rigid, and there is less sexual guilt, yet the incidence of mental disorders remains about the same. Sexual conflicts are not the only cause of personality disorders—and might not even be a major cause.
• Freud based his theory of personality on his observations of emotionally disturbed people, and it might not be an appropriate description of normal, healthy personality development.

> *"Whereof one cannot speak, thereof one must be silent."*
> —*Ludwig Wittgenstein, 1922*

• Freud's work was based on small sample sizes that would not be sufficient for scientific examination.
• There have been strong accusations of sexism in concepts such as penis envy and the Oedipal complex. So-called penis envy, for example, might have had more to do with women's inferior financial and social status compared with that of men in Freud's day than with sexual conflict.

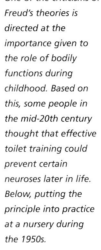

One of the criticisms of Freud's theories is directed at the importance given to the role of bodily functions during childhood. Based on this, some people in the mid-20th century thought that effective toilet training could prevent certain neuroses later in life. Below, putting the principle into practice at a nursery during the 1950s.

• Psychoanalysis does not recognize the importance of thought in neurosis: It is less concerned with the thoughts themselves than with the hidden meaning that, it claims, underlies them.
• Psychoanalysis and psychotherapy in general are expensive and time-consuming —a luxury that only certain people can afford. However, this is now changing, and many types of psychotherapy are subsidized, time-limited, and available to people from all walks of life.

BEHAVIOR THERAPY

Behaviorism is concerned with observable behavior (*see* Vol. 1, pp. 74–89). A strict behaviorist would not consider people's conscious experiences but rather the reports that they made about their responses or their observable behavior. Behavior is public; consciousness is private. Behaviorists think that the scientific study of psychology should deal with public facts. For example, a person might feel angry and report this or exhibit angry behavior, but the behaviorist would not speculate about the person's internal mental activity or state. Today, few psychologists would regard themselves as strict behaviorists. Nevertheless, many modern developments in psychology and psycho-therapy have been based on behaviorism.

Conditioning

Behaviorism formed the basis of learning theory or what is also known as stimulus–response (S–R) psychology. Stimulus–response psychology studies conditioning: the stimuli, or triggers, that cause responses, the rewards and punishments that maintain certain responses, and the changes in behavior that can be observed when the pattern of rewards and responses is altered. There are two types of conditioning:

Classical conditioning The study of classical conditioning began in the early part of the 20th century with Pavlov's experiments on dogs. Animals salivated when given food paired with a light, but eventually came to salivate when only

are potty-trained and are given a reward each time they use the toilet. Much real-life behavior is like this: We learn responses because they operate on our environment. Operant conditioning is sometimes called instrumental conditioning because the subjects or persons themselves are instrumental, or active, in obtaining reinforcement. For example, if left alone in a cot, babies might spontaneously pick up various toys to play with. They are not responding to the start of specific stimuli, like the food or food plus light, in classical conditioning; rather, they are operating on the environment. Whether they repeat the behavior will depend on whether the behavior meets with favorable or unfavorable results.

seeing the light. The salivation caused by the food alone is called an unconditioned response. The salivation caused only by the light is called a conditioned response. The animal has been taught—or conditioned—to salivate on seeing a light. The unlearning of this response is called extinction.

Operant conditioning In classical conditioning the conditioned response (for example, a dog salivating in response to a light) typically resembles the unconditioned response (salivation in response to food). But if you want to teach a new trick, you cannot use classical conditioning. To train a dog, for example, you must first persuade it to perform a behavior—or wait until it spontaneously performs a behavior—and then reward it afterward. If you keep doing so, the dog will eventually learn the trick or behavior. Acts that are rewarded—reinforced—are likely to be repeated; acts that are not reinforced are likely to die out. An important point in operant conditioning is that the behavior must be rewarded immediately. Too much delay between action and reward will not result in learning.

This type of conditioning or learning can be seen, for example, when toddlers

Operant conditioning is a form of stimulus–response learning used in training animals. Its principles, applied in behavior therapy, are based on reward and punishment. Above, a lab rat learns to find its way around a maze when its successful attempts are rewarded with a favorable result—a way out. But an animal must quickly receive reinforcement, such as a reprimand (right), if it is to learn new behavior.

Differences from psychodynamic therapy
In contrast to psychodynamic therapy, behavior therapy does not try to understand how people's past conflicts influence behavior; rather, it focuses directly on the behavior itself. The insights that psychodynamic therapies seek to achieve can be useful for the clients'

understanding of the causes of their problems; however, the understanding does not automatically result in a change in their behavior.

There might still be reasons why clients will not or cannot change their behavior. For example, they might understand that they fear speaking in public because, as a child, they were criticized by a parent when they expressed contrary opinions. But just understanding the cause will not remove the fear. Also, in contrast to psychodynamic therapy, behavior therapy concentrates on specific goals and changing behaviors in specific situations. Finally, it is more concerned than psychodynamic therapy with obtaining scientific validation of its techniques.

Therapeutic methods

Behavior therapy includes a number of different therapeutic methods based on learning theory. Essentially, behavior therapy sees disorders as the result of previous learning experiences. Often, they will be the result of a blend of classical and operant conditioning. For example, some children might be startled when they see the frightened response of their mother to a spider (a harmless stimulus). The children then withdraw from spiders or avoid such situations, which provides negative reinforcement. After this the fear of encountering a spider might increase to such a point that they feel frightened by merely thinking about a spider. It is how a phobia of spiders is acquired.

Behaviorists think that people develop problem behaviors as a way of coping with stressful situations. They think that behaviorist techniques used in experiments on learning can be applied to unlearning maladaptive behavior and learning more adaptive behavior.

Classical conditioning Maladaptive behavior in humans can be cured by classical conditioning. For example, in 1965 the eminent British psychologist Hans Eysenck (1916–1997), in the *International Journal of Psychiatry*, gave an example in which a man's impotency was triggered by a reaction to a certain wallpaper. If the stimulus can be removed—in this case the wallpaper—then so can the reaction (the impotence).

Desensitization is based on classical conditioning. It can be viewed as a "deconditioning" process for people who have become sensitized. Sensitization is a form of learning through which a person (or animal) learns to strengthen (intensify) his reaction to a weak stimulus if it is followed by a threatening or painful stimulus. For example, we learn to respond more intensely to the sound of a piece of equipment if it is followed by a crash. Desensitization is effective for treating fears or phobias. Arachnophobic people learn to be afraid of spiders and on this basis can unlearn their fear.

Systematic desensitization A behavioral technique based on classical conditioning can be used to treat phobias. The treatment involves weakening the established response (for example, fear of spiders) by strengthening the opposite response (relaxing when near a spider). The process works on the basis that it is impossible to feel two opposite things at the same time—in this instance it is impossible to be both anxious and relaxed at the same time. Therefore, one way of systematically

A child learns through sensitization to handle a frog that he might previously have learned to fear—associating frogs (a weak response) with another (strong) response, such as an unpleasant experience. He can unlearn his fear through reversing the process, or desensitization— touching the animal without any ill effect.

desensitizing people is to teach them to relax first before either imagining or being shown a picture of the feared situation. Sometimes the therapist can use drugs and hypnosis to help people who cannot otherwise relax.

Symbolic desensitization Behavior therapy distinguishes symbolic, or imaginal, desensitization from actual desensitization. In symbolic or imaginal desensitization the client does not encounter the feared situation, while in actual desensitization the client meets the feared situation in reality and so undergoes behavioral changes at the time. An example of this would be a man with agoraphobia (a fear of being alone in open spaces). He has perhaps been afraid to go shopping for many years. This is considered a dysfunctional and avoidant coping strategy that has strengthened, or reinforced, his fear of open spaces.

In symbolic desensitization the client and therapist would draw up a list of all feared stages of the journey to, say, the store. It would form a hierarchy of fear and might range from standing outside the front door to entering a large supermarket. Having taught the client how to relax, the therapist would talk through the various stages until at each stage the client could remain relaxed. If anxiety arose at any one stage, the client would be returned to that stage until the anxiety abated. When the client could visualize entering the supermarket without any tension or fear, he would be said to be systematically desensitized. In effect, he would have overcome the anxiety with relaxation.

By presenting milder forms of the stimulus and allowing clients slowly to accustom themselves to it, usually combined with relaxation techniques, it is possible gradually to make the stimulus like the original. Eventually, the client becomes desensitized to the stimulus, the reaction is lost, and the fear is removed.

Actual desensitization Actual desensitization is usually more effective than symbolic desensitization. In actual

KEY TERMS

- **Actual desensitization**—weakening a negative response by facing it in small doses.
- **Classical conditioning**—changing behavior through conditioned responses.
- **Conditioned response**—a learned response to a stimulus.
- **Flooding**—facing the negative situation with assistance.
- **Modeling**—teaching a positive response through a role model.
- **Operant conditioning**—teaching new behavior through rewards or punishment.
- **Sensitization**—a reaction to a weak stimulus that is followed by a strong stimulus.
- **Symbolic desensitization**—weakening a negative response by imagining positive responses.
- **Systematic desensitization**—weakening a negative response by strengthening a positive response.
- **Unconditioned response**—a naturally occurring response to a stimulus.

desensitization clients are exposed to the feared situation through a series of carefully graduated steps. Only when they have managed to tolerate each small step until the anxiety subsides do they move on to a more anxiety-provoking stage. Whenever possible, the behavior therapist aims to combine actual and symbolic desensitization.

Flooding In flooding clients are forced right away to confront the object triggering the fear response. For example, people with a fear of heights might be taken to the top of a tall building and prevented from escaping until the fear dies down. By preventing the client from avoiding or escaping from the feared situation, the anxiety is meant to be extinguished. However, although effective with some types of phobia, the increased anxiety for some people is too much. As a result, therapists use this type of technique with extreme caution.

Modeling An effective way of changing behavior is through modeling. In 1977 psychologist Albert Bandura (born 1925) showed in his social learning theory the importance of the role of models (such as parents) in transmitting to the other (the child) both specific behaviors and emotional responses. It is not unusual for a child to develop the same phobia as the parent. In treatment, observing the behavior of a model has proved successful in reducing fears and teaching new skills, and studies have shown that modeling successfully treats phobias.

Take, for example, a fear of snakes. Imitating a model in progressively feared behaviors with the snake, for example, touching it, the person gains a sense of mastery over the situation—a feeling that effective performance is the result of their own actions. This sense of mastery, personal effectiveness, or self-efficacy is a goal of most therapies.

Operant conditioning In practice the distinction between classical and operant conditioning is blurred in behavior therapy. For example, treating maladaptive behaviors through deconditioning or desensitization includes operant conditioning. Broadly speaking, however, classical conditioning tries to establish a new reaction that can then be reinforced (for example, replacing fear with relaxation), and operant conditioning tries to change how often an existing response occurs. This existing response can then be shaped to establish another response.

Behavior therapy makes good use of operant conditioning. The therapy is carefully constructed so that clients are encouraged, usually without their being aware of the encouragement, to respond in a certain way. These responses are immediately reinforced and, therefore, repeated more often.

Operant conditioning techniques have been used to help autistic children speak. Autistic people are unresponsive to the environment and show a marked lack of interaction with others. The work builds on existing sounds, such as grunts that the children already make (an existing response). The children are at first rewarded (reinforced) and then shaped, using food or some other special treat as an incentive. Eventually words can be strung together to form sentences (*see* pp. 71–80).

Limitations of behaviorism
• Behaviorism has traditionally paid little attention to thinking and reasoning. Behaviorists thought that taking any belief and attitude into consideration was a return to the kind of unscientific introspection that was criticized at the beginning of the last century (*see* Vol.1, pp. 74–89).

Modeling is a form of behavior therapy based on the fact that we find it safer to imitate someone we trust or respect. Left, a boy holds a python because he has seen his mother do the same thing.

- Learning, or stimulus–response, theory is based on animal experiments. But the laws of learning are not necessarily the same across all animal species, let alone readily transferable to people.
- Cognitive theorists have criticized behaviorism on the grounds that there is more to learning than associating a stimulus with a response. Learning cannot be understood solely through studying environmental factors. We first mentally encode external material and then operate on these mental representations rather than on actual external stimuli.
- One consequence of only looking at behavioral changes is that the client can substitute one symptom for another, for example, fear of snakes for fear of heights. Punishment might extinguish one behavior, but it is likely to resurface unless substituted with a more adaptive strategy. Sometimes behavior therapy is not substantial enough even for disorders such as phobias, where it has a good success rate, and a more "thinking" therapy that looks at underlying causes might be necessary.
- Historically, behavior therapy has tended to avoid ethical issues. For example, therapists play an authoritarian role: They can be manipulative and bullying. They also take control by choosing all the rewards or reinforcements for behavioral change. Insight, and therefore intellectual empowerment, is not encouraged. In particular, it is important to consider the ethical issue of punishment when considering treatment with children.
- Some early cognitive studies showed that even monkeys are not just the sum total of their observable behaviors: They can solve problems by trial and error and grasp concepts such as similarity, difference, and cause and effect.
- Behaviors learned under one set of conditions do not generalize to other situations, and changes in behavior therefore do not necessarily apply to more than one situation. Therapists must therefore work on making generalizable changes in behavior so that the person can show a variety of flexible behaviors.

COGNITIVELY BASED THERAPY

The term "cognition" comes from the Latin *cognoscere*, meaning to get to know. Cognition, as used in psychology, refers to the mental processes of perception, memory, and information processing through which we gain knowledge, solve problems, and plan for the future.

Cognitive psychology followed behaviorism in the late 1950s and early 1960s (*see* Vol. 1, pp. 104–117). It developed largely as a reaction to the narrow stimulus–response view of the behaviorists. Cognitive psychologists are concerned with the scientific study of mental processes, but they do not deal only with thought and knowledge; their approach has expanded to all areas of psychology, including clinical psychology. They do not believe, as behaviorists did, that our personality is the sum total of our responses to stimuli; rather, we have a mental model of reality and can think, plan, and make decisions on the basis of our stored memories.

In particular, cognitive psychologists note that even animals can learn to predict and control events. For example, a rat will soon learn that if a shock is paired with a sound, the sound will come to predict the shock. Dogs will learn not to jump a hurdle to avoid a shock if they have learned that they have no control over the shock. Predictability refers to a belief that something will happen. Beliefs are part of the mental world: They are made up of thoughts and perceptions—or cognitions. Both cognitively based therapies and cognitive behavior therapy focus on belief.

Cognitive theory

Cognitive theory concerns how we learn. It states that we do not passively respond to external events but actively develop our own explanations and give meaning to the world around us. These mental reconstructions of external events have been called "mental schema." Intelligence is defined by our mental representations of the world and how we subsequently operate on the representations, as opposed simply to reacting to the world itself. It allows us to think hypothetically, or on suppositions, without concrete items, or "reality," in front of us.

In 1955 U.S. psychologist George Kelly (1905–1967) presented his personal construct theory, which viewed people as scientists who try to predict and control events that take place in their everyday environment. Constructs are our concepts or beliefs about the world; they do not have a physical existence and, therefore, exist only in our minds. Since our constructs represent the events of our personal environment, Kelly refers to them as personal constructs.

Cognitions and the self

Cognitive psychologists are concerned with how we perceive, code, and categorize events. They look for how external events influence our memory so as to develop a theory that will predict our behavior. Among the main concepts they focus on in this area are the notions of the self, the schemata, and self-constructs.

The self is considered to be a system of self-concepts that organize and guide information relating to ourselves.

Schemata are theories or generalizations about the self that we gain from past experience. Evidence of schemata can be seen in automatic thoughts or behavior, or in stable cognitions, which remain the same despite external changes. When we face a particular situation, a schema related to the situation is activated. We categorize and measure our experiences through a set of schemas, or schemata. Normally, a person would match an appropriate schema to a particular external event. However, someone prone to depression would typically upset this orderly pattern and respond with one that is biased or overly negative. For example, when faced with an exam failure, the person might think, "I've always been a failure, there's nothing I can do about it, and it's always going to be the same." American psychologist Aaron Beck referred to this as a negative

cognitive triad because it involved three negative assumptions: about the past, the present, and the future (*see* p. 44).

Self-constructs are made up of how we think: They are coded as general and abstract representations of events, objects, and relationships in the real world. We become experts about our personal constructs and seek feedback that confirms our beliefs about ourselves, rather than that which contradicts them. We also go as far as to twist or distort information that does not support our self-construct. It is not surprising then that people's opinions of themselves are often not as others see them. For example, when faced with a situation in which we can speak up for ourselves but don't, we might either regard ourselves as tactful or cowardly depending on the view we have constructed about our core self and the information that we have gathered about that particular construct.

Theory and practice

The cognitive model sees mental disorders as resulting from distortions in cognitions (thoughts and beliefs). The aim of cognitively based therapies is to show clients that their distorted or irrational thoughts mainly contribute to their difficulties. If faulty modes of thinking can be modified or changed, the disorders can be alleviated.

Cognitive therapy is based on cognitive theory. It is concerned with how we see ourselves and how we give meaning to the world around us. We do so through mental representations that we make of things outside ourselves, which allow us to make suppositions about them.

CASE STUDY

A Cognitive Therapy Self-Monitoring Sheet

Cognitive therapy works through clients recognizing and changing beliefs—such as fear of flying—that cause problem behavior. By keeping a thought record during situations that cause problem behavior, they can monitor their thoughts and modify them.

Situation

Who? What? When? Where?

Sunday evening, in the airplane, on the runway, waiting for the plane to take off.

Moods

What did you feel? Rate intensity of mood 0–100%

Fear (98%)

Automatic thoughts (Images)

What was going through your mind just before you started to feel this way?

- I'm feeling sick.
- My heart is starting to beat harder and faster.
- I'm starting to sweat.
- I'm having a heart attack ("hot thought," the one that produces the most anxiety, depression, etc.).
- I'm going to die.

Evidence that supports the "hot thought"

- My heart is racing.
- I'm sweating.
- These are two symptoms of a heart attack.

Evidence that does not support the "hot thought"

- A rapid heartbeat can be a sign of anxiety.
- My doctor told me that the heart was a muscle, using a muscle is not dangerous, and therefore a rapid heartbeat is not dangerous.
- A rapid heartbeat does not mean that I am having a heart attack.
- I have had this happen to me before in airports, on airplanes, and when thinking about flying.
- In the past my heartbeat has returned to normal when I read a magazine, practiced deep breathing, did thought records, or thought in more calm ways.

Alternative/balanced thoughts

- My heart is racing, and I am sweating because I'm anxious and nervous about being on an airplane (95%).
- My doctor assured me that a rapid heartbeat is not necessarily dangerous, and in all likelihood my heartbeat will return to normal in just a few minutes (85%).

Rerate moods now

Fear (25%)

COGNITIVE THERAPY

Cognitive therapy aims to help people choose actions that are likely to change unhelpful ways of thinking—"learning from experience." It is not simply enough to help clients change the content of a particular thought; it is essential that they recognize and change the reasoning process that led to the false conclusion (the underlying belief) in order to avoid making similar errors in the future.

Since the beliefs have usually been present from an early age, they tend to be resistant to change. There are no simple ways of highlighting these faulty assumptions, but a useful start is to identify recurring stressful situations in the client's life.

The best way for the therapist to help

clients break the patterns is to encourage them to act against these deep assumptions.

In other words, cognitive therapy helps us see that there are many ways we give meaning to feelings and events and how these meanings might either make us feel better or worse. It is based on the principle that certain types of thoughts that we have about ourselves, for example, whether we are lovable or wanted, despised or boring, have a major effect on how we see the world. People are not disturbed by events but by the view they take of them. This type of therapy is called "cognitive" because it is primarily about changing our thoughts about ourselves, the world, and the future. In contrast to behavior therapists, cognitive therapists focus not so much on what people do as on how they think. They emphasize how we view ourselves and the world.

Cognitive theorists have identified two major factors that are likely to cause people to feel depressed, namely, a self-critical attitude, as outlined by Aaron Beck, and a sense of helplessness. While a behaviorist might encourage a depressed person to go out and be more social, a cognitive therapist would first look at the way that the person

> "Cogito ergo sum." ("I think therefore I am.")
> —René Descartes, 1637

would process this experience. For example, the behavioral change of going out to social events more often might be used by depressed people to confirm that they were unattractive since they are likely to "find" people who will confirm this. In other words, cognitive therapists suggest that depressed people might simply reinforce their view of themselves as inadequate. Before acting, they must first identify the faulty thinking that underlies the depression.

Cognitive therapy is based on Aaron Beck's cognitive restructuring therapy

CT BASICS

Cognitive therapy is based on the following principles:

- An ever-developing formulation of clients and their problems in cognitive (thinking) terms.
- A strong therapeutic alliance (a warm and trusting relationship between therapist and client).
- Collaboration between client and therapist and active participation by the client.
- Goal-oriented and problem-focused therapy.
- Initial emphasis on the present.
- Teaching clients to be their own therapist and emphasizing ways of preventing a relapse when therapy has ended.
- Structured sessions and generally time-limited therapy.
- Teaching clients to identify, evaluate, and respond to their dysfunctional thoughts and beliefs using a variety of techniques to change thinking, mood, and behavior.

FOCUS ON

(1976) and Albert Ellis's rational emotive therapy, or RET (1955). It also draws on Martin Seligman's theory of learned helplessness. Beck and Ellis were originally avid practitioners of psychoanalysis but became frustrated by what they considered the limitations of the psychodynamic approach.

AARON BECK
When practicing psychoanalytically, Aaron Beck (born 1921) tried to trace his clients' problems to sexual conflict arising from problems in childhood. However, he began to find that his clients applied certain patterns of thinking to their problems that he believed helped maintain the problems. For the first time, he felt he was getting inside his clients' minds and seeing the world as they saw it—something

he could not do using a psychoanalytic model. He based his work on the systematic study and clinical observation of depressed clients.

Beck's cognitive model of therapy makes three assumptions. Depressed people suffer from a cognitive triad of negative beliefs about themselves, their future, and their past experiences (*see* p. 105). The concept of underlying schemas can explain why clients maintain their pain-inducing and self-defeating attitudes despite positive factors in their lives. That is why depressed people are said to have a persistent cognitive, or thinking, negative bias.

Cognitive errors are faulty ways of thinking or processing information that maintain clients' belief in their negative schema despite evidence to the contrary. These errors are systematic and include "catastrophizing" or "all-or-nothing"

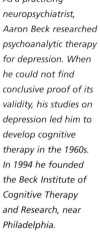

As a practicing neuropsychiatrist, Aaron Beck researched psychoanalytic therapy for depression. When he could not find conclusive proof of its validity, his studies on depression led him to develop cognitive therapy in the 1960s. In 1994 he founded the Beck Institute of Cognitive Therapy and Research, near Philadelphia.

thinking. Beck's therapy aims to identify the implicit and self-defeating assumptions a depressed person makes about themselves, change the way the person values these statements, and substitute more positive and adaptive assumptions. Beck's depression inventory (BDI) is now a widely used questionnaire in the measurement and monitoring of depressive symptoms.

Negative thinking

Beck believed that people prone to depression have developed a self-critical and negative way of looking at events. They expect to fail rather than succeed. They play down their successes and emphasize their failures. They also tend to blame themselves rather than external circumstances when things go wrong.

Rather than suggesting the existence of a subconscious, Beck suggested that automatic thoughts of which the client was unaware are operating to maintain problems. These thoughts develop into core beliefs such as "I am unlovable" or "I am only conditionally loved for being good." In other words, we are our thoughts, and the contents of our thoughts have a major effect on our emotions. For example, if we think we were or are unloved, we will feel unlovable, the world will appear unloving, and our sense of being unloved will be confirmed. This characterizes depression. These types of thoughts are called automatic because they operate on the margins of our consciousness as a continual internal monologue. If these thoughts can be identified, then the state of mind that they promote, be it anxiety or depression, can begin to be addressed. Beck based his work on depressed clients. However, since the end of the last century cognitive therapy has been successfully used to help clients with depression, panic disorder, phobias, anxiety, anger, stress-related disorder, relationship problems, drug and alcohol abuse, eating disorders, and most of the other difficulties that bring people to therapy.

ALBERT ELLIS

During his psychoanalytic training Albert Ellis (born 1913) was reluctant to accept the passive stance of the traditional psychoanalyst and became one of the most active psychoanalytically based therapists in the field. By 1955 Ellis had formed the basic theory and practice of rational emotive therapy (RET), and he was able to give a stimulating account of his conversion from psychoanalytic thinking to rational therapy.

Ellis believed that faulty thinking lay at the root of all psychological disorder and based his RET model on this. Like behaviorists and psychoanalysts, he believed that resolving people's early conditioning processes would give them the freedom to recondition themselves— that is, it would bring about change. Most importantly, he built on the behavioral and psychoanalytic models by stating that both approaches needed to stimulate clients to question and combat fear and hostility.

Rational emotive therapy

Rational emotive therapy has played a large part in cognitive behavioral therapy as we know it today. Ellis argued that many emotional difficulties are due to the irrational beliefs people bring to their experiences, and he showed how repetition reinforces these beliefs. Basically, rational emotive therapy looks at the way we worry about being worried.

Ellis believed that self-consciousness— or thinking about thinking—maintained emotional distress. Some people had learned to fear their own self-talk (see p.110). Once this was recognized, they could objectively define and analyze their own fears. For example, they could have been told that it was "terrible" or "horrible" or "awful" if they were unloved or disapproved of. They then kept telling themselves that being rejected or disapproved of was frightful. Ellis believed that this twice-told tale, in the great majority of cases, brought about neurosis. Very actively and energetically, people repeat this sort of message to

Albert Ellis had a difficult childhood that made him into "a stubborn and pronounced problem-solver." While practicing psycho-analysis, he found that clients he saw only once a week or less progressed as well as those he saw more frequently. He based his rational emotive therapy on his own experiences. In 1968 he founded the Institute of Rational Emotive Therapy, now known as the Albert Ellis Institute, in New York City.

themselves early on in childhood and internalize it as part of their character. Ellis strongly asserted that verbal repetition, or indoctrination, such as this was more important than the nonverbal cues and unconscious drives in which the psychoanalysts believed.

RET involves identifying the irrational ways in which we think about problems

> *"The best is the enemy of the good."*
> *—Voltaire, 1772*

and then helps us find less stress-provoking ways of dealing with them. Ellis used the A-B-C model of action, belief, and consequence to illustrate this. According to this process, a significant activating event A, such as being left by one's partner, is followed by a highly charged emotional consequence C, for example, feeling depressed.

Ellis stated that C, however, is usually thought to be a result of A because of the belief B that operates in between A and C. The belief might be "I am a worthless

10 IRRATIONAL BELIEFS EXAMINED IN RET

Albert Ellis and his colleagues have identified 10 common irrational beliefs that can lead to emotional distress:

1 I must be liked or accepted by every important person in my life for almost everything I do.

2 I must be successful and competent in everything I do if am to consider myself worthwhile.

3 It is awful and terrible when things are not the way I would like them to be. Things should be different.

4 I must feel anxious if something is, or might be, dangerous.

5 Events beyond our control cause human unhappiness, so we have no control over our negative feelings.

6 It is easier to avoid facing the many difficulties and responsibilities that come our way than to face them.

7 The past is all-important. If something once strongly affected our life, it cannot be altered.

8 When people act badly, inadequately, or unfairly, I blame them and view them as completely bad or pathetic—including myself.

9 Maximum happiness can be achieved by inertia and inaction or by passively enjoying oneself.

10 Everyone should be dependent on others, and I need someone stronger than myself on whom I can rely.

---

person because I have been rejected," or "I cannot accept being rejected," and will, in turn, affect future processes. Inappropriate emotions such as guilt and depression can only be alleviated if a change occurs in thinking and perception.

The central theme of RET is that we are uniquely rational as well as uniquely irrational. Our emotional or psychological disturbances are a result of our illogical or irrational thinking. If we learn to increase our rational thinking and decrease our irrational thinking, we can rid ourselves of most of our emotional or mental unhappiness. Ellis viewed neurosis as stupid behavior by a nonstupid person. According to him, a good deal of what we call thinking is in effect a type of appraisal that is strongly slanted or biased by previous perceptions or experiences, very personalized, often linked to physical changes (for example, a racing heart or sweating), and likely to involve some positive or negative action.

Theory of change in RET

Ellis believed that thinking causes the unwanted emotion in the first place, and that, by the same token, changing self-talk or internalized sentences would also change these emotions. Effective therapists should keep unmasking their clients' past and presenting the clients with their illogical thinking and self-defeating

internal sentences. They should do this by bringing the faulty thinking forcefully to the client's attention or consciousness, showing the clients how they are maintaining or causing their unhappiness, showing clients what are illogical links in their internalized sentences, and showing clients how to rethink, challenge, contract, and reword their sentences so that their internalized thoughts become more logical and efficient.

Ellis thought that autosuggestive (self-suggesting) thinking was an ingrained

During rational emotive therapy clients are encouraged to reassess their thinking about the situation that is causing distress. Faulty thinking might be influenced by the clients' way of thinking and might have been established in childhood.

and unreflected pattern. The thinking was acted out in external behavior that was self-defeating and neurotic. He agreed with psychoanalysts to the extent that most faulty thinking and beliefs were instilled by people's parents. Clients clung to them because of attachment reasons—that is, for fear of losing the parent on whom they were dependent. He added that these ideas also became part of the person's core beliefs or thinking patterns because they were internalized at a time in childhood before rational thought was possible.

COGNITIVE BEHAVIORAL THERAPY

Cognitive behavioral therapy (CBT) is a structured, problem-focused therapy incorporating cognitive, behavioral, and emotional change. CBT acknowledges the influence of behavior on thinking, but aims at behavioral as well as cognitive change, or insight. Unlike psychodynamic therapies, however, insight is not derived from examining clients' unconscious conflicts but rather their faulty thinking. Since it is based on the cognitive model, it seeks to change maladaptive behavior by changing the way we think.

The combination of cognition and behavioral change can be used to treat disorders such as phobias and posttraumatic stress disorder. Cognitive techniques, such as challenging negative automatic thoughts, and behavioral techniques, such as graded exposure and activity scheduling, are used to relieve symptoms by changing dysfunctional thoughts, beliefs, and behavior.

Cognitive behavioral therapy has also been widely applied to the so-called affective disorders: depression and anxiety. In addition, anxiety disorders with marked symptomatic anxiety (including panic disorder, agoraphobia, social phobia, obsessive-compulsive disorders, and generalized anxiety disorder) are likely to benefit from CBT. It is also effective in treating chronic fatigue and pain.

CBT differs from psychodynamic therapies in many ways:

KEY TERMS

• **Automatic thoughts**—negative thoughts that develop into core beliefs.
• **BDI**—Beck's depression inventory, a measurement of depressive symptoms.
• **Cognitive errors**—faulty thinking that maintains negative schemas despite contrary evidence.
• **Hot thought**—the thought that produces the most anxiety in a stressful situation.
• **RET**—rational emotive therapy, created by Albert Ellis.
• **Schemata**—beliefs about the self gained from past experiences.
• **Self-construct**—our view of events, objects, and relationships.
• **Self-talk**—internalized sentences or speech that reinforces negative or positive thoughts.
• **The A-B-C model**—the action, belief, and consequence that result in negative beliefs.
• **The self**—a system of beliefs through which we understand information about ourselves.

• CBT is not simply a talking cure on the part of the client, and the therapist is not a blank, silent screen but is continuously active and deliberately interacts with the client.
• Clients need to be actively engaged in the practice of therapy—for example, by keeping a diary and monitoring moods.
• CBT addresses the present and does not try to make conscious any unconscious conflicts from the past.
• CBT systematically investigates the client's automatic thoughts, core beliefs, and conclusions.
• Behavioral goals are set and monitored.
• CBT is usually time-limited.

CBT was developed and applied to depression during the 1970s, and many research studies report its effectiveness. It has become the treatment of choice for a wide range of mental-health problems and is said to be the best-researched form of psychological treatment.

Cognitive behavioral therapists suggest that it is important to alter people's beliefs to bring about durable changes in behavior. However, they also agree that changing beliefs alone is not enough; behavioral changes are ultimately more powerful than strictly verbal ones in affecting cognitive processes. The greatest change and sense of empowerment or self-efficacy come from successfully testing behaviors.

As we saw earlier, Beck's theory states that depressed people tend to appraise events from a negative and self-critical viewpoint. In treating depression, cognitive behavioral therapists try to help their clients recognize the distortions in their thinking and to bring the thinking and behavior more in line with reality—what can be observed objectively or inferred from observation. Most cognitive behavioral therapists agree that it is important to alter people's beliefs about themselves in order to change behavior. However, most also maintain that behavioral successes are more powerful than simply verbal changes in affecting cognitive processes—a sense of successful accomplishment ultimately comes from personal mastery of situations.

Theory and practice

CBT combines thinking and behavioral techniques to relieve psychological problems such as depression and anxiety. It is a general term for treatment methods that try to modify behavior with a view to changing maladaptive beliefs. It assumes two basic principles: The way that we feel depends on our thoughts and beliefs ("cognitions"); and the way we feel is influenced by what we do (our behavior).

The behavioral part of the treatment comes into play after clients devise alternative ways of viewing their situation, and the therapist encourages them to test these new alternatives in their daily life. The therapist uses a number of techniques to challenge negative thinking or "faulty beliefs." They include mood monitoring and diary keeping. For example, a woman

who believed she could not be happy without her husband would be asked to monitor how she felt before and after she was with him. If she felt more depressed afterward, the belief that she could not be happy without him would be challenged in therapy. Alternatively, behavioral techniques, such as desensitization for claustrophobia by gradually building up to going into a tunnel, would be combined with positive self-instruction to replace self-defeating internal dialogues, such as "I'm so nervous, I know I'll faint as soon as I get into the tunnel."

Limitations of cognitive therapies
• Complex psychological problems cannot be explained or changed by a simple concept like changing thinking. Cognitive theory has been seen as reductionist and mechanical because clients are reduced to the mechanics of their thinking and information processing. The person, or self, is thought to be made up of thinking and behavioral patterns. This view does not allow for philosophical dimensions when considering what constitutes a person.

Cognitive behavioral therapy works on thinking and behavior. The behavior strategy might be to desensitize someone who is afraid of heights by going up in an elevator in gradual stages (below). The cognitive strategy would be to replace fear-inducing thinking with a positive outlook.

THE ROLE OF FORMULATION IN CBT

Cognitive behavioral therapy usually lasts between 6 and 20 sessions. The formulation of a problem at the beginning is very important. Typically, it is made up of:

The problem list

This is a list of all the client's problems stated in concrete terms. The therapist takes note of all symptoms—including mood, thoughts, behavior, degree of motivation, and bodily symptoms (somatization), such as irritable bowel syndrome, inexplicable pains, or backache. The social situation is also noted: relationships, occupation, accommodation, finances, hobbies. Much of the information might be useful in describing core beliefs learned during childhood.

A typical problem list has 5–8 items and no more than 10. Usually one or two words describe the basics of the problem, for example, work difficulties, as well as cognitive, behavioral, and emotional components—for example, "I can't cope with my boss bullying me" (cognition); "I'll go in late tomorrow" (behavior); "but I'm still terrified of him" (emotion). Questionnaires such as the Beck depression inventory (BDI) can give therapists a baseline score by which they can measure progress later in the therapy.

The client outlines the problem and development of the problem, including triggers to anxiety states, for example. Predisposing factors might include the fact that panic attacks run in the family. A detailed description of the problem behaviors then follows, for example: where, when, how often, with whom, how distressing? Coping strategies are noted, as well as the context in which the problem occurs (What makes it better? What makes it worse?).

The therapist makes a note of the history of the client's development (familial, social, educational, and psychiatric) and relationships with parents, siblings, peers, authority figures, significant others, and major life events.

Core beliefs

The therapist makes a cognitive profile of the client to note typical and recurrent automatic thoughts. Therapists often structure this with the A-B-C formulation (activating event–belief–consequence). The therapist might suggest conditional beliefs to which the clients' symptoms are linked. For example, people with anxiety might hold beliefs such as "If I do this, then that will follow," or "If I get what I want, then I or others will suffer." These are called conditional assumptions. The therapist often draws them

out by offering hypotheses (theories) about the clients' views of themselves, of others, and of the world that seem to maintain their problems. For example, people with an anxiety state might view themselves as weak, helpless, and vulnerable, and the world as uncertain and frightening.

Triggers and activating situations

The therapist aims to identify external events that might act as triggers for core beliefs to be activated and for symptoms to occur. External events can reinforce a problem. For example, a businessman who had been promoted might find that the amount of public speaking involved in the new job triggers his anxiety. The public speaking as well as his fear of public speaking would be a trigger for his anxiety.

A working hypothesis

This part of the case formulation is the most important. The therapist "tells a story" to the client that ties together the problems on the problem list, the core beliefs, and the activating events and situations. The story tries to account for all the problems on the problem list. The working hypothesis can be one that explains and describes how core beliefs are activated by life events.

Origins of problem

In contrast to psychoanalysis, CBT does not focus on the origin of the problem. Instead, the therapist briefly describes episodes in the client's early history involving parents or other caretakers that might explain how the client came to learn the core beliefs. The original causes of problems can include how the client has failed to learn behaviors, such as social skills, or has not been able to copy (model) a parent successfully.

Treatment plan

The first step in a treatment plan is to set goals for therapy. The problem list is narrowed down to areas on which the client wants to concentrate. Generally, most only have one or two that become goals for therapy. The goals should be clearly defined, for example, "Make John more assertive" or "Decrease John's anxiety in social situations," rather than "Decrease John's chronic anxiety state." In this way treatment can be more effectively monitored. Asking the client questions such as "How would your life be different if you no longer had this problem?" also helps define and list treatment goals.

• Some people have challenged the assumption that feelings follow thoughts. For example, a negative thinking style does not necessarily precede depression but might be part of or accompany the depression itself. Research shows that in severely depressed clients, once the depression lifts, so does the negative thinking. Therefore, a predisposition to depression because of a cognitive (thinking) style is questionable. Most psychiatrists believe that the negative thinking found in depression is a symptom rather than a cause of depression.

• Beck's negative triad could be considered a particular type of depression (a subtype) rather than reflecting all types of depression.

• Like psychoanalytic notions of the unconscious, schemas are loosely defined.

• Cognitive therapy and CBT are "top-down" in that they are directed by the therapist. While the focus is on the internal world of the client, the approach contrasts with therapies where the therapy is client led.

• There is a danger the CBT approach can become technique driven and forget that successful therapy depends on a good therapeutic relationship.

• Studies show drugs work as well as cognitive therapies.

• Cognitive-based therapies have been particularly useful with depression and anxiety, but their usefulness in other problems, such as obsessive-compulsive disorder, has been questioned.

• Underlying causes such as early relationships are often ignored, and CBT might benefit from integrating some psychoanalytic ideas.

• In order to use CBT successfully, clients need to be relatively motivated, articulate, and literate, since they must keep a diary, fill in questionnaires, and engage in active hard work during therapy.

• Goals and time limitations put pressure on the client to "perform" in ways that psychoanalysis would not.

• The focus in therapy is on the client's problems, and so, like many therapies, it can be seen to have a negative bias.

• Cognitively based therapy works best on clients who have a clearly defined problem or diagnosis, such as generalized anxiety disorder, depression, specific phobia, or posttraumatic stress disorder. Those with less clearly defined problems or who are unable to clearly articulate their problems would not be considered suitable for cognitive-based therapy.

A CBT TREATMENT EXAMPLE

FOCUS ON

CBT aims to help people identify the kinds of stressful situations that produce their symptoms and to alter the way they cope with the situations. This applies to both physiological symptoms, such as headaches, and psychological symptoms, such as depression. For example, a man who suffers from tension headaches would be asked to begin by keeping a record of their occurrence and rating the severity of each headache, as well as the circumstances in which it occurred. Next, he is taught how to monitor his responses to these stressful events and is asked to record his feelings, thoughts, and behavior at three stages: before, during, and following the event. After a period of self-monitoring, certain relationships are often noticeable between situational variables, his thoughts, and his emotional, physical, and behavioral responses. For example, the following pattern might be observed:

•**Criticism at work by a supervisor:** situational variable.
•**Thoughts:** "I can't do anything right."
•**Emotional, behavioral, and physical responses:** depression, withdrawal at work, headaches.

The next step is to identify the beliefs or expectations that might explain the headache reaction: for example, "I expect to do everything perfectly and get upset by any criticism" or "I judge myself harshly, become depressed, and end up with a headache." Links might also have been made between having headaches as a child and feelings of helplessness. The final—and most difficult—step is to try to change something about the stressful situation, his way of thinking about it, or his behavior. The behavioral options might include finding a different job (change of situation), recognizing that the need to perform perfectly creates unnecessary anguish over errors (change of thinking or belief), or acting more assertively in relationships instead of withdrawing (change of behavior). This should lead to a decrease in headaches.

Cognitive behavioral therapy encourages thought monitoring. This might take the form of keeping a diary in which the client records the situations that caused anxiety, the thoughts that accompanied the anxiety, and the progress the client made in rethinking the situation.

OTHER THERAPIES

Most psychotherapists are eclectic—that is, they use a combination of elements from the numerous therapies that have developed since Freud's time. Below are some of the better established and widely used therapies:

Humanistic therapy (*see* p. 116).

Gestalt therapy is based on gestalt theory (*see* Vol. 1, pp. 46–51), which states that we think in terms of whole situations rather than a combination of separate elements. It was created by Fritz and Laura Perls in the 1940s.

Existential therapy was created by Ludwig Binswanger (1881–1966), who based it on the existentialist philosophy of Martin Heidegger (1889–1976). It tackles

major philosophical issues in the client's life, such as death, freedom, and isolation.

Feminist therapy explores gender and other social roles that contribute to the client's psychological distress. It does not cater solely to women and can also be beneficial to men.

Systemic and family therapies Systemic therapy is not concerned with the origins of problems; rather, it seeks to influence the dynamics of various relationships. Family therapy is a systemic therapy that focuses on interaction between family members (*see* also pp. 38 and 49–50).

Art therapy uses creating or viewing art as a way to express feelings. The goal is not to create a finished piece but to use the creative process to help clients with their problems—the end product might never be viewed outside the therapeutic situation.

Drama therapy uses aspects of the theater to explore the client's "story." Clients can use verbal and nonverbal ways to enact their own drama, which can help

> *"What one truly understands clearly articulates itself, and the words to say it come easily."*
> —Nicolas Boileau, 1674

them dissipate psychological tensions and understand their situation.

Solution-focused therapy seeks to find effective ways in which clients can solve their problems in a fixed period of time. It can take many forms and focuses on the present rather than the past.

Group therapy is conducted by a qualified therapist with a group of clients. Each member of the group benefits through interaction with the others.

Transactional analysis, also known as TA, is a psychoanalytically based group therapy created by Eric Berne (1910–1970). It works on three ego states (parent, child, and adult) through which we relate to others (*see* also Infant Attachment, Vol. 4, pp. 112–129).

Humanistic therapy

In contrast to the other approaches outlined in this chapter, humanistic therapy seeks to understand people's personal perception of events without imposing any theory or preconceptions.

Humanistic theories are also called phenomenological (*see* Vol. 1, pp. 66–73), since the phenomenological approach focuses on subjective experience (how people experience their lives). Very simply, it states that to understand people, we have to see the world through their eyes. Unlike approaches that aim to develop theories and predict behavior, the phenomenological approach is simply interested in a person's self-concept, feelings of self-esteem, and self-awareness. The method assumes that clients are experts on their own experience and hold the key to their own cure. Emphasis in therapy is on the therapist's genuineness, or "unconditional positive regard," that is, unconditional acceptance by another—a feature that is likely to have been missing in the client's upbringing.

Humanistic therapies emphasize qualities that distinguish people from animals, such as free will and the drive toward self-actualization. Humanists believe that we have a strong motivational force, or drive, toward developing our potential. Although environmental and social obstacles might stand in our way, our natural tendency is to progress beyond where we are now. The humanistic approach is more aligned with literature and the humanities than with science. In fact, some humanists reject scientific psychology, claiming that its methods have little to contribute to our understanding of human nature.

Rogerian therapy (*see* Vol. 1, pp. 67–71) is an example of this approach. It is based on people's reports of their subjective experiences, rather than on measurable behavior or on observations by others. Carl Rogers (1902–1987) believed that psychological problems lie in the "gap" between people's real or spontaneous self and that which they present to the world.

The gap is thought to be the result of conditional love by parents in childhood. A child's need for love and acceptance is paramount, and, when unmet, leads to inner confusion and conflict. Self-criticism and perfectionism are typical outcomes of this type of upbringing, and clients are likely to feel at odds with, or unaccepting of, their real selves.

The main features of this type of therapy are the therapist's acceptance and empathy, through which Rogers believed that positive change was possible. Since therapy is client-centered, measures of success are taken from clients' descriptions of their "real" versus their "ideal" self at various points during therapy.

Overcoming the odds. Humanistic therapy believes that humans are motivated to reach their full potential. It does not try to understand people through any particular line of thinking, but seeks to view their situation through their own eyes.

COMMON FACTORS IN THERAPIES

Psychotherapy shows benefits for a wide range of mental disorders compared to no treatment. However, studies cannot show which therapy works best for which disorder. David Shapiro of Leeds University, England, called this the equivalence paradox, since all therapies are considered to be generally equivalent, or of the same value. Also, some disorders, such as anxiety, might improve without any treatment at all.

The main features of long-lasting success in therapy are:
• A confiding relationship.
• Instillation of hope and acceptance of the client's feelings.
• Explanation of the rationale that underlies the treatment
• Exchange of information.
• Venting emotion.
• Acquiring understanding and insight.
• Learning new behaviors.
• Reassurance and support.
• Desensitization. All therapies are said to desensitize the client. Repeatedly discussing distressing experiences in the security of a therapeutic setting might gradually extinguish the anxiety associated with them.
• Reinforcement of adaptive responses, or behavioral change.

The key relationship

When all treatments are pooled, the effectiveness of different types of therapy depends primarily on the client and the therapist forming a good working relationship. Empathy, genuineness, reassurance and support, and reinforcement by the therapist of the client's newly learned adaptive responses tend to be more important in producing change than the specific therapeutic method.

KEY POINTS

• **Psychoanalysis** seeks to make conscious unacceptable feelings we repress in our unconscious.
• It works on the client's resistance, transference, and fixations.
• Freud's followers developed other psychodynamic therapies that emphasize social, cultural, and spiritual factors or the role of the ego rather than sexuality.
• The main criticisms of psychodynamic therapies include lack of scientific proof, emphasis on childhood sexuality, cost, and its appeal mainly for articulate and motivated clients.
• **Behavior therapy** is based on stimulus–response learning and classical and operant conditioning.
• It only focuses on the behavior that causes problems.
• Desensitization is based on classical conditioning.
• It can be symbolic or actual.
• Operant conditioning is used to help autistic children speak.
• Two other methods are flooding and modeling.
• Limitations of behavior therapy include ignoring the role of thinking, applying theories based on animal experiments to people, and avoiding ethical issues.
• **Cognitive therapies** are based on the cognitive theories and therapies developed by Aaron Beck and Albert Ellis.
• **CBT** works through changing behavior and thought.
• It has proved highly successful in treating many disorders.
• **Other major psychotherapies** include humanistic, gestalt, existential, feminist, systemic and family, art, drama, solution-focused, and group therapies, and transactional analysis.
• **Humanistic therapy** views clients' problems through their own eyes rather than any particular school of thought.
• It provides unconditional positive regard, which clients probably did not have in their childhood.
• **Rogerian therapy** is client-centered. It focuses on the gap between the client's true self and the one they show the world.
• Chief factors for success in any form of psychotherapy include an understanding by clients of the basis of the therapy, a trusting relationship between clients and therapist that allows clients to express their emotions, acceptance of the client's problems by the therapist, understanding and insight on the part of the client, and support and reassurance from the therapist that encourages new adaptive behavior from the client.
• The most crucial factor—and the one on which all psychotherapies are founded—is the client–therapist relationship.

CONNECTIONS

• Mental Disorders: pp. 20–67
• Abnormalities in Development: pp. 68–91
• Gestalt Psychology: Volume 1, pp. 46–51
• Psychoanalysis: Volume 1, pp. 52–65
• Behaviorism: Volume 1, pp. 74–89
• Cognitive Psychology: Volume 1, pp. 104–117

Physical Therapies

Treating the body to relieve symptoms of mental disorders

Psychotherapeutical approaches, such as the "talking cures," are not the only treatments available for mental disorders. Many people diagnosed with mental disorders find it difficult to get counseling or psychotherapy unless they have good access to private practitioners. The majority will be treated by a "physical" therapy, or medication, either by their family doctor or a psychiatrist, or if their symptoms are severe, even in a hospital.

Despite the fact that since the late 20th century successive governments both in the United States and Europe have taken steps to close down psychiatric hospitals and introduce services outside of them known as "community care" (*see* pp. 142–163), many mental-health patients are still treated within medical settings such as hospital clinics and wards. The majority of staff working in the medical services of mental health are medically trained as doctors or nurses, and the

number of nonmedically trained psychologists will probably be in a minority.

Why is it that people with mental disorders are prescribed physical therapies rather than psychological ones? Often it is because physical therapies are the only options that might have an effect on a disorder. The answer is complex, however, and involves how services for mental-health problems have evolved, the power and influence of different professional groups, and economic and

There is a large variety of drugs available to treat many mental disorders. Doctors often prescribe medication since psychological services might not be readily available or entirely suitable for certain disorders.

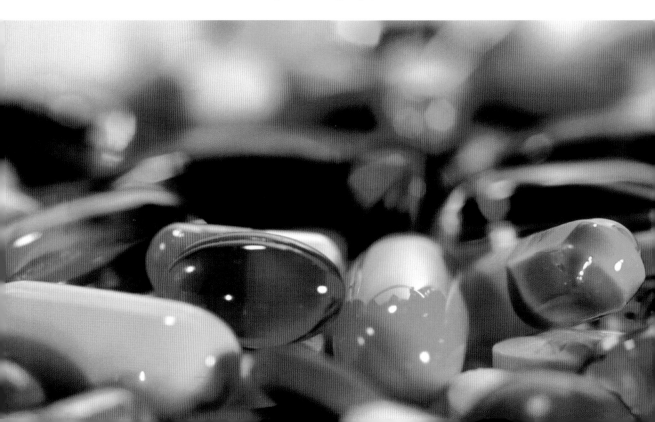

political interests involved in the funding of treatment for mental disorders. The choice between physical and nonphysical treatments is not just restricted to western society but can be found in many cultures. Many nonwestern societies have explained mental disorders in religious or spiritual terms, and care for people with mental-health problems is frequently seen as a duty for the family or as a charity offered by religious leaders. In contrast, other cultures have attempted primitive physical treatments for these conditions in the past, including trephining, whereby a hole is cut into the skull to release evil or malevolent spirits.

PHYSICAL APPROACHES

The treatment of mental-health problems as a medical illness and the provision of hospital care and drugs is largely a product of the west (*see* Vol. 1, pp. 16–21, and Vol. 6, pp. 20–67). Even within western countries it has only been in recent times that the care of people who experience mental-health problems has been dominated by medicine and psychiatry.

During the 17th and 18th centuries mental institutions used some forms of physical treatment, such as harnesses and restraints, to pacify the most disturbed and distressed patients. Other inhumane treatments, such as revolving chairs and blindfolds, were also used to shock people out of their madness.

Some institutions also used more psychologically based treatments, such as mesmerism and hypnosis, adopted in France in the 18th century. However, many institutions were purely custodial and did not seek to treat or cure their inmates.

Birth of psychiatry

By the beginning of the 19th century some doctors, such as Philippe Pinel in France (1745–1826), and social reformers,

A skull dating from 2200–2000 B.C. excavated from near Jericho, Israel, shows that physical approaches to mental health date back several millennia. Holes were trephined, or bored in the skull, probably with the intention of letting out spirits that caused the illness. The patient must have survived, since the holes show signs of healing.

like William Tuke (1732–1822) and his brother Samuel (1784–1857) in England, were questioning the inhumane treatment of inmates of mental institutions. This was the beginning of the medical discipline of psychiatry: Doctors believed that mental disorders were no different than any other medical problem and originated from a disease of the brain and the nervous system. It was widely believed that there was a strong link between mind and body, and that psychological functioning might be related to the shape of the skull: A common representation of psychology even today is the phrenologist's head, which links our faculties to regions mapped on the skull.

Medicine and mental health

After World Wars I and II (1914–1919 and 1939–1945) many people suffered from psychological problems resulting from shell shock and brain injuries sustained in combat. This placed even greater pressures on the old asylums. In addition, the institutions were then very much run by medically qualified staff and included nurses and care staff to look after the inmates.

As more drugs were developed during the 1950s, scientists hoped that many of the most serious mental disorders could be cured or their symptoms suppressed by medication. This would also lead to the closure of many of the old and large mental institutions. Similarly, as scientists discover more about the brain and neurotransmitters (*see* Vol. 2, pp. 20–39), some of them hope that certain mental disorders might sometime in the near future be eliminated.

The medical model

The application of the medical model to mental-health problems (*see* pp. 16–17 and 23, and box p. 120) was the most

THE MEDICAL MODEL

FOCUS ON

• Doctor interviews patient to find out what the problem is and the nature of the symptoms.
• Where appropriate, the doctor arranges for diagnostic tests to record measurable signs of the illness.
• Doctor makes a differential diagnosis: It identifies the most likely cause of the illness.
• Doctor suggests a prognosis: It predicts the course of the illness.
• Doctor prescribes a choice of treatment based on the diagnosis.

A doctor and patient discuss the nature of the patient's symptoms. The doctor might send the patient for tests to arrive at a diagnosis. The procedure forms the basis of the medical model of illness.

influential approach in the treatment of mental disorders in the 20th century. This was despite the breakthroughs of Freud and psychoanalysis at the beginning of the century (*see* Vol. 1, pp. 52–65), which, although they might have reshaped our thinking about the mind, did not necessarily lead to widespread changes in the care and treatment of people with mental disorders.

Essentially, the medical model assumes that mental disorders are caused by some malfunctioning, or pathology (disease), of the brain, and that this shows up in two ways: signs and symptoms. For physical illness signs are objective indicators that the body is malfunctioning, for instance, high blood pressure as a result of some underlying pathology or disease, such as

renal failure or kidney disease. Symptoms are feelings and sensations that the patient has because the body is not functioning normally, such as sickness and nausea or flashing before the eyes when blood pressure is raised.

For mental disorders, however, there are very few objective tests that could detect reliable signs of an illness. Psychiatrists rely either on their patients to describe their problems, or they consider the observations and reports from others, such as relatives and nursing staff. Symptoms, such as hearing voices, being depressed, or feeling anxious, are used by psychiatrists to make a diagnosis. The diagnosis is a judgment based on the doctor's knowledge and experience as to the underlying pathology, or disease, that might be affecting the patient.

Once psychiatrists make a diagnosis, they select a treatment that they think will reduce the patient's symptoms. The diagnosis also helps predict the future course, or prognosis, of the disorder—whether the patient will get better and how long that process might take.

The reliability problem

Psychologists are frequently critical of the medical model and psychiatric diagnoses (*see* pp. 6–19). Many psychiatric diagnoses have suffered problems in the past because of poor agreement between psychiatrists as to the actual diagnosis. This is called the reliability problem because not all psychiatrists reach their diagnoses in the same way (*see* pp. 35–36). Even if a diagnosis was reliable, it might not be very helpful in either deciding on the treatment or knowing the patient's prognosis. Many different mental disorders are treated with similar drugs or other forms of treatment. For example, antidepressants are frequently prescribed to people diagnosed with depression, obsessional-compulsive disorder, eating disorders, anxiety disorder, or post-traumatic stress disorder.

Finally, many psychologists stress that mental disorders can have several causes and are very skeptical about the ability of a solely medical-based model of physical disease to account for their origins. Very few, if any, so-called mental disorders have a specific biological cause or pathology that can be identified within an individual patient and is known with certainty to the psychiatrist. Doctors and psychiatrists now generally accept that explanations of mental disorders need to include physical, psychological, and cultural factors.

> *"The desire to take medicine is one feature that distinguishes man, the animal, from his fellow creatures."*
> —William Osler, 1890

Similarly, an effective treatment for a severe mental disorder will also include a combination of physical treatments, psychological interventions, and also good social care.

Principal physical interventions
This chapter looks at the more common medical, or physical, treatments used to relieve the suffering and symptoms of mental disorders, including drugs, such as anxiolytics and antidepressants and antipsychotic and mood-stabilizing drugs, and physical interventions such as electroconvulsive therapy (ECT) and psychosurgery.

ANXIOLYTICS
Everybody feels anxious sometimes. Doctors regard anxiety as clinical when it is more severe or persistent than normal, or when it occurs in situations that cause some incapacity to the person. In practice, people ask for help with anxiety when they can no longer tolerate it, but this might vary in terms of the actual level of anxiety as assessed by the doctor or psychologist.

Three main types of anxiety are recognized: generalized anxiety disorder (GAD), panic disorder, and phobic anxiety. Other types of phobia include specific ones that are very common, such as fear of spiders and snakes, and social phobia, which is shown by extreme anxiety in social situations (*see* pp. 23–30).

Drugs that doctors commonly prescribe to treat anxiety are known as anxiolytics. "Anxiolytic" literally means dissolving anxiety. The drugs are also often called tranquilizers. Anxiolytics are widely used to treat most types of anxiety, including anxiety that is associated with depression. Specific phobias are not normally treated with medication, except in special circumstances, such as severe flying phobia. Anxiolytics are also widely used to treat sleep problems, although doctors only recommend this as a short-term treatment.

Benzodiazepines
The most commonly used anxiolytics are called benzodiazepines, the best known of which are diazepam (Valium) and lorazepam (Ativan). Benzodiazepines act at specific receptor sites in the brain for the neurotransmitter GABA (gama-amino butyric acid) by increasing its activity. Scientists think that abnormalities of some GABA receptors might underlie certain anxiety disorders.

Before the 1960s doctors treated anxiety with barbiturates, which are addictive. Benzodiazepines were introduced as the nonaddictive alternative and soon became extremely popular. At the time, however, doctors did not know that benzodiazepines can also lead to addiction, and millions of people were prescribed the drugs. Although such drugs are very effective in damping down the symptoms of anxiety, when people try to stop taking them after using them for a long time, some develop withdrawal symptoms worse than the original anxiety.

Withdrawal symptoms include many that are very similar to those experienced in anxiety, such as panicky feelings, sleep problems, irritability, shakiness, and agitation. The symptoms gradually wear off over a period of weeks or months,

Other treatments

Most modern treatment guidelines for anxiety emphasize that psychological methods of treatment should be tried before medication. There is a great deal of research showing that quite simple psychological therapies can be very effective in treating the common types of anxiety (*see* pp. 20–67).

Stimulants Just as tranquilizers can dampen anxiety, so stimulants can worsen it. A widely used stimulant is caffeine, which is contained in tea, coffee, and cola drinks. People who are prone to anxiety should cut down on or avoid it. Alcohol can be a stimulant and a depressant. Although it can quickly reduce anxiety, long-term use can lead to dependence and withdrawal symptoms that actually worsen the feelings of anxiety.

ANTIDEPRESSANTS

When doctors think it essential to use drug treatment for anxiety, they usually recommend an antidepressant. This might seem paradoxical: Antidepressants are used for treating depression. That was their original use, but there is now a great deal of evidence that antidepressants, particularly the selective serotonin reuptake inhibitor, or SSRI, types of drugs (*see* p. 124), effectively treat generalized anxiety disorder, social phobia, agoraphobia, and panic disorder.

The advantage of using antidepressants is that they are not addictive. But the disadvantage is that they have side effects. Also, many mental-health professionals feel that people can get to rely on drugs to treat their symptoms when it would be better to learn new psychological ways of coping. Anxiety symptoms often stay with a person for years, and long-term drug treatment should be avoided whenever possible. Where drugs are thought necessary, they should be combined with psychological treatment. Treatment of anxiety should never depend on drugs alone.

Other conditions classified under anxiety include obsessive-compulsive disorder (OCD) and posttraumatic stress

although in rare cases they can be more severe and include confusion or even epileptic fits.

Because the withdrawal symptoms are so similar to the anxiety for which the drugs were prescribed in the first place, it took nearly 20 years before doctors fully realized that benzodiazepines can be addictive. Some feel that the problem has been exaggerated because the majority of patients do not get addicted to benzodiazepines even after prolonged use.

Benzodiazepines are still available and are quite widely used, but now doctors are much more careful to prescribe them for a shorter time and in lower doses to reduce the risk of addiction.

The majority of people experience anxiety or depression at some stage of their lives. If a point is reached at which the patient's life is severely affected, a doctor might prescribe anxiolytics or antidepressants to alleviate the symptoms.

disorder (PTSD). OCD is normally treated by cognitive-behavioral therapy (*see* pp. 111–114); but if it does not work or is not practical, then an antidepressant of the SSRI type is an effective second choice of treatment. Due to the disadvantages of medication, psychological treatment is the preferred approach to PTSD, but antidepressants can also help.

Depression
Like anxiety, depression is a normal human emotion and is regarded as clinical only when it becomes particularly severe and has some specific characteristics (*see* pp. 39–44). The type of depression that is now called major depression is characterized by a persistent depressed mood and a loss of interest or pleasure in anything, together with other signs and symptoms, such as weight loss, sleep disturbance, lack of energy, feelings of guilt, and thoughts of suicide.

Much more common are the less severe forms of depression, such as those that follow the breakup of a relationship, and that do not have all the characteristic features of major depression. This form of depression is known as adjustment disorder with depressed mood. Drugs are mostly prescribed for major depression rather than for adjustment disorder.

Anxiety is usually treated with tranquilizers. Doctors recommend that people with a tendency to acquire an anxiety disorder should avoid stimulants such as caffeine, which is found in coffee.

Tricyclics and MAOIs
Antidepressants, as the name implies, are used for treating patients with clinical depression. Two types of the drug were discovered—by chance—in the 1950s: the tricyclic antidepressants and the monoamine oxidase inhibitors, or MAOIs.

Tricyclic antidepressants derive their name from their chemical structure. The first such drug was imipramine. Psychiatrists gave it to patients diagnosed with schizophrenia because they thought that it might be a useful treatment. Swiss psychiatrist Roland Kuhn, one of the doctors on the ward where the research was being carried out, realized that although the drug was not treating the schizophrenia, it was improving the mood of people who were depressed. There are now more than 20 different types of tricyclic antidepressants available.

MAOIs are so called because they act on monoamine oxidase. The MAOI drug iproniazid was being used to treat tuberculosis when in the mid-1950s it was again observed that people who were depressed showed improvement when they were treated with it. MAOIs are not much used now because they have side effects, including a rapid rise in blood pressure, which might lead to bleeding in the brain if certain foods that contain

naturally occuring amines, such as cheese, are eaten along with the drug. MAOIs are also dangerous when taken with some treatments for colds.

Mood and neurotransmitters

Neurotransmitters (*see* Vol. 2, pp. 20–39) are contained in vesicles (tiny vessels) in nerve endings. When a nerve impulse travels along a nerve cell, the transmitter is released into the synaptic gap, the space between two nerve cells. The transmitter activates specific receptors on the next nerve cell, generating another nerve impulse. Excess transmitter is actively taken back by the first nerve cell.

Certain neurotransmitters, particularly noradrenaline and serotonin, play an important part in controlling mood.

A nerve impulse traveling along a nerve cell releases the neurotransmitter into the synaptic gap between two nerve cells. Normally, appropriate receptors on another nerve would absorb some of the neurotransmitter, and the rest would be taken back into the original nerve. An SSRI blocks this reabsorbtion, so the neurotransmitter stays longer in the gap and has greater effect on mood.

After the discovery of tricyclics and MAOIs scientists recognized that the drugs were acting through their effect on these neurotransmitters. A lot of research went into finding new drugs that would act on only one neuro-transmitter, particularly serotonin, which was thought to be the most important in relation to depression.

The research led to a whole new group of drugs called the selective serotonin reuptake inhibitors (SSRI). Tricyclic and SSRI antidepressants act by blocking the reuptake of neurotransmitters so that more remains in the synapse (the junction of two nerve cells) for a longer period of time and has a prolonged effect. Tricyclic antidepressants block both noradrenaline and serotonin reuptake, but SSRI drugs are selective serotonin reuptake inhibitors and govern the reuptake of serotonin more than that of noradrenaline. MAOIs work by blocking the enzyme monoamine oxidase, which breaks down the neurotransmitters inside the cells. This means that more of the neurotransmitter is available for release. Both types of antidepressants, therefore, work by increasing the effect of neurotransmitters.

Prozac

The most well known of the SSRIs, and the most widely used, is fluoxetine, best known as Prozac. It is no more effective than other antidepressants, but in general it has fewer side effects. Because Prozac and the other SSRI drugs have fewer harmful effects on the heart and other body organs, these drugs are safer in overdose than the older tricyclic antidepressants. This is an important safety factor because people with severe clinical depression might take an overdose in an attempt to end their life. Despite this, the SSRI drugs do have some disadvantages. A small number of people develop nausea or even vomiting while taking these drugs. There are also reports of increased aggression and suicidal impulses in a few people taking Prozac, but this is disputed and controversial. Tricyclic antidepressants

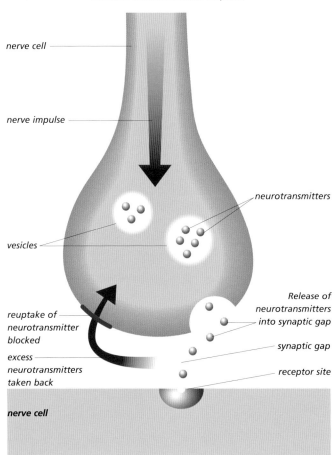

Selective neurotransmitter reuptake

nerve cell

nerve impulse

neurotransmitters

vesicles

Release of neurotransmitters into synaptic gap

reuptake of neurotransmitter blocked

synaptic gap

excess neurotransmitters taken back

receptor site

nerve cell

Prozac Nation

The widespread prescription of SSRIs gives rise to the question "To what degree do you need to be clinically depressed to either benefit from or receive prescribed medication?" It is suggested that many people receiving SSRIs are doing so to lift their mood (gain happiness) rather than to diminish their depression, and that people who are not clinically depressed are prescribed SSRIs to enhance their mood. Is this any different than some people taking street drugs or other illegal substances to "get their kicks"? It raises the possibility of lifestyle or mood-altering drugs that could be legally prescribed in addition to those traditionally used, such as caffeine, alcohol, and nicotine (*see* pp. 51–57). Until the SSRIs came along, this was not a major problem since people were resistant to taking psychoactive medications because of side effects, while SSRIs seem to have fewer of them.

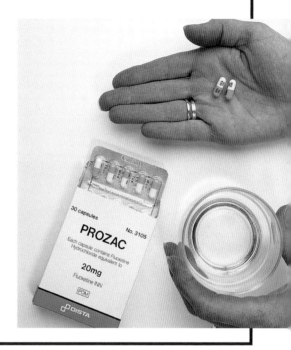

A pack of 20-mg capsules of Prozac, a brand of fluoxetine. After its introduction in 1986 this SSRI antidepressant became so popular that annual sales up to 2001 were said to exceed $2 billion.

have other side effects, including a dry mouth, weight gain, and effects on blood pressure and heart rate.

Treatment with SSRIs

It takes two or three weeks for an antidepressant to have full effect. Even then, only about two-thirds of patients will see significant benefit. Interestingly, about a third will improve if they are given a placebo, an inactive tablet made of chalk or some other inert substance. In some cases treatment for as long as four or six weeks might be necessary to get any benefit. If the first antidepressant does not work after that length of time, then the doctor will normally try a different antidepressant. Once the patient responds to it, treatment is normally continued for around six months after a single episode of acute depression. This is called continuation treatment. Without this prolonged treatment depression will return in

around 50 percent of patients, while that only happens in 15 percent of patients who are given continuation treatment. Some people who develop chronic or recurring depression might need antidepressant treatment for much longer periods of time.

> **"It is estimated that Prozac has treated more than 40 million patients worldwide since its introduction in 1986."**
> **—Prozac.com**

It is seldom enough to use antidepressants as the only way of treating depression. Many people with milder forms of the disorder will do well with a simple explanation, support, and reassurance without the need for medication at all. Even more serious forms of depression can often be treated using a form of

ANTIDEPRESSANT SIDE EFFECTS

TRICYCLIC
- Dry mouth
- Blurred vision
- Constipation
- Rapid heartbeat
- Palpitation
- Low blood pressure
- Drowsiness
- Weight gain

SSRI
- Nausea
- Indigestion
- Loss of appetite
- Diarrhea
- Headache
- Insomnia
- Sweating

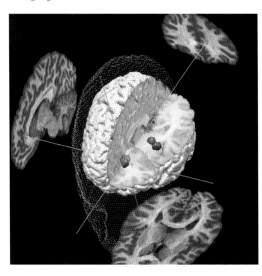

Antidepressants take a while to have full effect. A graphic developed from a brain scan shows areas (marked red) that were activated after several weeks' use of medication.

psychotherapy known as cognitive therapy (*see* pp. 106–111). Also, many bouts of depression are caused by an adverse life event, such as losing a job or the breakup of a relationship. After time many people might get over such adverse events either by coming to terms with their loss, or some other event might happen in their life that compensates for the original negative event, for instance, they might get a new job, meet a new partner, or get together with their original partner after a broken relationship. It is, therefore, necessary to discuss this with the patient, as well as to give antidepressants

to relieve symptoms. Most often a combination of antidepressant treatment with suitable psychological therapy is the preferred way of treating moderate to severe degrees of depression.

ANTIPSYCHOTIC DRUGS

Antipsychotic drugs, or neuroleptics, are used to treat psychotic disorders such as schizophrenia or schizoaffective disorder. Schizophrenia is a diagnostic term that probably covers a range of disorders that psychiatrists also describe as psychosis. The disorders are characterized by major disturbances of thinking and perception—including hallucinations and delusions—together with emotional disturbances that make social contact difficult (*see* pp. 30–39).

Whether or not schizophrenia is a useful diagnostic concept is a controversial subject for many psychologists. Even if it is considered a useful category in which to think about the psychoses, it is commonly held that several different types of schizophrenia exist, all with different causes and outcomes. Accordingly, it is likely that no single treatment approach will be successful for schizophrenia, and that different types of treatment might be necessary depending on the exact type of disorder and its causes.

Typical antipsychotics

Antipsychotic drugs to treat schizophrenia were discovered in the 1950s (*see* p. 144). They are now known as typical antipsychotics. The first drug of this kind was called chlorpromazine. Another commonly used drug of this type is haloperidol, marketed as Haldol. The drugs are commonly taken as tablets. Because people who have psychotic symptoms might be very disturbed in their behavior and might not be willing to take tablets, injections are also available. If treatment is given against a person's wishes, it is normally done after detention in hospital under the appropriate state law. In the great majority of cases, however, patients voluntarily accept treatment. A type of injection whose effect lasts for as long as a month is particularly useful for long-term treatment of people who are not reliable at taking regular oral medication. This type of injection is known as a depot antipsychotic.

The dopamine factor

Typical antipsychotic drugs are thought to work by blocking dopamine D2 receptors in the brain (*see* Vol. 2, pp. 20–39). Scientists used to think that schizophrenia was caused by overactivity of dopamine systems in the brain. They came to believe this because antipsychotic drugs block dopamine receptors; and drugs, such as amphetamines, that stimulate dopamine activity can cause symptoms similar to those experienced in schizophrenia. Also, when they studied brain tissue taken from schizophrenic patients after their death, they found that there were an excessive number of dopamine receptors. However, it now seems that this increased number of dopamine receptors was mainly caused by the drugs. If you block dopamine receptors, then your body responds by making more.

Modern studies using brain-imaging techniques in living patients suggest that changes in brain dopamine function are very small in people with schizophrenia who are not taking drugs, although there does appear to be an increased response to amphetamines (*see* box p. 128). That is why the use of amphetamines—and some other drugs, such as cannabis—is usually detrimental to the mental health of people who are predisposed or vulnerable to schizophrenia (*see* box p. 139).

Atypical antipsychotics

Newer antipsychotic drugs, which are known as atypical, have less effect on dopamine receptors and also act on other receptors, including those for serotonin. Commonly used atypical antipsychotic drugs include risperidone and olanzapine. Many doctors claim that atypical antipsychotics are more effective treatments and cause fewer side effects; but despite this, there is controversy about their use because they are significantly more

Striking examples of psychotic art produced by patients hospitalized for schizophrenia. The disorder is mainly treated with typical or atypical antipsychotic drugs.

expensive, and not everyone agrees that they are more effective.

Using antipsychotics

Antipsychotic drugs are used in three ways. First, large doses of antipsychotic drugs are sometimes given to control very disturbed behavior. This type of use of the drugs has been called a chemical baton or chemical straitjacket by those who oppose the use of drugs to treat psychiatric disorders. However, in the days before such drugs existed, behavior was controlled by more physical means, such as a straitjacket

TECHNOLOGY AND DOPAMINE

Much of the research into mental disorders has been stimulated by technological breakthroughs that allow the brain to be "X-rayed" using techniques known as functional magnetic resonance imaging (fMRI) or positron emission tomography (PET). The techniques allow neuroscientists to study the brain's activity while the person being studied performs psychological tasks and undergoes assessments. Scientists hope that such advances in technology will help localize within the brain normal psychological processes, which, in turn, will help identify areas of the brain that might be dysfunctional in psychological disorders. One example was the use of PET to assess the number of dopamine receptors in people with schizophrenia.

In 1974 Burton Angrist and others proposed in the *American Journal of Psychiatry* that an excess of the neurotransmitter dopamine might be responsible for some of the symptoms and dysfunctions known as schizophrenia. This was based on knowledge that:

• Substances that increased dopamine in the brain, such as amphetamines, often made the symptoms worse.

• The extent to which different neuroleptic drugs were effective seemed to be related to the manner in which they chemically interacted with dopamine receptors in the brain.

• An excess of dopamine in animals might produce behaviors that some scientists thought resembled symptoms of schizophrenia.

However, studies that tried to measure dopamine directly in the blood or brains of people diagnosed with schizophrenia failed to provide evidence to support the idea that they had an excess of dopamine in their brain.

On the other hand, recent PET studies that use radioactive chemicals that bind to dopamine receptors in the brain suggest that while the amount of the dopamine neuotransmitter might not be increased, some people with schizophrenia might have more sensitive receptors. This would mean that their nervous systems would be more reactive to the influence of dopamine. The research has also suggested that there are many different types of dopamine receptor in the brain, and that this could provide a basis for developing different types of medication for schizophrenia. The advantage of this modern technology is that it can be used to investigate people who have never been given medication, so that changes caused by medication do not confuse the results.

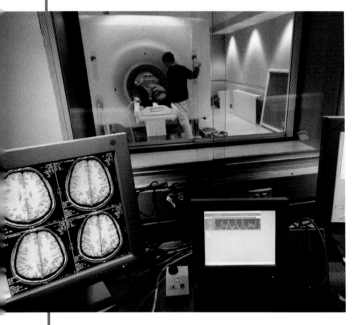

Monitors show real-time changes in the brain's chemistry brought about by the psychological responses of a person undergoing a brain scan.

and a padded cell, to which the use of medication is preferable.

The straitjacket was designed to keep patients' arms bound around their body to prevent them lashing out or harming themselves. Today, physical forms of restraint, such as confining someone to their own room or to a special seclusion room, are rarely used and are strictly regulated and supervised.

The next phase of treatment lasts for a month or so, when antipsychotic drugs are given on a regular basis to reduce the severity of positive symptoms such as delusions and hallucinations. This is the main method of treating what is called the acute phase of schizophrenia, when patients are actively experiencing positive symptoms. Usually, patients are treated within a hospital setting, especially if it is their first episode or breakdown. While in the hospital they are in a place of safety, and staff can observe the nature of their illness. The choice of drug treatment and the dosage can also be explored when the patient is admitted. However, in less severe episodes of psychosis or schizophrenia medication is given without the patient being hospitalized. It is worth emphasizing that it is usually the positive symptoms that mostly respond at this stage of treatment, and that the negative symptoms, such as lack of drive and motivation and reduced emotional responses, slowly become more disabling and might prevent the person from making a full recovery. Unfortunately, negative symptoms are less easily treated by medication.

Despite the impression given by the movies and other media, straitjackets are not commonly used to restrain people with mental disorders. However, very occasionally some patients have to be restrained to protect themselves and other people from harm.

The third stage is long-term treatment with medication that is aimed at reducing the risk of relapse. This form of treatment is known as prophylaxis. It is a very important, if unusual, stage. The purpose of taking the drug even though many of the symptoms have gone is to protect against future relapses of psychosis or schizophrenia. It is similar to people going on vacation to the tropics who have to continue taking antimalarial medication for a while to prevent them getting malaria. Antipsychotic medication taken on a long-term basis is prescribed on the same grounds: It is to prevent further outbreaks of psychotic symptoms. Unfortunately, this does not fit with our usual view of medication and why we take pills. Normally, if we have a headache, we might take an aspirin or paracetamol tablet to relieve the symptoms. We might take several doses until the symptoms get better. However, when the symptoms go, we usually stop taking the drug. Most people with psychosis understandably apply this "aspirin model" to their own illness. When their psychotic symptoms get better, they want to stop taking the medication. That is usually because they want to reduce the side effects and because most people are very reluctant to take medication continually throughout their lives. Unfortunately, stopping medication usually results in a relapse in the disorder at some time over the following few months.

Not all people benefit from antipsychotic medication, however, nor do they necessarily relapse when it is stopped. Nevertheless, the way psychiatric patients view their medication and how they perceive its benefits and side effects are very important. This issue is sometimes known as drug adherence, or compliance.

A long-term patient of antipsychotic drugs shows signs of tardive dyskinesia, one of the side effects associated with such medication. It involves loss of control mainly over the mouth and facial muscles, resulting in the patient twitching or grimacing.

Side effects of antipsychotics

Antipsychotic drugs have a variety of unwanted effects. The main side effects of the older, typical antipsychotic drugs are muscle stiffness and shaking similar to Parkinson's disease (*see* pp. 60–61). Long-term treatment, over a period of years, can cause a disorder known as tardive dyskinesia. It is a disorder that mostly affects the mouth and face, with involuntary movements such as grimacing or twitching, but can also affect other parts of the body.

Some people with schizophrenia develop these movements without any medication, but patients on long-term medication are more likely to be affected. Because of such side effects many psychiatrists prefer to use the newer, atypical antipsychotic drugs that are much less likely to cause such problems. However, the newer drugs have side effects of their own, such as weight gain.

Generally, the newer, atypical antipsychotic drugs are no more effective than the older, typical antipsychotics, with one exception: clozapine. Clozapine has been shown to be the most effective antipsychotic drug. Unfortunately, it carries the risk of reducing the white cell count in the blood to a level at which patients can get infections that, in rare cases, can be fatal. Because of this doctors treating patients with clozapine very carefully monitor them with regular blood tests and only use the drug if other antipsychotics have not worked.

Limitations of antipsychotics

Even with the most effective use of drug treatment many people with schizophrenia have long-term disability that is caused by continuing symptoms, particularly the so-called negative symptoms. In fact, the long-term outcome of schizophrenia in terms of this residual (remaining) disability has not changed substantially since antipsychotic drugs were introduced. The advantage of using the drugs, however, is that they allow patients to be treated without being hospitalized because the drugs damp down the more obvious symptoms that lead to disturbed behavior.

Despite treatment with antipsychotic drugs, many patients will eventually show a relapse of the acute psychotic symptoms that might lead to further hospital admissions. Antipsychotic drugs are not curative: They mainly suppress symptoms and delay relapse. About a third of patients do not respond adequately to standard antipsychotic drugs and are termed treatment resistant. Such patients are normally treated with clozapine, although, again, not all will respond.

Antipsychotics and therapy

As with all mental-health problems, it is important to recognize that medication is not the only way to help people diagnosed with schizophrenia or their families and carers. For example, psychologists realize that the way in which members of a family behave toward each other can have a substantial effect on the risk of relapse. In particular, those families in which there is a lot of emotion, whether it is positive (overprotective) or negative (critical), are much more likely to promote relapse.

Psychologists have developed psychosocial therapies to help families deal more effectively with their relative who might be experiencing schizophrenia.

Psychologists also use other forms of psychosocial therapy to help patients' negative symptoms, such as lack of social skills, apathy, and motivation. These treatments are usually referred to as psychiatric or psychosocial rehabilitation. They focus on helping patients learn the skills needed to survive in the community, such as shopping and cooking, as well as skills useful for employment.

More recently, psychologists have tried to use psychological treatments such as cognitive therapy to treat positive symptoms like hallucinations and delusions. Although the therapies are very experimental and in the early days of development, carefully controlled treatment trials, particularly those conducted in the United Kingdom and Europe, seem to show that such therapies can help some patients control their symptoms despite their having been treatment resistant in the past to medication.

MOOD-STABILIZING DRUGS

Doctors prescribe mood-stabilizing drugs to help patients who show mood swings either upward (mania) or downward (depression) on a regular basis. Typically, these kinds of mood swings last for weeks or months, with periods of normality in between (see pp. 39–46). Such severe mood swings are very disruptive and prevent sufferers from living a normal life. When depressed, they are withdrawn, apathetic, and unable to work or interact with people—even with their family and friends. There is a substantial risk of suicide at this time. When manic, they are severely elated and overactive, often going without sleep for long periods of time. Although to be highly elated superficially appears to some as a good thing, people with mania often behave in disruptive and damaging ways to themselves and their families.

Lithium

In the past the most commonly used drug for treating the mood swings of bipolar 1 disorder was lithium, first used by Australian psychiatrist John Cade in 1949. Lithium is generally given as the salts lithium carbonate or lithium citrate. There is good evidence that long-term treatment with lithium will reduce the frequency of mood swings, particularly in bipolar 1 disorder. Scientists do not know exactly how lithium works because its actions are complex, but they think

Psychosocial therapy, or psychiatric rehabilitation, can help people develop a variety of social and practical skills, such as how to work with computers. Patients with schizophrenia would not otherwise feel motivated to develop these skills because of the negative symptoms of the condition.

that it probably affects the biochemical mechanisms of neurotransmission.

Lithium, however, does have side effects: If its level in the blood gets too high, then symptoms such as shakiness and diarrhea become more common, and very high lithium levels can cause toxicity leading to convulsions and even death. Because of this problem lithium levels in the blood have to be measured on a regular basis. If this precaution is observed, the use of lithium is very safe. The small risk involved in using lithium is more than offset by the fact that one in six people with this kind of mood disorder will eventually kill themselves if they are not properly treated.

Lithium is still widely used, but other treatments are now finding favor with psychiatrists. For recurrent depression most patients will now be treated with long-term antidepressants rather than lithium. For bipolar 1 patients doctors prefer anticonvulsant drugs, which are normally used for epilepsy. The drug most commonly used in the United States for this purpose is disodium valproate (depakote), but other anticonvulsants have also been shown to be beneficial.

PHYSICAL INTERVENTIONS

Insulin shock therapy, or insulin coma therapy, was widely used for schizophrenia until the use of tranquilizers became more common. In 1933 Polish psychiatrist Manfred Sakel (1900–1957) found that certain symptoms of schizophrenia could be alleviated by first putting patients into a coma. They were given increasing doses of insulin, which lowered blood sugar levels and put them into a coma (an unconscious state). Patients were kept in this state for about an hour, after which they were revived with warm saline (salt solution) sent directly into the stomach through a tube or by glucose injections. The treatment seemed to work best for patients who had suffered

from schizophrenia for less than two years—however, spontaneous remission (disappearance) of schizophrenia can occur anyway within the first two years.

Another method of treating psychotic symptoms was devised by Hungarian psychiatrist Ladislaus von Meduna (1896–1964) in 1935. Meduna found that patients with psychotic symptoms who also suffered from epilepsy showed reduced psychotic symptoms after an epileptic fit. He therefore induced convulsions in the patients by giving them a brain convulsant, cardiazol, to mimic epilepsy in the belief that one disorder would chase out the other. The trouble was that during the part of the treatment when the patients were conscious, they felt as if they were about to die.

Electroconvulsive therapy (ECT)

In 1938 two Italian psychiatrists Ugo Cerletti (1877–1963) and Lucio Bini (1908–1964) came up with an alternative to Meduna's shock therapy. Following a visit to an abattoir where the animals were stunned electrically before slaughter, they

Professor Kay Redfield Jamison, an authority on bipolar 1 disorder, and a sufferer herself, revealed in An Unquiet Mind *(1995) her experience of being treated with lithium.*

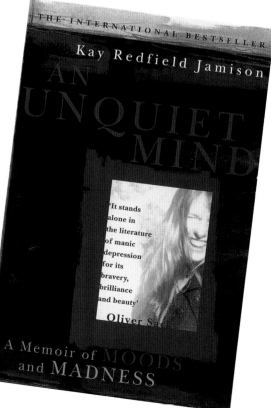

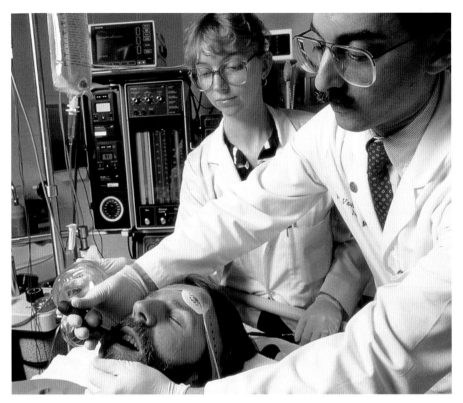

A patient is prepared for electroconvulsive therapy. The patient is anesthetized, and muscle relaxants keep body movements to a minimum. The electric current is applied to the temples through padded electrodes. The therapy is controversial and is only used to treat severe depression that might threaten a patient's life.

were inspired to bring about convulsions in patients by applying an electric current across the temples. This treatment now known as electroconvulsive therapy, or ECT.

When doctors first used ECT in the 1940s, the procedure was done without any kind of anesthetic. This was very frightening for the patient and sometimes led to fractures and other injuries. Modern use of ECT is much more sophisticated. Patients are given an anesthetic injection into a vein so they are not conscious during the procedure, and then given a further injection to relax the muscles. Because of this the body does not convulse, even though the brain shows signs of epileptic activity after the electric shock has been administered. Often six or eight electric shocks are given in total, spaced out at a rate of two or three times per week.

ECT is probably one of the most controversial treatments used widely in modern psychiatry. Psychiatrists vary

in the extent to which they use it, and some patient groups protest that the treatment is barbaric. In general, the use of ECT has been steadily declining in popularity with the development of more effective drug and psychological treatments. Some psychiatrists now do not use ECT at all.

Despite the misgivings, there is evidence that ECT can be effective for severe depression. In the most severe kind of depression patients' lives might be threatened, not only from suicide but also if they lapse into a stupor and cannot eat or drink. ECT is potentially lifesaving in such situations. It is often true, however, that more effective treatment could have been given earlier in the depression to prevent it from reaching such severity.

Some psychiatrists will also use ECT for less severe forms of depression when other treatments such as medication have not been effective. One problem with

- **Antipsychotics**—drugs that treat psychotic disorders.
- **Anxiolytics**—drugs that treat anxiety disorders.
- **Atypical antipsychotics**—antipsychotic drugs that work on receptors for several neurotransmitters.
- **Benzodiazepines**—anxiolytics that work on GABA receptors.
- **Capsulotomies**—removing brain tissue through electrodes.
- **Cingulotomy**—cutting through the cingulum bundle in the brain.
- **Disodium valproate**—anticonvulsant used for epilepsy and also bipolar 1 disorder.
- **ECT**—electroconvulsant therapy. Applying electric shocks to the scalp as treatment for severe depression.
- **Frontal leucotomy**—or frontal lobotomy. Cutting through the deep white matter of the brain.
- **Insulin shock therapy**—or insulin coma therapy, whereby the patient is briefly put into a coma when blood sugar levels are lowered with insulin.
- **GABA**—gamma-amino butyric acid, a neurotransmitter.
- **Lithium**—the salts lithium carbonate and lithium citrate, used to treat bipolar 1 disorder.
- **MAOIs**—antidepressant drugs that inhibit monoamine oxidase.
- **SSRIs**—selective serotonin reuptake inhibitors, or drugs that leave more of the neurotransmitter serotonin in synapses in the brain.
- **Standard leucotomy**—a refined version of frontal leucotomy.
- **Transorbital leucotomy**—incising an arc in the brain with a needlelike instrument inserted through the eye socket.
- **Tricyclics**—antidepressant drugs named for their chemical structure.
- **Typical antipsychotics**—antipsychotics that work on receptors in the brain of the neurotransmitter dopamine.

using ECT in this way is that it generally brings only short-term benefit. It is still necessary to use medication on a longer-term basis in order the prevent the depression from returning.

Also, it is not known how ECT works. Studies comparing sham ECT (in which the anaesthetic is given without the electroshock) have shown that much of the benefit occurs with the sham treatment, and after three months there is no difference in the outcome between the real and the sham procedures.

> *"ECT remains the most reliably effective treatment for serious depression."*
> —*Charles Kellner, 1997*

There is also controversy about the potential long-term harmful effects of ECT. Sometimes ECT treatment can be followed by a short period of poor memory and mental confusion immediately after treatment. Some patients claim that their memory and other intellectual functions have been permanently impaired. However, when this has been investigated by research workers, they have not been able to find any difference between patients who have had ECT in the past and those with the same disorder who have never had ECT. Current evidence suggests that ECT does not have any permanently damaging effects. Nevertheless, for many patients it is still a deeply distressing form of treatment that is frequently vehemently resisted.

PSYCHOSURGERY

Sometimes doctors perform surgery on the brain to modify the symptoms of a psychiatric disorder. The procedure, known as psychosurgery, was devised by Portuguese neurologist António Moniz (1874–1955) in the 1930s. Moniz was inspired by work done on the frontal lobes of chimpanzees. He persuaded a young neurosurgeon, Almeida Lima, to devise an operation that consisted of an extensive cut in the white matter that lies beneath the cortex (top layer) in the frontal lobes of the brain. The idea was that the connection between "thinking," processed in the frontal lobes, would be severed from "emotion," originating in the lower brain, and so reduce excessively irrational aggressive behavior. The procedure was known as a frontal leucotomy or lobotomy. It was later modified by Walter

> *"Shock treatment, when you strip off all the pretensions, is cruel, and no amount of expression of good intentions will make it otherwise."*
> *—Phyllis (an ECT patient)*

Freeman (1895–1972) and neurosurgeon James Watts into the so-called standard leucotomy, in which smaller cuts were made in the frontal lobes. Although Freeman was not a surgeon, he devised another form of lobotomy, the transorbital leucotomy, in which a

needlelike instrument is hammered through the eye socket and then rotated in the frontal lobe to cut an arc.

Modern forms of lobotomy are called capsulotomies. Two radioactive electrodes are inserted through tiny holes in the forehead, and brain tissue is destroyed by beta rays. In thermocapsulotomies computer-operated electrodes, heated to 155°F (68°C), are applied to interrupt neural pathways between the hypothalamus and the limbic system (*see* pp. 87–88). In a cingulotomy surgeons cut the cingulum bundle of nerve fibers that connects the prefrontal cortex to parts of the limbic system.

Limitations of psychosurgery

Although doctors have used psychosurgery, it commonly led to adverse effects, including intellectual impairment, loss of control of the emotions, incontinence of urine, and epilepsy. It is also irreversible. Before long, research brought about other methods of treatment, including drug treatments, and the use of psychosurgery rapidly declined. This form of treatment is now used only rarely. Modern operations produce much smaller lesions in the brain that are

LICENSING DRUGS

PSYCHOLOGY & SOCIETY

The manufacturing and supply of medicines is a multibillion-dollar industry. Developing and marketing a particular drug might result in large profits for a drug manufacturer and its shareholders. Drug companies apply considerable pressures both on governments and individual doctors to sanction and use particular drugs for the treatment of mental disorders. But what proof is there that the drug is more effective than another produced by a competitor drug company? How safe are these drugs? What are their long-term side effects? Which drugs are the cheapest or the best value for money in treating a particular illness? All such questions could potentially be answered by scientific research.

For many years clinical scientists have conducted drug trials to assess the effectiveness of individual drugs and

also to measure their side effects. Usually these trials are conducted "double blind," so that neither the patient nor the clinician knows what type of medication the patient is receiving. A new drug is usually tested against an existing treatment or against a control or placebo treatment that is not expected to yield any positive effects.

The results of the randomized control trials, as they have become known, now greatly influence the choice of particular treatments for individual disorders. Politicians argue that money should only be invested in treatments that have been scientifically proven to be effective. In the United States it is part of the managed care movement: Doctors need to account for their choice of treatments to an insurance company, which usually picks up the bill for the patient's treatment.

have failed. In practice, this means that psychosurgery is now rarely used, and most psychiatrists will never have referred a patient for treatment of this kind.

CHOOSING TREATMENT

For people suffering from a mental-health disorder there seems to be a potentially baffling range of treatments available. Even if the choice is medication, there is a range of different types of medication designed to combat the wide variety of disorders. However, for nearly every physical treatment for a mental disorder there are also alternative psychosocial interventions. How should patients, their relatives, or carers decide which treatment is best for them?

The most important consideration when choosing treatment is evidence and proof that it is helpful in resolving the problem. That is why the prescribing of medication is closely regulated in the United States to minimize any harm that drugs might do and also to show that they are effective treatments.

Efficacy and effectiveness

It is important that treatments for mental health problems are shown to be effective—but what does that mean? For many double-blind randomized control trials it probably means that one type of drug has successfully reduced a group of patients' symptoms when compared with another drug or a placebo (*see* box p. 135).

However, some important factors must be taken into account: First, the results are usually based on group findings, and care should be taken when applying the overall results to individual cases. What works on average might not work for everyone. In fact, usually only a certain percentage of people show improvement over a fixed period of time. Second, often a significant number of people—perhaps up to 50 percent—might not benefit, or they might even get worse after taking the new medication. Some of them will continue to take the medication but will not show any improvement. It means that

accurately placed in specific areas that are thought to be related to the development of psychiatric symptoms.

The older procedures were generally used for schizophrenia. Although it might seem surprising that doctors were prepared to cause brain damage to their patients in this way, we should remember that there were no other treatments available for schizophrenia in those days, and patients used to spend their whole lives locked up in a mental hospital. Any treatment that had some success was regarded positively by doctors despite the side effects. Modern psychosurgical procedures, if they are used at all, are only considered for severe chronic obsessional and depressive disorders, when all other possible treatment approaches

Compliance is a major factor in the effectiveness of drug treatment. If patients do not take their medication as prescribed—perhaps because they do not understand how it works—they will not fully benefit from it.

this particular medication is just not for them; perhaps there is a different cause for their mental-health problem that cannot be helped by that particular medication.

Third, it is also likely that some of the people who show no improvement stopped taking the medication before the trial was completed. This is very common and reflects the fact that for a whole range of both physical and mental disorders, people do not necessarily follow medical advice and treatment. How many of us who have been prescribed a course of antibiotics have stopped taking them once the first signs of the problem have disappeared? It is no different for people taking medication for mental-health problems. Many reasons might account for why they stop taking their medication.

Noncompliance

Even when patients are prescribed suitable medication, it will not be very effective unless they take it as prescribed. There are many reasons why they might not do so:

• They might not believe in the effectiveness of the medication.
• They might not be willing to tolerate its side effects.
• They might not believe that they have a mental disorder that needs treating.
• They might lack motivation because of the cost of the medication, or they might feel ashamed to take it.
• They might not remember to take the medication regularly.

Such problems lead to what psychiatrists have termed noncompliance, or poor adherence, which is an important factor in determining the effectiveness of particular treatments. Highly effective drugs may exist, but they are no use if they produce negative side effects to the extent that patients stop taking them. Such a treatment when used clinically will prove totally ineffective. The balance between benefits and side effects is very important in determining whether patients should

PSYCHIATRY AND HUMAN RIGHTS: A BRIEF HISTORY

19th century: Unmarried mothers and women who had many sexual partners were often detained for the rest of their lives in institutions either for the insane or the mentally retarded on the grounds that they were "morally incapable."

1920s: The eugenics movement in the United States advocated the compulsory sterilization of people with certain mental disorders.

1930s and 1940s: In Nazi Germany people with serious mental disorders or retardation were put to death within medical institutions.

1950s: Homosexuality was considered a mental disorder and included as a psychiatric diagnosis.

1950s–1980s: In many communist regimes prior to the 1990s political dissidents were detained in mental hospital and treated against their will.

1990s: In the United Kingdom it was found that many young men from poor and ethnic minority backgrounds were frequently and forcibly treated for psychosis. It raised the whole issue of prejudice within mental-health services.

Jewish prisoners with mental disorders are lined up at Buchenwald concentration camp in Germany to be photographed for anti-Semitic Nazi propaganda.

patients have little insight or understanding as to what is happening to them because of their mental disorder.

It is very common for people with severe mental-health problems to deny that they have them and to refuse any form of treatment or psychiatric help. Because of this there are comprehensive laws and procedures to detain such patients and take them to a place of safety where psychiatric treatment might be administered. Such laws should also protect the human rights of the patients and ensure that they are not inappropriately detained or treated against their will. This is not always the case, and it is not just people living under totalitarian regimes who have been denied their liberties and forcibly treated with psychiatric drugs (*see* box p. 137). Informed consent for treatment implies choice.

Information and choice
Today the users of psychiatric services tend to be more and better informed about their condition. There are many self-help books and organizations designed to inform patients about their rights and also the treatments they might expect to be available to them. Much of the information is also now available on the Internet. A consequence of this is that the more informed people are, the more they wish to exercise choices and decide for themselves which type of treatment they want to receive. Although this could mean patients exercising a preference between one drug and another, it is more likely that they will want to choose between physical and psychological treatments. For nearly all the conditions discussed and their medications, psychotherapists and psychologists can claim to treat the same conditions equally effectively. What is the basis of these claims, and how should patients exercise their choices?

stick with their treatment and reap the benefits.

A patient's understanding of medication and insight into their illness are also very important. Research shows that in the past many people receiving medication for schizophrenia and their relatives were unable to name the drugs that they were taking or why they were taking them. The better informed that patients are and the more involved they have been in deciding for themselves whether or not they wish to take a particular medication, the more likely they are to continue to take it and experience its benefits. This has led to important developments in education packages for patients and their relatives about their individual illnesses and the treatments available to them.

Agreeing to treatment
Another important area when considering treatment is informed consent (*see* pp. 152–153). It might be that many people with a mental-health problem might not consider that they in fact have a problem that requires treatment. Psychiatrists often refer to this as a lack of "insight." The dividing line between illness and well-being might sometimes appear quite arbitrary. Most of the time, however, this problem occurs when

Self-help booklets, such as these published by the National Institute of Mental Health, help educate patients about their problems. Well-informed patients might be better prepared to make choices between physical and psychological therapies.

MULTIFACTOR MODELS

Nearly all forms of mental disorders are likely to be caused by a combination of different factors, including upbringing and close family relationships, the effects of physical and emotional trauma, genetics (inheritance), and physical damage to the brain from alcohol or other substance abuse. Theories that stress the interaction of a whole range of factors are termed multifactor models.

Psychosocial factors

Even within severe forms of mental disorders, such as schizophrenia, psychological and social factors are critically important. For example, whether people diagnosed with schizophrenia make good progress and recover from the disorder to continue with their life depends as much on the influence of family and carers around them as it does on their medication. These other, nonmedical factors are often called psychosocial because they include both psychological and social factors.

Vulnerability model

Many recent models of mental disorders are called vulnerability models because they emphasize the importance of interactions between two types of factors: those that might increase the risk that someone might develop a mental disorder, and triggering factors that actually lead to the disorder.

The vulnerability factors might be a combination of physical and psychosocial factors, while the triggering factors are often psychosocial stresses, perhaps caused by life events, such as arguments within the family or financial difficulties (*see* box right).

CHOICE OF TREATMENT

If mental disorders are caused by a variety of physical and psychosocial factors, it follows that the treatments for them are also directed at the different factors. Medication and physical treatments can correct some of the physical problems

experienced by patients and reduce their symptoms: Psychosocial solutions can help them deal better with their stress and manage their lives more effectively.

Alternatives to physical treatments

It is true that for many mental disorders, such as anxiety disorders and depression, psychological therapies developed since the 1970s claim to be at least as effective as routine drug treatment. Although there have been psychodynamic forms of therapy for many years, particularly in the United States, the research evidence for the effectiveness of psychological therapies has only really accumulated since the 1980s because of the requirements of evidence-based practice and managed care.

New forms of therapy, such as cognitive behavior therapy (*see* pp. 111–114), have been scientifically validated as effective for a range of psychological problems. A major body of research has been accumulated to support the effectiveness of cognitive therapy for a wide range of disorders, including panic disorder, certain phobias, posttraumatic stress disorder, depression, obsessive-compulsive disorder, sleep disorders, and more recently, applications to psychotic disorders, including schizophrenia and bipolar disturbances.

Physical versus psychological treatments

How should a patient choose, therefore, between physical and psychological treatments? The answer will depend on

A VULNERABILITY MODEL

The vulnerability model, as applied to schizophrenia, shows that people with
- **predisposing vulnerability factors**, including genetic, family, biological, are at
- **increased risk for developing schizophrenia** sometime within their life if the vulnerability factors combine with
- **triggering stresses**, such as family arguments, life events, substance abuse, which might result in
- **symptoms of schizophrenia**.

who is making the choice and why. Patients might easily arrive at a decision opposite to either that of their clinician or perhaps those responsible for paying for the treatment. All parties need to consider several important issues:

Treatment efficacy How good is the evidence from scientific studies that a treatment will benefit the patient and usually lead to a decrease in symptoms? This is known as treatment efficacy.
• If improvements take place, do they also affect the quality of life of the patients?
• Are they really better off on this treatment?
• What side effects do they experience, and are positive effects outweighed by negative effects?
• How stable and consistent are the benefits over time?
• Do patients relapse, or fall ill again, after receiving the treatment?

Practice If we can identify an effective treatment on the basis of the scientific evidence, what is this treatment like in practice? Do family physicians understand the drug that they are prescribing, or are psychotherapists competent and trained in a particular therapeutic approach? The

Certain mental disorders, such as depression, might ultimately be better treated with psychotherapy than medication. While drugs might alleviate symptoms more rapidly, insight and new behavior acquired through successful psychotherapy might in the longer term help the patient cope better.

process of translating the results of scientific research into day-to-day practice is known as assessing the effectiveness of a particular treatment, as opposed to its scientific efficacy.

Resources Are there the resources needed to support a particular treatment, and which ones are more cost effective? Would just providing the money to the patient bring about a better clinical improvement? Although some medications are in relative terms very expensive, many are also very cost effective. For psychotherapy, on the other hand, you usually need a highly trained and experienced therapist. Not only is this likely to be expensive, there might not be enough therapists. The access that patients have to treatment, therefore, is a very important factor in the treatments they receive.

Patients' choice There is a whole set of factors that might determine which therapy patients have a preference for. The information and attitudes that they have prior to treatment might determine which ones they believe to be effective or ineffective. Much research has shown that expectations about treatment and patients' faith in their therapist or the therapy considerably contribute to the effectiveness of the treatment. Sometimes just the belief in an ineffective or sham treatment, such as a drug placebo, will lead to highly credible therapeutic changes.

Psychological therapies Many doctors and psychiatrists recognize the importance of psychotherapies and psychosocial interventions. However, drug treatments might be more widely available and bring about clinical improvement more quickly. An important difference between medication and psychotherapy is that drug treatment appears only to relieve the symptoms for an episode of illness but does not help patients overcome their problems if the symptoms return. There is evidence, particularly for depression, that psychotherapies reduce the chances of the disorder recurring in the future. Medication does not appear to have this important beneficial effect. Nevertheless, there are

Medication has proved helpful in relieving the symptoms of many mental disorders. However, it can have disadvantages, such as side effects and dependency. It is important, therefore, for patients to be able to make well-informed choices about the treatments available to them.

many disorders for which psychotherapy is only used after medication has been effective or is used in combination with it. This is particularly true for more serious disorders. Even here, recent studies suggest that some people who never responded well to medication make improvements with psychological treatments—although they are probably important exceptions that do not necessarily prove the rule.

Physical treatments for mental disorders are necessary and very helpful; however, many of them involve side effects that can be uncomfortable. That is why many mental-health professionals advocate combining physical with psychosocial therapies. Above all, they recommend that all patients should be aware of the nature of their treatments and be able to make informed choices about them.

KEY POINTS

- Since the 1950s an increasing number of drugs have been developed to treat mental disorders.
- There are many ways of looking at mental disorders, including the medical and multifactor models.
- The vulnerability model is a multifactor model that looks at possible risk factors.
- **Anxiolytics**, or tranquilizers, are prescribed for anxiety disorders.
- Benzodiazepines are anxiolytics that act on GABA receptors. They include diazepam (Valium) and lorazepam (Ativan).
- They can be addictive.
- **Antidepressants** are also prescribed for anxiety disorders.
- MAOI antidepressants block monoamine oxidase.
- Tricyclic antidepressants block serotonin and noradrenaline uptake.
- SSRI antidepressants only block serotonin reuptake.
- **Antipsychotics**, or neuroleptics, are prescribed for schizophrenia.
- Older, typical antipsychotics block dopamine receptors.
- Newer, atypical antipsychotics also work on other receptors.
- Antipsychotics have side effects.
- **Lithium** is a mood-stabilizing drug used for bipolar 1 disorder.
- **ECT** is controversial but can help in severe depression.
- **Psychosurgery** involves cutting into the brain. It is rarely used.
- **Compliance** involves continuing to take the drugs as prescribed for full effectiveness.
- Most clinicians prefer to combine psychological and physical therapies.

CONNECTIONS

- Mental Disorders: pp. 20–67
- Psychotherapies: pp. 92–117

- Mental Disorders and Society: pp. 142–163
- Cognitive Psychology: Volume 1, pp. 104–117
- Neuropsychology: Volume 1, pp. 90–95
- Emotion and Motivation: Volume 2, pp. 86–109

Mental Disorders and Society

"It is better to prevent than to cure."

Peruvian folk wisdom

Since the beginning of the 20th century society has viewed mental disorder in many different ways: as a brain disease, as the product of early childhood trauma, even as a consequence of faulty learning experiences. The story of mental disorders in modern society is a vivid tale of therapists and scientists wrestling with complex problems that have no easy solutions.

On June 20, 2001, Andrea Yates drowned all five of her children one at a time in a bathtub. She then wrapped each child's body in a sheet and placed it carefully on her bed. When she was done, she called her husband at work.

"You need to come home," she said, in a matter-of-fact tone.

"What's wrong?" asked her husband. "Anyone hurt?"

"Yes," replied Andrea. "The children. All of them."

The trial opened on February 18, 2002, and some people regarded it as an open-and-shut case. But throughout the trial many had nagging doubts. Was Yates really responsible for what she had done, or was she suffering from a mental disorder and unable to control her actions?

On the surface it certainly seemed as if Yates had a mental disorder. She had been diagnosed with a severe case of postnatal depression, and she was being treated for the condition with medications. But Yates's actions on that day were so well planned that it was hard to see how they could have been products of this. The jury believed that she had a mental disorder, but decided that the murders had been premeditated—essential for a murder conviction—that she was in control of her actions at the time, and that she knew that what she was doing was wrong. On March 12 Andrea Yates

Andrea Yates did not deny murdering her children. However, the defense claimed that she was suffering from depression after the loss of her sixth child by miscarriage.

was found guilty of two counts of capital murder and sentenced to life imprisonment.

Although Yates is now being punished for what she did, the question remains: Should she have been hospitalized and treated instead? To begin to answer this question and other questions raised by similar cases, we must first look at how mental-health professionals think about mental disorders—how they explain the causes and treat the symptoms.

FROM BRAIN TO MIND

For the greater part of the 20th century psychoanalytic theory about mental disorders was most influenced by the work of Sigmund Freud (1856–1939) (*see* Vol. 1,

CAN WE REALLY KNOW WHO HAS A MENTAL DISORDER?

EXPERIMENT

In 1973 psychologist David Rosenhan published a study in the periodical *Science*. His piece, entitled "On Being Sane in Insane Places," shocked the mental-health profession and has kept it talking ever since. The study was simple. Rosenhan recruited a group of graduate students and professional colleagues, and asked them to present themselves for admission at 12 different psychiatric hospitals throughout the United States. The pseudopatients were told to report they were hearing voices that kept repeating three words: "empty," "hollow," and "thud." Apart from that, they were to provide accurate life histories and answer the psychiatrists' questions as honestly as possible. The unexpected result was that all 12 were admitted to the hospitals, and all but one were diagnosed with schizophrenia. On entering the hospital, all the pseudopatients resumed acting normally and no longer reported hearing voices or experiencing any unusual symptoms. Still, the average length of stay was 19 days (one patient was not discharged for 52 days).

Did any of the hospital staff detect the deception? According to Rosenhan: no. Everything the pseudopatients did (for example, taking notes, making conversation with the nurses) was interpreted by the staff as further evidence of their mental disorder. Some of the other patients apparently figured out the ruse, but none of the doctors or nurses did. All but one of the patients was discharged with a diagnosis of schizophrenia in remission (schizophrenia that has been treated successfully).

Rosenhan reached the alarming conclusion that mental-health professionals cannot distinguish the sane from the insane. Many psychologists and psychiatrists were offended by this attack on their clinical skills. Some psychologists pointed out that Rosenhan's conclusion was unfair—the same thing would have happened if someone showed up at a hospital faking physical symptoms such as chest pain. Wouldn't they be admitted too—and shouldn't they be, just to be on the safe side? According to Rosenhan's critics, the admitting psychiatrists did the proper thing—the conservative thing.

The study made the important point that mental-health professionals are human, just like the rest of us, and just like the rest of us, they make mistakes. They can be fooled or misled—and so can we.

pp. 52–65). According to Freud, all psychological disorders are rooted in unconscious conflicts—internal mental battles that occur outside of awareness and eventually lead to depression, phobias, eating disorders, and even severe mental disorders, such as schizophrenia. Freud's work was revolutionary in many ways. But from the perspective of mental disorders and society one aspect of his theory stands out: Freud was the first researcher to develop a model of mental disorders that was almost entirely psychological. Freud's psychoanalytic theory shifted scientists' attention from brain to mind as the source of psychological disorders.

Impact of Freud's theories

Although Freud's first papers on psychoanalysis were published in 1895, it was not until 1909, when he delivered a series of lectures at Clark University in Worcester, Massachusetts, that his work

The Nightmare *(1781)* *by Swiss artist Henry Fuseli (1741–1825) vividly captures a turbulent dream state. Freud's theories of the unconscious, based on the interpretation of dreams, were among the earliest and most influential psychological explanations of mental disorders.*

began to make an impact on physicians, psychologists, and the general public. By the early 1920s virtually every educated person in Western society was familiar with the basic propositions of psychoanalytic theory. By World War II (1939–1945) Freud's ideas had been so widely disseminated that even people with no real knowledge of psychology had heard of concepts such as repression, dream analysis, the Oedipus complex, and the Freudian slip (parapraxis). Freud's ideas changed the world, and virtually every field of social study—from psychology and psychiatry to anthropology and literature—was influenced by his theories.

Today only a minority of mental-health professionals (about 15 percent) describe themselves as strict Freudians. However, the majority—60 percent or more in some surveys—report that they still incorporate at least some of Freud's ideas into their research and clinical work. Freud's legacy lives on, but in recent years it has been overshadowed by new biological perspectives on mental disorders (*see* Vol. 1, pp. 90–95).

Rise of drug treatments

The first psychotropic drugs (medications used to treat mental disorders) became available long ago—even before Freud was constructing his revolutionary model of the mind. But it was not until the early 1950s, with the release of a medication called haloperidol, that drug treatments assumed a major role in the treatment of mental disorders (*see* pp. 118–141). Haloperidol was the first widely prescribed antipsychotic medication—it is still used to manage the symptoms of schizophrenia and other severe mental disorders. By removing the hallucinations (false perceptions) and delusions (false beliefs) caused by schizophrenia, haloperidol has given many severely disturbed patients their first real opportunity to live on their own outside the confines of a hospital ward.

To understand the impact that haloperidol and other antipsychotic drugs have had on society, consider a simple but telling fact: in 1950, before the first of

these drugs were widely available, more than 500,000 U.S. citizens were confined in mental hospitals. By 1990 the number had fallen to fewer than 50,000. The

> *"Approximately one third of the estimated 600,000 homeless people in the U.S. have a severe mental illness. However, only one in 20 people with a severe mental illness are homeless."*
> —*National Alliance for the Mentally Ill, 2001*

widespread use of antipsychotic medications resulted in a 90 percent reduction in the mental hospital population. But where did all these patients go—and were they cured? Ex-patients found follow-up services hard to come by, and without guidance and supervision many with serious mental

Down and out in New York City. Many homeless people take refuge in densely populated urban areas. Some have mental disorders and take to the streets. After the discovery of antipsychotic drugs in the 1950s the number of patients in mental hospitals was considerably reduced.

disorders simply stopped taking their medication. They drifted onto the fringes of society, too confused (and sometimes too ashamed) to seek medical and psychiatric help on their own. Many of the patients released from mental hospitals during the 1950s through to the 1970s ended up on the streets.

The problem has worsened over the years. A walk through the downtown neighborhoods of any large city reveals large numbers of homeless people. Not all of them are former mental patients—homelessness has many possible causes, including poverty, discrimination, and addiction. Yet research shows that 30 percent or more of the homeless suffer from at least one serious mental disorder.

The decline of mental hospitals and the resulting increase in homelessness illustrate one of the fundamental truths about mental disorders—there are no ideal social solutions. Instead, therapists and researchers look for trade-off strategies that alleviate existing problems without creating too many new ones.

CURRENT PERSPECTIVES

Under the influence of Freud the first decades of the 20th century saw the rise of mind theories of mental disorders. The latter part of the century saw the increased use of drug treatments and biologically based brain theories. At first they were seen as alternatives, but increasingly they are regarded as complementary parts of a single whole.

Psychiatrists are physicians with special expertise in the biological aspects of mental disorders. Like other doctors, they complete four years of medical school, but then move on to specialize in diagnosis and treatment of mental disorders.

Until the 1970s psychiatrists provided both psychotherapy and medication, with different psychiatrists emphasizing different types of treatment depending on their own training and theoretical orientation. In fact, it was not unusual for psychiatrists to devote most—perhaps even all—of their efforts to psychotherapy, with very little time spent prescribing medication. Many used some version of Freud's theory in their therapeutic work.

A Right to Be Crazy?

In the late 1980s Joyce Brown lived on the Upper East Side of Manhattan in one of New York City's most exclusive and expensive neighborhoods. It was an ideal life in many ways. The problem was, Joyce Brown lived on the street. New York City has thousands of homeless people, and most of them never make the news. But Joyce Brown did because she refused to live quietly in the shadows, as many homeless people do. Instead, she made a scene. And she did it nearly every day. She talked to herself, paced the streets gesturing wildly, and urinated and defecated in public. She begged for money; and if anyone gave her a dollar or two, she burned the cash. Residents began to complain about Brown's behavior, and nearby businesses complained that she was driving away customers. Eventually the police arrested her, and she was committed to a psychiatric hospital. She was deemed legally incompetent and forced to receive treatment, including antipsychotic medication.

Everyone thought the problem was solved—until lawyers got involved. Joyce Brown found a sympathetic attorney who accepted her argument that she had a right to live her life however she wanted. If it meant living on the street, or if she wanted to burn money, it was her business. Brown brought suit against the City of New York for violating her civil rights by forcing her off the street and onto medication—and she won. Although she was not permitted to behave antisocially (urinating in public is illegal), the courts found that otherwise she did indeed have the right to live however she wanted—even on the street—as long as she did not interfere with other people's right to live peacefully as well.

The case of Joyce Brown has important implications for the civil rights of people with serious mental disorders. It points out that simply because some people have a mental disorder—and make what look like bad choices—it does not mean they can be told where (and how) to live.

Since then the picture has changed dramatically. Psychiatrists now devote most of their time to prescribing and managing medications. Meanwhile, psychotherapy is provided by psychologists and psychotherapists.

General practitioners (family physicians) also play a greater role in the process than ever before, treating mental disorders with medication. They now

Drugs are used increasingly to treat a variety of mental disorders. Psychiatrists and general practitioners can prescribe medication for certain mild disorders, such as depression.

receive extensive training in pharmacology (the scientific study of drugs and their effects). Because of this they are better able to treat mental disorders without the help of a psychiatrist. The latest medication has fewer side effects than earlier products and is therefore easier to manage. Patients are more willing to take their medicine, and fewer discontinue their drugs against doctors' orders. Financial pressures from managed care organizations, such as insurance companies, have forced family physicians to handle by themselves some milder forms of mental disorders, such as moderate depression or anxiety, that 10 or 20 years ago they might have referred to a psychiatrist.

For all the help that physicians now provide, most nonextreme mental disorders are handled by psychologists. Unlike psychiatrists, they rely on therapy alone—what Freud termed "the talking cure." It may appear unstructured, but in fact there are various approved methods and guidelines, the most important of which are contained in the

A DAY IN THE LIFE OF A HOSPITAL PSYCHIATRIST

Dr. Albert Henden's day begins early, with 7 a.m. rounds. He arrives at the hospital's psychiatry unit around 6:30 a.m. so he has time to chat with nurses, who always have a good feel for how different patients are doing. He takes a quick look at his patients' charts, and then he goes from room to room, chatting for a few moments with each of his patients. He notes their progress and their setbacks as well. Rounds usually end before 8:00 a.m., although that depends on the number of patients Dr. Henden has to see that day, and on how well or poorly they are doing.

After rounds comes the daily team meeting, a forum for the exchange of observations and ideas that is attended by everyone involved in patient care. Dr. Henden leads the meeting, soliciting the opinion of psychologists, nurses, social workers, and others. It is here, in the team meeting, that treatment plans get updated, and discharge plans begin to take shape.

Most of Dr. Henden's morning is taken up with patient work, consultations with other units in the hospital, and

hospital committee meetings. Dr. Henden sits on the hospital's ethics committee, which must meet to decide how to handle tricky questions, such as whether or not information may be revealed about a patient who is in a coma and who is not able to give formal consent for personal data to be released.

On this particular day much of Dr. Henden's afternoon is taken up with a consultation in the hospital's cardiac unit, where an agitated, confused woman with chest pains has been admitted. After that he goes to the emergency room, where there is some question about the mental condition of a man who has been in a car accident.

Dr. Henden's hospital day usually ends around 4 p.m. but he's not done yet. He also has a small caseload of private patients whom he sees in his office across town. By 7 p.m. the last patient has left, and Dr. Henden finally heads home—at the end of a 12-hour day. The following day's rounds begin at 7 a.m., when the whole process begins anew.

FOCUS ON

Diagnostic and Statistical Manual of Mental Disorders. Through a combination of tests and careful listening psychologists are able to make judgments about their patients' mental state and then, if necessary, refer them to a psychiatrist.

Psychologists typically undergo four years' graduate training, plus a one- or two-year internship in a hospital or similar establishment. They also receive extensive training in conducting and evaluating scientific research to keep abreast of the latest findings in their field. Some clinical psychologists continue to conduct research in hospitals and other treatment settings.

Different clinical psychologists have different theoretical orientations—they apply different models of the mind to psychotherapy. Three theoretical orientations are most popular among clinical psychologists—they are the psychodynamic, the behavioral, and the cognitive (*see* pp. 92–117).

The psychodynamic orientation is essentially a modern version of Freud's psychoanalysis that emphasizes talking about patients' problems and helping them gain insight into the source of their current difficulties. About 15 percent of psychologists are psychodynamicists.

The behavioral orientation focuses on helping the patient learn how to replace self-defeating behaviors with more adaptive behaviors. About 10 percent of psychologists are primarily behavioral.

The cognitive orientation emphasizes changing patients' thought patterns so that they are more optimistic and realistic in their thinking. About 12 percent of practitioners describe themselves as cognitive psychologists.

In addition to these long-standing, well-established schools of psychotherapy many clinical psychologists describe themselves as eclectic—they use bits and pieces of different theories in treating different patients, modifying their approach to suit each patient's needs. The eclectic therapist might use a combination of cognitive and behavioral techniques with one patient but employ psychodynamic techniques with another depending on what works for the patient and the patient's problem. It is hard to obtain reliable figures for the number of eclectic psychologists, but some studies indicate that over 50 percent of clinical psychologists have this type of orientation.

The role of therapists

Clinical psychology and psychiatry go back 100 years or more. Since World War II numerous other types of psychotherapist have appeared on the scene. In general these therapists have less extensive training than clinical psychologists or psychiatrists and handle a narrower range of patient problems. Some specialize in marriage guidance counseling and family therapy; others treat only people with addictive disorders, such as alcohol or drug addiction.

Clinical social workers often deal with cases of mental disorders in which factors such as financial and housing difficulties play a prominent role. In addition to doing traditional psychotherapy, social workers may help their patients gain access to social services such as housing assistance that they might not otherwise get.

As scientists have learned more about the factors that cause mental disorders,

Psychiatrists are physicians who specialize in the physiological aspects of mental disorders. They are qualified to treat the symptoms with drugs, if necessary. Most psychiatrists work in hospitals, but many also see patients in private practice.

A Day in the Life of a Clinical Psychologist

Dr. Paula Wiggins usually schedules her first patients for 10 a.m., but she gets to the office at least an hour earlier. There are always a few phone calls to return—from patients, professional colleagues, and managed-care companies. Dr. Wiggins likes to get through them before her first patient arrives. Like many clinical psychologists, she does not have a full-time secretary, so she must do a fair amount of organizational work on her own. Her part-time secretary comes in two days a week on her busiest days.

From 10 a.m. until 5 p.m. Dr. Wiggins sees patients. Each session lasts 50 minutes, so she should get a break every hour. In reality many sessions overrun by a few minutes, so she usually has to move directly from one patient to the next. Some days she schedules a patient session during the noon hour; on other days she leaves that hour open and grabs a quick lunch.

After work one day a week Dr. Wiggins works at a local shelter for battered women. She is usually there from 6 p.m. until 9 p.m. or so, talking with new residents and running her weekly therapy group. She is not paid for her time at the shelter. She does this work voluntarily, to give back to the community. This is known as *pro bono* work, and most psychologists do it.

On days when she comes home directly after work, Dr. Wiggins has time to read some scientific journals to keep up on the latest findings. She subscribes to a half dozen such publications, and she feels that keeping abreast of the scientific literature is one of her most important professional activities. On evenings when she does not read journals, she catches up on her paperwork—patient notes, reports on testings and assessments she completed during the week, and detailed descriptions of new patients and their problems, known as "intake reports." She usually spends at least an hour or two a day on paperwork—not what she had imagined when she entered graduate school, but the reality of private practice in clinical psychology today.

psychologists have developed new treatment approaches. The methods do not always involve working one-on-one with a patient, as traditional treatments do. Instead, they are guided by the principle that where mental disorders are concerned, anything and everything is worth a try if it might improve the patient's life.

The role of self-help programs

The first self-help program for a mental disorder, alcohol addiction, was Alcoholics Anonymous (AA), founded in 1935. AA is now so well established that virtually every city and most smaller communities have at least one active AA chapter. Like all self-help programs, AA emphasizes the need for individuals to take responsibility for their own recovery and supports other people who are going through a similar struggle.

A clinical psychologist can have many roles: conducting diagnostic tests, teaching, and as a therapist (as here) in a hospital, private practice, and often doing pro bono *(free) work.*

Studies confirm that self-help programs of this type can be very effective in helping people recover from addiction. In recent years other drug-related self-help programs based on AA principles have taken root, such as Cocaine Users Anonymous and Marijuana Users Anonymous. The programs can be very helpful in treating other forms of drug addiction.

The self-help movement has branched out beyond addiction. There are groups for people who suffer from depression, anxiety, and eating disorders. They are also available for parents who are grieving the loss of a child and for children who are grieving the loss of a parent. Victims of physical and sexual abuse, people who care for relatives with Alzheimer's disease, children and adults with learning difficulties—all now have specialized self-help support groups available that focus on their particular problem.

> "All successful therapy has two things in common: It is forward looking and it requires assuming responsibility."
> —Martin E. P. Seligman, 1994

The role of the community

Of course, not everyone has access to mental-health services, even in the developed world. People living in extreme poverty have little chance of receiving even basic medical care, let alone cutting-edge mental-health treatment. Recent immigrants living in new and unfamiliar countries do not always know how to obtain mental-health services and might lack the language skills needed to benefit from treatment even if they knew where to get it.

For such people community outreach programs are critical. These initiatives—which are staffed by teams of mental-health professionals and located near the communities that need them most—do not wait for people to come and ask for help. Instead, they make the first

Self-help groups are another form of therapy available for mental disorders. Participants gain support from each other and learn from the experiences of group members.

contact themselves, through flyers, radio advertisements, even by going door-to-door. They want to make sure that everyone who needs their services knows how to get them. Community outreach programs try to ensure that people with limited financial resources can get the basic mental-health care they need.

The primary prevention movement

Mental-health professionals have long known that stressful events, such as living in poverty, place people at increased risk of mental disorder. In the early 1960s George Albee (born 1921), a psychologist at the University of Vermont, proposed that, instead of waiting for disorders to strike and then treating them, mental healthcare professionals should employ preventive measures so that there would be fewer disorders in the first place.

The primary prevention movement—sometimes called the community psychology movement—was born. Now psychologists and other mental-health professionals work with entire communities, trying to find ways of making life for the people less stressful and more pleasant. Studies show that Albee's primary prevention strategy works: When community stress is

Stressful social conditions such as poverty and poor housing have been shown to be major contributors to mental disorders. The community psychology—or primary prevention—movement aims to improve social conditions to reduce the risk of mental disorders within a community.

reduced, fewer people develop mental-health problems, and fewer need treatment.

This does not mean that primary prevention can solve the problem completely and rid the world of mental disorders. Many mental illnesses, such as schizophrenia, reflect problems in the functioning of the brain. Reducing stress will not make them disappear. Primary prevention is an important component in mental-health treatment—one more weapon available for mental health professionals to do battle against mental disorders. But it is not the only solution, mainly because it is inconceivable that individuals can alter the fundamental socioeconomic problems of their lives.

The multipronged approach

The more we learn about different methods of treating mental illness, the easier it is to see that a given disorder might be treated in more than one way. Often a patient benefits most when several different forms of treatment are used contemporaneously in combination, rather than when one type of treatment alone is relied on (*see* pp. 118–141).

Today most disorders are treated using a multipronged strategy that addresses the biological, psychological, and environmental aspects of the disorder at the same time. Thus, for example, severely depressed people might receive antidepressant medication to deal with the biology of the disorder as well as traditional psychotherapy to address its psychological components. At the same time, psychologists and social workers will intervene wherever possible to change the patients' environment—to improve their living conditions and help them obtain better access to medical care and other social services.

Managed care

Managed care is an approach to treating medical and psychological disorders in which a person's treatment is arranged by organizations such as insurance companies that coordinate the different services a patient is receiving. The advantage of managed care is that it helps improve communication among the various professionals—physicians, psychologists, social workers, and others—who are involved in a person's treatment. As the lines of communication between these people improve, the person's care improves as well. Problems arise when some managed-care companies become too concerned with saving money. In the United States there have been several landmark legal actions in which patients have argued that they were prevented from receiving needed care because a managed-care organization refused to pay for it. In some such cases the courts found

A person undergoes a CT scan. Neuroimaging techniques have greatly benefited from advances in computer technology. Scientists can look into the functioning of the brain while the patient undergoes tests.

in favor of the patients, with the result that today managed-care organizations are more conscious than ever before of the need to place patients' needs ahead of financial self-interest.

The role of technology
Technology—especially computer-based technology—changed society as a whole during the last 10 years of the 20th century and had a particularly powerful impact in two areas of mental-health treatment. First, new neuroimaging techniques (sometimes termed "brain imaging") have become available, allowing physicians to peer inside a working brain and pinpoint problem areas. Computerized tomography (CT) is one well-known neuroimaging technique; another is magnetic resonance imaging (MRI). (For a more detailed description of these processes *see* Vol. 1, pp. 96–103.) In fact, there are many different neuroimaging techniques available, but they all have one thing in common: They allow scientists to get a real-time image of the brain in action even while the patient is engaged in some other task, such as talking about troubling feelings or trying to recall childhood events (*see* pp. 118–141).

Technology has not only helped psychiatrists delve deeper, it has also enabled psychologists to reach out and connect with people who might not otherwise be able to obtain access to mental-health services. It is now possible for patients to receive psychotherapy over the Internet, conversing with psychologists who may be thousands of miles away. Housebound elderly and disabled people, and people living in isolated, rural areas have benefited tremendously from Internet-based therapy.

RIGHTS OF PATIENTS
For most people the image of mental hospitals is not a pleasant one—we see them as dirty, dangerous places, full of frightened, confused patients and uncaring, sadistic staff. This perception has been shaped at least in part by popular

A Day in the Life of a Mental-Health Researcher

When Professor Sandra Davis arrives at her university office, there are usually at least a dozen e-mails awaiting her attention. Dr. Davis is a mental-health researcher: She conducts scientific studies of mental disorders. Her specialty is eating disorders, and her recent work examines the personality traits of anorexic college women.

Like many mental-health researchers, Dr. Davis spends part of her time teaching. Today she will give a lecture on child development to her introductory psychology class. After answering her e-mails, she goes over her lecture notes, updating the information as needed, and making sure she has her lecture well organized and planned.

When class is done at 10:15 a.m., Dr. Davis spends some time talking with her students. She does this most days, and it is the part of her job she enjoys the most. By talking informally with them after class, she feels more connected with them, and they with her. Most days she holds a meeting with her research group—advanced psychology students who help her plan and conduct her own studies. In the meetings they discuss the progress of ongoing projects and talk about upcoming research. Her students give her progress reports, and she fills them in

on the latest findings reported by other researchers. After today's lab group meeting Dr. Davis heads across campus for a meeting with the director of the university's counseling center. She is collecting data at the center for one of her studies, so she periodically meets with the center's director to make sure everything is going smoothly.

By the time her meeting is done it is midafternoon, and Dr. Davis heads back to her office to grab a quick bite and work on a paper. It describes her most recent study—an investigation of personality changes in women who are successfully treated for anorexia. She hopes to present the results at an upcoming psychology conference and then submit the paper for publication in a professional psychology journal. On some days she takes work home with her; other days she does not. Today she must—the deadline for submitting the paper to the conference is just two days away, and she wants to make sure she has the manuscript ready on time. Tomorrow she will distribute drafts of the paper to the members of her research group to get their feedback. She will have just enough time to incorporate their suggestions before the package must go in the mail.

films such as Milos Forman's *One Flew over the Cuckoo's Nest* (1975). In most cases the stereotype is not reality. There was indeed a time when people with mental disorders were treated very badly. But for the most part, they have a number of important legal rights that protect them from abuse both in hospitals and in society as a whole.

Confidentiality

Virtually everything that a patient says to a mental-health professional must be kept in strict confidence. It may not be revealed to anyone without the patient's permission—even to other treatment professionals or the patient's family. There are two exceptions to this rule, however. The first is when the patient reports that child abuse has occurred. In this case it does not matter whether the patient was the victim or the abuser, nor does it matter whether the abuse is

continuing to happen or took place in the past. Neither does it matter whether the abuse was sexual, physical, or emotional. Once the patient discloses child abuse, the therapist has to report it right away to the child-abuse authorities.

The other time that confidentiality must be broken is when a patient threatens to harm another person (*see* box on page 154). Here again, the rules are strict: The patient must make a realistic threat against an identifiable person. Implausible threats against unnamed people do not count; neither do vague statements such as "I'm so angry I don't know what I'm liable to do."

Informed consent

Patients have the right to be informed about the risks and benefits of any treatment. They must be given accurate, unbiased information, and they have a right to ask questions until they are

A scene from One Flew over the Cuckoo's Nest, *which was set in a 1950s' mental hospital in Portland, Oregon. Both the movie and the novel by Ken Kesey on which it was based exposed the authoritarianism of psychiatric hospitals of the time. Since then changes in mental-health services have ensured that patients are treated much more humanely than before.*

satisfied. The patient also has the right to be informed of other possible treatments, even if the psychologist or psychiatrist does not favor such treatments.

Patients must specifically consent to receive treatment after being informed of its potential benefits and risks, and they must give consent in writing before the treatment can begin. If patients choose not to receive a recommended treatment, that, too, is their right. Even after treatment has begun, they may change their minds and decide to stop it. The right holds regardless of whether patients are being treated in a doctor's office, in a clinic, or in a hospital. Simply because they are hospitalized, patients do not lose their right to refuse treatment.

Humane treatment

What happens when people's thoughts are so confused by schizophrenia or Alzheimer's disease, for example, that they cannot realistically give informed consent? In such cases another person (usually a family member) is appointed to do it for them. If patients should later regain the ability to give informed consent (for example, if the symptoms of schizophrenia lessen once medication takes effect),

then the other person steps aside, and the patients now have the right to give consent—or choose not to give it—for themselves. This means, ironically, that patients would then have the right to refuse the very treatment that improved their conditions; and if they do, the treatment must be stopped (*see* below, p. 156).

Patients with mental disorders also have the right to be dealt with humanely. They must be treated in the least restrictive environment possible—they may not be kept in locked wards unless keeping them in open wards would be dangerous. They may not be physically restrained unless they would otherwise do harm to themselves or other people. Under no circumstances may a patient be threatened, hit, or handled roughly. There are no exceptions to this rule.

The right to humane treatment extends to other areas as well. Patients must be allowed to receive visitors, to have social contact with other patients, to make and receive phone calls, and to attend religious services (which are held in most hospitals at least once a week). Patients have a right to wear their own clothes and to decorate their rooms as they like within reason—hate literature and pornography are forbidden.

WHEN CONFIDENTIALITY TAKES A BACK SEAT

There are very few circumstances in which the confidentiality between therapist and patient must be broken. One of the most important is when a patient makes a realistic threat against an identifiable person. But it was not until 1972—in the now famous California court case known as the "Tarasoff Decision"—that this rule became law.

Tanya Tarasoff and Prosenjit Poddar were students at the University of California at Berkeley. They became friends, and Poddar eventually developed a crush on Tarasoff. She refused his romantic advances, and over time his crush became an obsession. He became extremely frustrated and unhappy, and sought therapy at the university counseling center.

During one therapy session Poddar revealed to his therapist that he planned to hurt Tarasoff. The therapist recorded the student's threat on his chart but did nothing

about it. Several weeks later Poddar acted on his threat: He went to Tarasoff's house, confronted her, and killed her.

Tarasoff's parents sued the trustees of the University of California, and after a series of court cases a decision was finally reached: Prosenjit Poddar's therapist should have warned Tarasoff about the danger to her life, said the court, since Poddar had made a realistic threat and specifically identified her as his target. The university and the therapist were legally responsible for Tarasoff's death.

Since 1972 the Tarasoff Decision has been challenged many times, but it has weathered each challenge and has remained in effect. New cases continue to test the limits of the Tarasoff Decision—should a therapist break confidentiality if an HIV patient plans to have sex with her boyfriend without telling him of her condition? But the Tarasoff Decision remains a landmark in therapist–patient confidentiality law.

Conflicts of interest

Sometimes a conflict of interest might arise during treatment. For example, if physicians are being paid to take part in a research project evaluating a new drug, they might be tempted to prescribe the drug to as many patients as possible to further the study. They cannot do so, however, because the interests of the drug company might be different from those of the patients, and the physicians might be tempted to act in ways that serve the company not the patients. In such situations mental-health professionals must inform patients in advance about potential conflicts of interest so the patients can choose how to proceed. If necessary, they might have to be referred to a different psychiatrist or psychologist to avoid conflict of interest and to ensure they are getting the best possible care.

Conflicts of interest might also arise when mental-health professionals treat one member of a family, and another member of that family comes to them for treatment. Sometimes a mental-health professional can treat two or more members of a family without having a conflict of interest (for example, a psychiatrist may prescribe antidepressant medications to parent and child). At other times, however, treating two people within the same family becomes too complicated to handle. For example, a psychologist cannot see both members of a married couple for individual therapy because a conflict might arise if marital difficulties turn out to be part of the problem.

The reception area of a modern psychiatric hospital. Patients with mental disorders have the right to receive visitors and socialize with other patients.

Cultural sensitivity

Statistical studies have shown that for many years members of ethnic minority groups in the United States, such as Asian and African Americans, were traditionally unwilling to seek treatment for mental disorders. This reluctance stemmed either from fear or from a cultural belief that such problems should be handled without professional help. Today, however, many more members of ethnic and racial minority groups seek treatment for mental disorders to get the help they need.

As psychologists and psychiatrists deal with an increasingly diverse patient population, they have had to become more sensitive to cultural values and cultural norms (*see* Vol. 1, pp. 152–161)—behavior that will pass without remark in one culture may be regarded as disturbed if done in another. It is important that mental-health professionals bear this in mind and do not try to force their own beliefs onto patients. Instead, they must respect the patients' right to handle their own problems however they choose.

PSYCHOLOGY & SOCIETY

CULTURE AND PSYCHOLOGICAL SYMPTOMS

Some psychological disorders, such as depression, turn up in almost every society. Other mental illnesses are found in some cultures but not in others. For example, bipolar 1 disorder was almost unheard of in Japan until the mid-20th century. Eating disorders such as anorexia and bulimia are extremely rare in many African nations. There is no doubt that culture affects mental disorders (*see* Vol. 1, pp. 152–161). In fact, some mental disorders are surprisingly culture specific. They turn up in one—and only one—society, and they seem to reflect something important about that society's traditions and values.

Here are a few examples of mental disorders that are highly culture bound:

• *Dhat* syndrome in India is characterized by weakness, dizziness, insomnia, and bodily aches. It is thought to be caused by excessive loss of semen in men (although there is no scientific evidence to support this theory).

• *Nervios* is a Latin-American disorder characterized by anxiety, palpitations (rapid heartbeat), trembling, and persistent worry. It is usually attributed to the loss of an important personal relationship.

• *Taijin kyofusho* is a Japanese syndrome characterized by an intense fear that one's physical appearance, facial expression, and body odor are offensive to other people. It appears to stem from a deep-seated belief that one is not living in sufficient harmony with other members of the community.

Japanese people greeting each other with deep bows. Behavior is often defined by a society's culture, and so, too, are certain mental disorders. Japanese culture places great importance on a person's position within the social order, and fears of nonconformity could result in specific culture-bound disorders.

LEGAL ISSUES

People with mental disorders have many legal rights that, most of the time, are very carefully protected. But sometimes circumstances arise when legal and mental-health professionals must balance the rights of the individual patient against those of society. When this happens, society's mental-health system and legal system work together to try to do what is best for the patient and for society as well. That usually involves compromise.

People with mental illnesses have the right to make informed decisions about themselves and their care. But there are exceptions to this rule. The main one occurs when patients are so seriously impaired by the symptoms of their disorder that they cannot make reasonable, informed decisions on their own behalf (*see* page 153 above). When this occurs, they may be declared legally incompetent, and others will be designated to make decisions for them. Such another person—known as a guardian—is appointed by the courts through a formal legal process known as a "competency hearing."

In many ways the relationship between a guardian and a legally incompetent patient is similar to that between a parent and a child. Like a parent, the guardian makes decisions on the other person's behalf, and like a parent, the guardian is expected to make decisions that are in the other person's best interests.

Having a person declared legally incompetent is not a simple matter. Under U.S. law a person is considered competent until proven otherwise. Evidence of legal incompetence must be compelling, and courts are usually reluctant to declare someone legally incompetent unless failure to do so would clearly put the person at risk. Competency hearings can be lengthy, expensive, and complicated, with psychologists and psychiatrists presenting evidence on both sides.

From a mental-health perspective incompetence is not necessarily permanent. Simply because people are declared incompetent today does not

mean they will still be incompetent next week or next month. Follow-up court hearings must be held periodically to give them the chance to demonstrate that they have regained their competence and can now again make informed decisions on their own. In practice it is quite common for people who have been declared incompetent to regain their competency later on.

People cannot be declared incompetent simply because their beliefs are strange or unusual. If they keep all their money hidden under the mattress because they think banks cannot be trusted, that is their right—it does not mean they are incompetent. However, if they do not trust banks because they think the tellers are all Martians, that might be evidence of legal incompetence. Similarly, if people refuse lifesaving medical treatment on religious grounds, they are entitled to do so—it does not mean they are incompetent. But

> "*I called them mad, and they called me mad, and, damn them, they outvoted me!*"
> — *Nathaniel Lee, 1684*

if they refuse medical treatment because they think the doctors are all plotting to kill them, that might be taken as evidence of incompetence.

The concept of competency is complex, and decisions regarding it are rarely easy to make. Many think that is just as it ought to be—declaring a person legally incompetent is serious business and not something to be taken lightly.

Involuntary commitment

Involuntary commitment—sometimes known as civil commitment—occurs when people are hospitalized against their will. Although some movies and TV shows might make it seem as if this is easy, it is not. People may be involuntarily

THOMAS SZASZ AND THE MYTH OF MENTAL ILLNESS

U.S. psychiatrist Thomas Szasz (born 1920) is famous but not very popular among certain members of the mental-health profession. In 1960 he published a paper, "The Myth of Mental Illness," in which he argued that mental illness does not really exist—it is an idea made up to explain behavior that seems irrational ("crazy") to most members of society. According to Szasz, when people report hearing voices or try to kill themselves, it seems irrational, and it makes us uncomfortable. Instead of simply accepting that the person is making choices we do not understand, we find it easier to label their behavior a symptom of mental illness. In this way we convince ourselves that:

• The behavior is indeed "crazy" (after all, it is a symptom).

• Those who display such symptoms are not responsible for what they are doing (because they are mentally ill).

• We have the right to stop them from doing it (because we are mental-health professionals).

According to Szasz, some odd behaviors, such as Tourette syndrome, stem from brain diseases—but they are physical diseases, not mental diseases. If people exhibit strange behavior and there is no biological cause, then according to him, it is just that—strange behavior. It is their choice and their responsibility. We all have a right to be as strange as we please, he argues, as long as we do not interfere with anyone else. Mental-health professionals have no right to force people to give up their strange behaviors no matter how self-destructive those behaviors might be.

Few mental-health professionals agree completely with Szasz's radical view, but his emphasis is on personal choice and responsibility. It questions fundamental assumptions that psychologists and psychiatrists make about mental disorders. For example, his personal responsibility perspective suggests that:

• People should never be hospitalized against their will: After all, they have a right to act however they want.

• Mental-health professionals should not force suicidal people into treatment because suicide, like other self-destructive behavior, is nobody else's business.

• All drugs should be legal: If people want to use cocaine or heroin, that is their choice.

• The insanity defense should be abolished since insanity does not exist.

Szasz's view might be controversial, but it has practical implications—implications that have kept mental-health professionals arguing for more than 40 years.

committed only under certain very specific circumstances. In fact, for people to be hospitalized against their will, at least one of two conditions must be satisfied: They must be a clear and immediate danger either to themselves or to other people (and the risk of danger must be real and immediate, not just possible or likely somewhere down the line); alternatively, they must be unable to care for themselves—they must be acting in such a way as to jeopardize their health and well-being by, for example, living in filthy and unsafe conditions.

Once people have been involuntarily committed to a psychiatric hospital, steps must be taken to ensure that they are treated fairly and humanely. For example, civil commitment lasts only for a short time—48 or 72 hours in most states—and at the end of the period patients have the right to be released from the hospital unless staff can prove that they are still a danger to themselves or others. People who are involuntarily hospitalized have exactly the same rights as people who go in voluntarily. They have the right to therapist-patient confidentiality, to make informed decisions regarding their care, to refuse treatment they do not want, and to be treated with respect and dignity. Regardless of whether they entered the hospital willingly or under orders, they are there for the same reason: to be cared for, not punished.

THE INSANITY DEFENSE

One of the most well-publicized areas in which the mental-health and legal systems meet is the insanity defense. Most of us have heard something about this controversial topic, and media messages might lead us to the conclusion that defendants plead insanity all the time. In fact, insanity pleas are entered in fewer than two percent of all murder trials. And only a very small percentage of those insanity pleas—fewer than 10 percent overall—are successful.

Just how does a person "plead insanity"? And legally what does it mean to be declared "insane"? To answer such questions, we must look at the landmark court cases and legal decisions that shaped today's insanity defense. Four stand out: the M'Naghten Rule, the Durham Decision, the American Law Institute guidelines, and the Insanity Defense Reform Act.

The M'Naghten Rule

The first modern version of the insanity defense arose from an 1843 trial in which Daniel M'Naghten, a Scotsman, was put on trial for attempting to assassinate British Prime Minister Robert Peel. M'Naghten claimed that he committed the crime because the prime minister was plotting against him—he believed he had to assassinate Peel to protect himself.

After a long and controversial trial the court declared M'Naghten insane and not legally responsible for his actions because he did not understand that what he had done was wrong. This is the basic principle of the M'Naghten Rule: A person is legally insane if he cannot tell right from wrong. The M'Naghten Rule formed

In the movie Suddenly Last Summer *(1959)* Catherine Holly *(played by Elizabeth Taylor) is hospitalized against her will as a psychiatric patient. Montgomery Clift plays John Cukrowicz, a neurosurgeon who investigates her case to determine whether she should be forced to undergo a lobotomy.*

The trial of Daniel M'Naghten in 1843 in London, England, found him insane and not legally responsible for his actions even though he had tried to kill the British prime minister. The resulting M'Naghten Rule formed the basis of the first legal plea of insanity.

the basis of the insanity defense for more than 100 years in both Britain and the United States.

The Durham decision

The 1954 Durham decision firmly established psychiatry in the court systems of America. On July 13, 1951, Monte Durham, a 23-year-old with a long criminal and psychiatric history, was convicted of housebreaking despite his insistence that he was not guilty by reason of insanity. The U.S. Court of Appeals overruled the original verdict on the grounds that "an accused is not criminally responsible if his unlawful act was the product of a mental disease or defect." This was a landmark in legal history. Henceforth a defendant who could be shown to be mentally ill or mentally defective could not be convicted—the question of whether he had committed the crime became irrelevant. The Durham decision superseded the M'Naghten Rule not only in the United States but also across much of the world and was effectively the law's formal recognition of modern psychiatry.

The American Law Institute guidelines

The next major shift in insanity law came in 1962, when the American Law Institute (ALI) developed a new definition of insanity. According to ALI guidelines, people are insane if they cannot understand or control their actions. In other words, they are not legally responsible if they do not understand

> **"If a man is a minority of one, we lock him up."**
> —*Oliver Wendell Holmes, 1838*

what they did. But even if they understand what they did, they cannot be held legally responsible if they cannot control their actions, that is, if their actions stemmed from what legal scholars describe as an "irresistible impulse."

Over the years many criminal defendants have used this aspect of the ALI guidelines to try to escape punishment, arguing that they knew what they were doing was wrong, but still could not stop themselves. This might be the case in a crime of passion—for example, if

AN ILL-PLACED PASSION

"Dear Jodie,

There is a definite possibility that I will be killed in my attempt to get Reagan. It is for this very reason that I am writing you this letter now. By sacrificing my freedom and possibly my life I hope to change your mind about me. This letter is being written an hour before I leave for the Hilton Hotel. Jodie, I'm asking you please to look into your heart and at least give me the chance with this historical deed to gain your respect and love.

I love you forever."

Expert Witness 1: [John Hinckley suffers from] schizophrenia.
Expert Witness 2: Hinckley does not suffer from schizophrenia.
Expert Witness 3: [Hinckley suffers from] a severe depressive disorder.
Expert Witness 4: There is little to suggest [Hinckley is] seriously depressed.

A twisted love letter. An eerie photograph (right). Four expert witnesses with four contrasting conclusions. It is not surprising that when a jury declared John Hinckley not guilty of attempted murder by reason of insanity on June 21, 1982, no one knew what to think.

Some people were outraged. After all, he had clearly attempted to assassinate President Ronald Reagan—the whole incident had been captured on film. He had bought the weapon, learned how to use it, planned his attack carefully, and carried it out just as he said he would. This had to be the work of a cold, calculating person, albeit one with strange ideas and motives.

Others disagreed: Hinckley's diary and letters to actress Jodie Foster (which became part of the public record during the trial) were clearly the rantings of an insane man. He shot the president to impress a stranger—a woman he had never met. No, argued the critics, if ever there was a clear-cut case of insanity, this was it.

The Hinckley case is important because it helped reshape the insanity defense. In fact, it took Congress only three days after the Hinckley verdict to convene a special committee to strengthen the insanity law. But equally important, the case altered public opinion. No longer was the insanity defense something abstract and unseen—almost everyone in the United States witnessed its consequences right there on the evening news.

People still disagree about the insanity defense, and whether it should be allowed in cases such as this one. Decades after the event John Hinckley remains hospitalized in the forensic (legal) unit of Saint Elizabeth's Hospital in Washington, D.C. He has periodically petitioned for release from the hospital, but his requests have been denied.

a woman came home to find her husband cheating on her, became so enraged that she lost control, and shot him. She knew that shooting her husband was wrong, but she just could not stop herself and was thus not responsible for her action.

> *"I feel the insanity defense should be retained. I bear no grudge against John Hinckley, but I sure don't hope he wins the Irish Sweepstakes."*
> —*James Brady, wounded by John Hinckley, 1982*

The Insanity Defense Reform Act

In the spring of 1981 John Hinckley shot and wounded U.S. President Ronald Reagan on the street outside the Hilton Hotel in Washington, D.C. Hinckley was arrested immediately, and over time it became clear that his motive for shooting the president was quite strange (*see* box p. 160). Eventually he was acquitted of all charges against him on the grounds of insanity. The public outcry against this verdict was so great that in 1984 Congress passed the Insanity Defense Reform Act (IDRA), which set a higher threshold for proving insanity. Before IDRA became law, a defendant such as John Hinckley was considered insane until proven otherwise; now he would be presumed sane unless he could convince a judge and jury that he was genuinely insane.

Diminished capacity

In the United States today the insanity defense has largely been replaced by a plea of "diminished capacity." In such cases the defendant pleads guilty to the crime, but presents evidence that he was not thinking clearly at the time it was committed. Perhaps the defendant was under great stress or suffering from some sort of mental disorder. In this situation the defendant would still be found guilty, but would receive a reduced sentence if the jury is convinced that "diminished capacity" was really an issue in the case.

PSYCHOLOGY & SOCIETY

ARE WE GETTING SICKER?

Research shows that your parents are more likely to develop serious depression than your grandparents were, and that you are more likely to become depressed than your parents. If current trends continue, your children will be at higher risk of depression than you are, and your grandchildren's risk will be even higher. No one knows why this should be the case, but the fact remains that the incidence of depression is increasing with each passing generation.

Neither is depression the only psychological illness that appears to be on the increase. Eating disorders and phobias are also becoming more common. Although no one is sure why, there is no shortage of theories. Some researchers contend that the increase in mental disorders is due to increased stress. After all, we know that stress tends to increase the risk of mental disorders (*see* pp. 118–141), and that life in the modern world is—or, at least, is perceived to be—more stressful than it was in earlier, more leisurely periods of history.

Some researchers take the view that increased rates of mental disorders reflect our increased contact with environmental toxins—everything from air and water pollution to chemicals in the home. This increased exposure to potentially harmful chemicals begins even before we are born.

Other experts contend that these data are misleading. Mental disorders are not getting more common; we are just getting better at identifying them. People are more willing to talk about psychological problems than they used to be, and mental-health professionals are better at diagnosing them.

The hectic pace of modern life can increase stress, which could trigger mental disorders such as depression.

THE FUTURE

How will mental disorders be viewed and treated in our society in the future? It was not that long ago that people with mental disorders were routinely discriminated against in the workplace. As recently as 1972, vice-presidential candidate Thomas Eagleton felt he had to resign from the Democratic ticket because it was revealed that he had undergone treatment for depression. People in the public eye at the time tried to hide the fact that they were receiving mental-health treatment for fear their careers would be jeopardized.

Since then things have changed. People with mental disorders are much more willing to talk about their experiences, and by doing so, they make it easier for others to talk about theirs too. Oprah Winfrey, Tipper Gore, Jonathan Winters, Carly Simon, Mike Wallace, Cathy Rigby—these are just some of the well-known people who have talked publicly about their experiences with mental disorders and their treatment experiences as well.

Things have also changed in the legal arena. With the passing of the 1990 Americans with Disabilities Act (ADA), it became illegal to discriminate on the basis of any type of illness, physical or mental. Increasingly, mental disorders have come to be seen as challenges, not weaknesses or flaws. And just as employers must accommodate workers who have physical challenges, they must accommodate those who have mental challenges to overcome.

Improved diagnosis and treatment techniques—along with landmark laws such as the ADA—have brought mental disorders out of the closet and into mainstream society. As public perceptions change, mental disorders are no longer seen as barriers to success. In fact, the more we learn about mental disorders, the clearer it becomes that sometimes a successful struggle against a mental disorder can actually work in a person's favor. Many people with mental disorders have done outstanding, creative work. And, as people

Society's attitudes to mental disorders can be slow to change. In 1972 Thomas Eagleton (left), the original running mate of the Democratic party's presidential candidate George McGovern (right), had to give up his candidacy after it was revealed that he had suffered from depression.

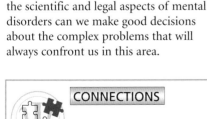

Vincent Van Gogh
(1853–1890) suffered
from severe mental
disorders, but they did
not inhibit his
creativity—indeed,
they may have inspired
and facilitated it.
Paintings such as this
1889 self-portrait are
now among the
world's most treasured
works of art.

KEY POINTS

• Many people who would once have been held in mental institutions are now released into the community, their conditions controlled by psychotropic drugs.

• Psychiatrists are medically qualified specialists whose training focuses on a biomedical approach to psychological problems. Unlike clinical psychologists (see below), they can prescribe drugs.

• Clinical psychologists are psychologists who have completed postgraduate training in the diagnosis and treatment of psychological problems, and served a period of supervised clinical practice.

• Therapists help people overcome psychological difficulties. They may, but need not, be psychologists. Psychotherapists generally discuss problems; somatic therapists propose medical or biological intervention.

• Clinical social workers help with practical problems, such as where to find the right care.

• Community programs aim to provide local psychiatric services and improve social conditions.

• Managed-care companies help coordinate the work of various services and provide payment.

• Rights of people with mental disorders include informed consent and humane treatment.

• The legal definition of insanity has changed greatly since the 19th century.

who have overcome the challenge of mental disorders point out, once you have battled serious depression (or addiction or anxiety), life's minor, everyday troubles do not seem so overwhelming.

We have made tremendous progress in dealing with mental disorders since the mid-20th century, but further challenges remain. Take the cases examined in this chapter. Should Andrea Yates be held responsible for what she did? Should John Hinckley be in a hospital or in prison? Should Joyce Brown (see box on page 145) be allowed to live life as she chooses no matter how poor her choices seem to us? There are no easy answers to such questions. The more we learn about mental disorders and accommodating them in society, the more we realize ideal solutions rarely exist. Society still has a responsibility, however, to find out as much as it can and to use the knowledge to deal more effectively with the disorders. Only by understanding the scientific and legal aspects of mental disorders can we make good decisions about the complex problems that will always confront us in this area.

CONNECTIONS

• Psychoanalysis: Volume 1, pp. 52–65
• Neuropsychology: Volume 1, pp. 90–95
• Brain-imaging Techniques: Volume 1, pp. 96–103
• Cross-cultural Psychology: Volume 1, pp. 152–161
• Talking Cures: pp. 92–117
• Physical Therapies: pp. 118–141

Set Glossary

abnormality Within abnormal psychology abnormality is the deviation from normal or expected behavior, generally involving maladaptive responses and personal distress both to the individuals with abnormal behavior and to those around them.

abnormal psychology The study and treatment of mental disorders.

acquisition The process by which something, such as a skill, habit, or language, is learned.

adaptation A change in behavior or structure that increases the survival chances of a species. Adjective: adaptive

addiction A state of dependence on a drug or a particular pattern of behavior.

adjustment disorder A mental disorder in which a patient is unable to adjust properly to a stressful life change.

affect A mood, emotion, or feeling. An affect is generally a shorter-lived and less-pronounced emotion than mood.

affective disorder A group of mental disorders, such as depression and bipolar 1 disorder, that are characterized by pronounced and often prolonged changes of mood.

agnosia A group of brain disorders involving impaired ability to recognize or interpret sensory information.

Alzheimer's disease A progressive and irreversible dementia in which the gradual destruction of brain tissue results in memory loss, impaired cognitive function, and personality change.

amnesia A partial or complete loss of memory.

amygdala An almond-shaped structure located in the front of the brain's temporal lobe that is part of the limbic system. Sometimes called the amygdaloid complex or the amygdaloid nucleus, the amygdala plays an important role in emotional behavior and motivation.

anorexia nervosa An eating disorder in which patients (usually young females) become obsessed with the idea that they are overweight and experience dramatic weight loss by not eating enough.

antidepressants A type of medication used to treat depression.

antianxiety drugs A type of medication used to treat anxiety disorders.

antipsychotic drugs A type of medication used to treat psychotic disorders such as schizophrenia. Sometimes known as neuroleptics.

anxiety disorder A group of mental disorders involving worry or distress.

anxiolytics *See* antianxiety drugs

aphasia A group of brain disorders that involve a partial or complete loss of language ability.

arousal A heightened state of awareness, behavior, or physiological function.

artificial intelligence (AI) A field of study that combines elements of cognitive psychology and computer science in an attempt to develop intelligent machines.

attachment theory A theory that describes how infants form emotional bonds with the adults they are close to.

attention The process by which someone can focus on particular sensory information by excluding other, less immediately relevant information.

attention deficit disorder (ADD) A mental disorder in which the patient (usually a child) is hyperactive, impulsive, and unable to concentrate properly.

autism A mental disorder, first apparent in childhood, in which patients are self-absorbed, socially withdrawn, and engage in repetitive patterns of behavior.

automatization The process by which complex behavior eventually becomes automatic. Such a process may be described as having automaticity or being automatized.

autonomic nervous system A part of the nervous system that controls many of the body's self-regulating (involuntary or automatic) functions.

aversion therapy A method of treating patients, especially those suffering from drink or drug addiction, by subjecting them to painful or unpleasant experiences.

axon Extension of the cell body of a neuron that transmits impulses away from the body of the neuron.

behavioral therapy A method of treating mental disorders that concentrates on modifying abnormal behavior rather than on the underlying causes of that behavior.

behaviorism A school of psychology in which easily observable and measurable behavior is considered to be the only proper subject of scientific study. Noun: behaviorist

bipolar I disorder A mental (affective) disorder involving periods of depression (depressed mood) and periods of mania (elevated mood).

body image The way in which a person perceives their own body or imagines it is perceived by other people.

body language The signals people send out to other people (usually unconsciously) through their gestures, posture, and other types of nonverbal communication.

Broca's area A region of the brain (usually located in the left hemisphere) that is involved with processing language.

bulimia nervosa An eating disorder in which patients consume large amounts of food in binges, then use laxatives or self-induced vomiting to prevent themselves putting on weight.

CAT scan *See* CT

causality The study of the causes of events or the connection between causes and effects.

central nervous system The part of the body's nervous system comprising the brain and spinal cord.

cerebellum A cauliflower-shaped structure at the back of the brain underneath the cerebral hemispheres that coordinates body movements.

cerebral cortex The highly convoluted outer surface of the brain's cerebrum.

cerebrum The largest part of the brain, consisting of the two cerebral hemispheres and their associated structures.

classical conditioning A method of associating a stimulus and a response that do not normally accompany one another. In Pavlov's well-known classical conditioning experiment dogs were trained so that they salivated (the conditioned response or CR) when Pavlov rang a bell (the conditioned stimulus or CS). Normally, dogs salivate

(an unconditioned response or UR) only when food is presented to them (an unconditioned stimulus or US).

clinical psychology An area of psychology concerned with the study and treatment of abnormal behavior.

cognition A mental process that involves thinking, reasoning, or some other type of mental information processing. Adjective: cognitive

cognitive behavioral therapy (CBT) An extension of behavioral therapy that involves treating patients by modifying their abnormal thought patterns as well as their behavior.

cognitive psychology An area of psychology that seeks to understand how the brain processes information.

competency In psycholinguistics the representation of the abstract rules of a language, such as its grammar.

conditioned stimulus/response (CS/CR) *See* classical conditioning

conditioning *See* classical conditioning; instrumental conditioning

connectionism A computer model of cognitive processes such as learning and memory. Connectionist models are based on a large network of "nodes" and the connections between them. Adjective: connectionist

consciousness A high-level mental process responsible for the state of self-awareness that people feel. Consciousness is thought by some researchers to direct human behavior and by others simply to be a byproduct of that behavior.

cortex *See* cerebral cortex

cross-cultural psychology The comparison of behavior, such as language

acquisition or nonverbal communication, between different peoples or cultures.

cross-sectional study An experimental method in which a large number of subjects are studied at a particular moment or period in time. Compare longitudinal study

CT (computed tomography) A method of producing an image of the brain's tissue using X-ray scanning, which is commonly used to detect brain damage. Also called CAT (computerized axial tomography).

culture-specific A behavior found only in certain cultures and not observed universally in all humankind.

declarative knowledge A collection of facts about the world and other things that people have learned. Compare procedural knowledge

declarative memory *See* explicit memory

defense mechanism A type of thinking or behavior that a person employs unconsciously to protect themselves from anxiety or unwelcome feelings.

deficit A missing cognitive function whose loss is caused by a brain disorder.

delusion A false belief that a person holds about themselves or the world around them. Delusions are characteristic features of psychotic mental illnesses such as schizophrenia.

dementia A general loss of cognitive functions usually caused by brain damage. Dementia is often, but not always, progressive (it becomes worse with time).

Dementia of the Alzheimer's type (DAT) See Alzheimer's disease

dendrite A treelike projection of a neuron's cell body that conducts nerve impulses toward the cell body.

dependency An excessive reliance on an addictive substance, such as a drug, or on the support of another person.

depression An affective mental disorder characterized by sadness, low self-esteem, inadequacy, and related symptoms.

desensitization A gradual reduction in the response to a stimulus when it is presented repeatedly over a period of time.

developmental psychology An area of psychology concerned with how people develop throughout their lives, but usually concentrating on how behavior and cognition develop during childhood.

discrimination In perception the ability to distinguish between two or more stimuli. In social psychology and sociology unequal treatment of people based on prejudice.

dysgraphia A brain disorder involving an ability to write properly.

dyslexia Brain disorders that disrupt a person's ability to read.

eating disorders A group of mental disorders that involve disturbed eating patterns or appetite.

echoic memory See sensory memory

ego The central part of a person's self. In Freudian psychology the ego manages the balance between a person's primitive, instinctive needs and the often conflicting demands of the world around them.

egocentric A person who is excessively preoccupied with themselves at the expense of the people and the world around them.

eidetic An accurate and persistent form of visual memory that is generally uncommon in adults (often misnamed "photographic memory").

electroconvulsive therapy (ECT) A treatment for severe depression that involves passing a brief and usually relatively weak electric shock through the front of a patient's skull.

electroencephalogram (EEG) A graph that records the changing electrical activity in a person's brain from electrodes attached to the scalp.

emotion A strong mood or feeling. Also a reaction to a stimulus that prepares the body for action.

episodic memory A type of memory that records well-defined events or episodes in a person's life. Compare semantic memory

ethnocentricity The use of a particular ethnic group to draw conclusions about wider society or humankind as a whole.

event-related potential (ERP) A pattern of electrical activity (the potential) produced by a particular stimulus (the event). EVPs are often recorded from the skull using electrodes.

evoked potential See event-related potential (ERP)

evolution A theory suggesting that existing organisms have developed from earlier ones by processes that include natural selection (dubbed "survival of the fittest") and genetic mutation.

evolutionary psychology An approach to psychology that uses the theory of evolution to explain the mind and human behavior.

explicit memory A type of memory containing information that is available to conscious recognition and recall.

flashbulb memory A very clear and evocative memory of a particular moment or event.

fMRI (functional magnetic resonance imaging) An MRI-based scanning technique that can produce images of the brain while it is engaged in cognitive activities.

functionalism An approach to psychology that concentrates on the functions played by parts of the mind and human behavior.

generalized anxiety disorder (GAD) A type of nonspecific anxiety disorder with symptoms that include worry, irritability, and tension.

genes A functional unit of the chromosome that determines how traits are passed on and expressed from generation to generation. Adjective: genetic

Gestalt psychology A psychology school that emphasizes the importance of appreciating phenomena as structured wholes in areas such as perception and learning, as opposed to breaking them down into their components. Most influential in the mid-1900s.

gray matter The parts of the nervous system that contain mainly nerve cell bodies.

habituation See desensitization

hallucination A vivid but imaginary perceptual experience that occurs purely in the mind, not in reality.

heritability The proportion of observed variation for a trait in a specific population that can be attributed to genetic factors rather than environmental ones. Generally expressed as a ratio of genetically caused variation to total variation.

hippocampus A part of the limbic system in the temporal lobe that is thought to play an important role in the formation of memories.

Humanism A philosophy that stresses the importance of human interests and values.

hypothalamus A small structure at the base of the brain that controls the autonomic nervous system.

hysteria A type of mental disturbance that may include symptoms such as hallucinations and emotional outbursts.

implicit memory A type of memory not normally available to conscious awareness. Sometimes also known as procedural or nondeclarative memory. Compare explicit memory

imprinting A type of learning that occurs in a critical period shortly after birth, such as when chicks learn to accept a human in place of their real mother.

individual psychology An approach to psychology that focuses on the differences between individuals. Also a theory advanced by Alfred Adler based on the idea of overcoming inferiority.

information processing In cognitive psychology the theory that the mind operates something like a computer, with sensory information processed either in a series of discrete stages or in parallel by something like a connectionist network.

ingroup A group whose members feel a strong sense of collective identity and act to exclude other people (the outgroup).

innate A genetically determined trait that is present at birth, as opposed to something that is acquired by learning.

instinct An innate and automatic response to a particular stimulus that usually involves no rational thought.

instrumental conditioning A type of conditioning in which reinforcement occurs only when an organism makes a certain, desired response. Instrumental

conditioning occurs, for example, when a pigeon is trained to peck a lever to receive a pellet of food.

internalize To make internal, personal, or subjective; to take in and make an integral part of one's attitudes or beliefs:

introspection A behaviorist technique of studying the mind by observing one's own thought processes.

language acquisition device (LAD) According to linguist Noam Chomsky, a part of the brain that is preprogrammed with a universal set of grammatical rules that can construct the rules of a specific language according to the environment it is exposed to.

libido The sexual drive.

limbic system A set of structures in the brain stem, including the hippocampus and the amygdala, that lie below the corpus callosum. It is involved in emotion, motivation, behavior, and various functions of the autonomic nervous system.

long-term memory A type of memory in which information is retained for long periods after being deeply processed. Generally used to store events and information from the past. Compare short-term memory

longitudinal study An experimental method that follows a small group of subjects over a long period of time. Compare cross-sectional study

maladaptive Behavior is considered maladapative or dysfunctional if it has a negative effect on society or on a person's ability to function in society.

medical model A theory that mental disorders, like diseases, have specific underlying medical causes, which must be addressed if treatment is to be effective.

mental disorder A psychiatric illness such as schizophrenia, anxiety, or depression.

metacognition The study by an individual of their own thought processes. *See also* introspection

mnemonic A technique that can be used to remember information or improve memory.

modeling The technique by which a person observes some ideal form of behavior (a role model) and then attempts to copy it. In artificial intelligence (AI) people attempt to build computers that model human cognition.

modularity A theory that the brain is composed of a number of modules that occupy relatively specific areas and that carry out relatively specific tasks.

morpheme The smallest unit of a language that carries meaning.

motor neuron *See* neuron.

MRI (magnetic resonance imaging) A noninvasive scanning technique that uses magnetic fields to produce detailed images of body tissue.

nature–nurture A long-running debate over whether genetic factors (nature) or environmental factors (nurture) are most important in different aspects of behavior.

neuron A nerve cell, consisting of a cell body (soma), an axon, and one or more dendrites. Motor (efferent) neurons produce movement when they fire by carrying information *from* the central nervous system *to* the muscles and glands; sensory (afferent) neurons carry information *from* the senses *to* the central nervous system.

neuropsychology An area of psychology that studies the connections between parts of the brain and neural processes, on one hand, and different cognitive processes and types of behavior, on the other.

neurotransmitter A substance that carries chemical "messages" across the synaptic gaps between the neurons of the brain.

nonverbal communication The way in which animals communicate without language (verbal communication), using such things as posture, tone of voice, and facial expressions.

operant conditioning *See* instrumental conditioning

outgroup The people who do not belong to an ingroup.

parallel processing A type of cognition in which information is processed in several different ways at once. In serial processing information passes through one stage of processing at a time.

peripheral nervous system All the nerves and nerve processes that connect the central nervous system with receptors, muscles, and glands.

personality The collection of character traits that makes one person different from another.

personality disorder A group of mental disorders in which aspects of someone's personality make it difficult for them to function properly in society.

PET (positron emission tomography) A noninvasive scanning technique that makes images of the brain according to levels of metabolic activity inside it.

phenomenology A philosophy based on the study of immediate experiences.

phobia A strong fear of a particular object (such as snakes) or social situation.

phoneme A basic unit of spoken language.

phrenology An early approach to psychology that studied the relationship between areas of the brain (based on skull shape) and mental functions. Phrenology has since been discredited.

physiology A type of biology concerned with the workings of cells, organs, and tissues.

positive punishment A type of conditioning in which incorrect responses are punished.

positive reinforcement A type of conditioning in which correct responses are rewarded.

primary memory *See* short-term memory

probability The likelihood of something happening.

procedural knowledge The practical knowledge of how to do things ("know-how"). Compare declarative knowledge

prosody A type of nonverbal communication in which language is altered by such things as the pitch of someone's voice and their intonation.

psyche The soul or mind of a person or a driving force behind their personality.

psychiatry The study, classification, and treatment of mental disorders.

psychoanalysis A theory of behavior and an approach to treating mental disorders pioneered by Austrian neurologist Sigmund Freud. Adjective: psychoanalytic

psychogenic A mental disorder that is psychological (as opposed to physical) in origin.

psycholinguistics The study of language-related behavior, including how the brain acquires and processes language.

psychosurgery A type of brain surgery designed to treat mental disorders.

psychotherapy A broad range of treatments for mental disorders based on different kinds of interaction between a patient and a therapist.

psychosis A mental state characterized by disordered personality and loss of contact with reality that affects normal social functioning. Psychosis is a feature of psychotic disorders, such as schizophrenia. Adjective: psychotic

reaction time The time taken for the subject in an experiment to respond to a stimulus.

recall The process by which items are recovered from memory. Compare recognition

recognition The process by which a person realizes they have previously encountered a particular object or event. Compare recall

reductionism A philosophy based on breaking complex things into their individual components. Also, an attempt to explain high-level sciences (such as psychology) in terms of lower-level sciences (such as chemistry or physics).

reflex An automatic response to a stimulus (a "knee-jerk" reaction).

reflex arc The neural circuit thought to be responsible for the control of a reflex.

rehearsing The process by which a person repeats information to improve its chances of being stored in memory.

representation A mental model based on perceptions of the world.

repression In psychoanalysis an unconscious mental process that keeps thoughts out of conscious awareness.

response The reaction to a stimulus.

reuptake The reabsorption of a neurotransmitter from the place where it was produced.

risk aversion A tendency not to take risks even when they may have beneficial results.

schema An abstract mental plan that serves as a guide to action or a more general mental representation.

schizophrenia A mental disorder characterized by hallucinations and disordered thought patterns in which a patient becomes divorced from reality. It is a type of psychotic disorder.

secondary memory *See* long-term memory

selective attention *See* attention

self-concept The ideas and feelings that people hold about themselves.

semantic memory A type of long-term memory that stores information based on its content or meaning. Compare episodic memory

senses The means by which people perceive things. The five senses are vision, hearing, smell, touch, and taste.

sensory memory An information store that records sensory impressions for a short period of time before they are processed more thoroughly.

sensory neuron *See* neuron

serotonin A neurotransmitter in the central nervous system that plays a key role in affective (mood) disorders, sleep, and the perception of pain. Serotonin is also known as 5-hydroxytryptamine (5-HT).

shaping A type of conditioning in which behavior is gradually refined toward some ideal form by successive approximations.

short-term memory A memory of very limited capacity in which sensory inputs are held before being processed more deeply and passing into long-term memory. Compare long-term memory

social cognition An area of psychology that combines elements of social and cognitive psychology in an attempt to understand how people think about themselves in relation to the other people around them.

social Darwinism A theory that society behaves according to Darwinian principles, with the most successful members thriving at the expense of the least successful ones.

social psychology An area of psychology that explores how individuals behave in relation to other people and to society as a whole.

sociobiology A theory that seeks to explain social behavior through biological approaches, notably the theory of evolution. *See also* evolutionary psychology

somatic Something that relates to the body as opposed to the mind; something physical as opposed to something mental.

stereopsis The process by which the brain assembles one 3-D image by combining a pair of 2-D images from the eyes.

stimulus A type of sensory input that provokes a response.

subject The person studied in a psychological experiment.

synapse The region across which nerve impulses are transmitted from one neuron to another. It includes the synaptic cleft (a gap) and the sections of the cell membranes on either side of the cleft. They are called the presynaptic and postsynaptic membranes.

synesthesia A process by which the stimulation of one sense (such as hearing a sound) produces a different kind of sensory impression (such as seeing a color).

thalamus A structure in the forebrain that passes sensory information on to the cerebral cortex.

theory of mind The realization by an individual (such as a growing child, for example) that other people have thoughts and mental processes of their own. It is universally accepted that humans have a theory of mind, and research has shown that some other animals, such as chimpanzees and dolphins, might also have a theory of mind, but this is still debated. Theory of mind is of interest to developmental psychologists since it is not something people are born with, but something that develops in infancy.

tranquilizers A type of medication with sedative, muscle-relaxant, or similar properties. Minor tranquilizers are also known as antianxiety or anxiolytic drugs; major tranquilizers are also known as antipsychotic drugs.

unconditioned stimulus/response (US/UR) *See* classical conditioning

unconscious In psychoanalytic and related theories the area of the mind that is outside conscious awareness and recall but that informs the contents of such things as dreams. In general usage *unconscious* simply refers to automatic cognitive processes that we are not aware of or the lack of consciousness (that is, "awareness") at times such as during sleep.

working memory *See* short-term memory

Resources

Further Reading

Altmann, G. T. M. *The Ascent of Babel: An Exploration of Language, Mind, and Understanding.* Cambridge, MA: Oxford University Press, 1999.

American Psychiatric Association. *Diagnostic and Statistical Manual of Mental Disorders, 4th edition, Text Revision.* Washington, DC: American Psychiatric Press, 2000.

Argyle, M. *The Psychology of Interpersonal Behaviour (5th edition).* London, UK: Penguin, 1994.

Asher, S. R. and Coie, J. D. (eds.). *Peer Rejection in Childhood.* Cambridge, UK: Cambridge University Press, 1990.

Atkinson, R. L. *et al. Hilgard's Introduction to Psychology (13th edition).* London, UK: International Thomson Publishing, 1999.

Barnouw, V. *Culture and Personality.* Chicago, IL: Dorsey Press, 1985.

Baron, J. *Thinking and Deciding.* Cambridge, UK: Cambridge University Press, 1994.

Barry, M. A. S. *Visual Intelligence: Perception, Image, and Manipulation in Visual Communication.* Albany, NY: State University of New York Press, 1997.

Beck, J. *Cognitive Therapy: Basics and Beyond.* London, UK: The Guildford Press, 1995.

Bickerton, D. *Language and Species.* Chicago, IL: The University of Chicago Press, 1990.

Blackburn, I. M. and Davison, K. *Cognitive Therapy for Depression and Anxiety: A Practitioner's Guide.* Oxford, UK: Blackwell, 1995.

Boden, M. A. *Piaget (2nd edition).* London, UK: Fontana Press, 1994.

Brehm, S. S., Kassin, S. M., and Fein, S. *Social Psychology (4th edition).* Boston, MA: Houghton Mifflin, 1999.

Brody, N. *Intelligence (2nd edition).* San Diego, CA: Academic Press, 1997.

Brown, D. S. *Learning a Living: A Guide to Planning Your Career and Finding a Job for People with Learning Disabilities, Attention Deficit Disorder, and Dyslexia.* Bethesda, MD: Woodbine House, 2000.

Bruhn, A. R. *Earliest Childhood Memories.* New York: Praeger, 1990.

Buunk, B. P. "Affiliation, Attraction and Close Relationships." *In* M. Hewstone and W. Stroebe (eds.), *Introduction to Social Psychology: A European Perspective.* Oxford, UK: Blackwell, 2001.

Cacioppo, J. T., Tassinary, L. G., and Berntson, G. G. (eds.). *Handbook of Psychophysiology (2nd edition).* New York: Cambridge University Press, 2000.

Cardwell, M. *Dictionary of Psychology.* Chicago, IL: Fitzroy Dearborn Publishers, 1999

Carson, R. C. and Butcher, J. N. *Abnormal Psychology and Modern Life (9th edition).* New York: HarperCollins Publishers, 1992.

Carter, R. *Mapping the Mind.* Berkeley, CA: University of California Press, 1998.

Cavan, S. *Recovery from Drug Addiction.* New York: Rosen Publishing Group, 2000.

Clarke-Stewart, A. *Daycare.* Cambridge, MA: Harvard University Press, 1993.

Cohen, G. *The Psychology of Cognition (2nd edition).* San Diego, CA: Academic Press, 1983.

Cramer, D. *Close Relationships: The Study of Love and Friendship.* New York: Arnold, 1998.

Daly, M. and Wilson, M. *Homicide.* New York: Aldine de Gruyter, 1988.

Davis, R. D., Braun, E. M., and Smith, J. M. *The Gift of Dyslexia: Why Some of the Smartest People Can't Read and How They Can Learn.* New York: Perigee, 1997.

Davison, G. C. and Neal, J. M. *Abnormal Psychology.* New York: John Wiley and Sons, Inc., 1994.

Dawkins, R. *The Selfish Gene.* New York: Oxford Universty Press, 1976.

Dennett, D. C. *Darwin's Dangerous Idea: Evolution and the Meanings of Life.* Carmichael, CA: Touchstone Books, 1996.

Dobson, C. *et al. Understanding Psychology.* London, UK: Weidenfeld and Nicolson, 1982.

Duck, S. *Meaningful Relationships: Talking, Sense, and Relating.* Thousand Oaks, CA: Sage Publications, 1994.

Durie, M. H. "Maori Psychiatric Admissions: Patterns, Explanations and Policy Implications." *In* J. Spicer, A. Trlin, and J. A. Walton (eds.), *Social Dimensions of Health and Disease: New Zealand Perspectives.* Palmerston North, NZ: Dunmore Press, 1994.

Eliot, L. *What's Going on in There? How the Brain and Mind Develop in the First Five Years of Life.* New York: Bantam Books, 1999.

Eysenck, M. (ed.). *The Blackwell Dictionary of Cognitive Psychology.* Cambridge, MA: Blackwell, 1991.

Faherty, C. and Mesibov, G. B. *Asperger's: What Does It Mean to Me?* Arlington, TX: Future Horizons, 2000.

Fernando, S. *Mental Health in a Multi-Ethnic Society: A Multi-Disciplinary Handbook.* New York: Routledge, 1995.

Fiske, S. T. and Taylor, S. E. *Social Cognition (2nd Edition).* New York: Mcgraw-Hill, 1991.

Franken, R. E. *Human Motivation (5th edition).* Belmont, CA: Wadsworth Thomson Learning, 2002.

Freud, S. and Brill, A. A. *The Basic Writings of Sigmund Freud.* New York: Modern Library, 1995.

Gardner, H. *The Mind's New Science: A History of the Cognitive Revolution.* New York: Basic Books, 1985.

Garnham, A. and Oakhill, J. *Thinking and Reasoning.* Cambridge, MA: Blackwell, 1994.

Gaw, A. C. *Culture, Ethnicity, and Mental Illness.* Washington, DC: American Psychiatric Press, 1992.

Giacobello, J. *Everything You Need to Know about Anxiety and Panic Attacks.* New York: Rosen Publishing Group, 2000.

Gazzaniga, M. S. *The Mind's Past.* Berkeley, CA: University of California Press, 1998.

Gazzaniga, M. S. (ed.). *The New Cognitive Neurosciences (2nd edition).* Cambridge, MA: MIT Press, 2000.

Gazzaniga, M. S., Ivry, R. B., and Mangun, G. R. *Cognitive Neuroscience: The Biology of the Mind (2nd edition).* New York: Norton, 2002.

Gernsbacher, M. A. (ed.). *Handbook of Psycholinguistics.* San Diego, CA: Academic Press, 1994.

Gigerenzer, G. *Adaptive Thinking: Rationality in the Real World.* New York: Oxford University Press, 2000.

Goodglass, H. *Understanding Aphasia.* San Diego, CA: Academic Press, 1993.

Gordon, M. *Jumpin' Johnny Get Back to Work! A Child's Guide to ADHD/Hyperactivity.* DeWitt, NY: GSI Publications Inc., 1991.

Gordon, M. A *I Would if I Could: A Teenager's Guide to ADHD/Hyperactivity.* DeWitt, NY: GSI Publications Inc., 1992.

Goswami, U. *Cognition in Children.* London, UK: Psychology Press, 1998.

Graham, H. *The Human Face of Psychology: Humanistic Psychology in Its Historical, Social, and Cultural Context.* Milton Keynes, UK: Open University Press, 1986.

Grandin, T. *Thinking in Pictures: And Other Reports from my Life with Autism.* New York: Vintage Books, 1996.

Greenberger, D. and Padesky, C. *Mind over Mood.* New York: Guilford Publications, 1995.

Groeger, J. A. *Memory and Remembering: Everyday Memory in Context.* New York: Longman, 1997.

Gross, R. and Humphreys, P. *Psychology: The Science of Mind and Behaviour.* London, UK: Hodder Arnold, 1993.

Halford, G. S. *Children's Understanding: The Development of Mental Models.* Hillsdale, NJ: Lawrence Erlbaum Associates, 1993.

Harley, T. A. *The Psychology of Language: From Data to Theory (2nd edition).* Hove, UK: Psychology Press, 2001.

Harris, G. G. *Casting out Anger: Religion among the Taita of Kenya.* New York: Cambridge University Press, 1978.

Hayes, N. *Psychology in Perspective (2nd edition).* New York: Palgrave, 2002.

Hearst, E. *The First Century of Experimental Psychology.* Hillsdale, NJ: Lawrence Erlbaum Associates, 1979.

Hecht, T. *At Home in the Street: Street Children of Northeast Brazil.* New York: Cambridge University Press, 1998.

Hetherington, E. M. *Coping with Divorce, Single Parenting, and Remarriage: A Risk and Resiliency Perspective.* Mawah, NJ: Lawrence Erlbaum Associates, 1999.

Higbee, K. L. *Your Memory: How It Works and How to Improve It (2nd edition).* New York: Paragon 1993.

Hinde, R. A. *Individuals, Relationships and Culture: Links between Ethology and the Social Sciences.* Cambridge, UK: Cambridge University Press, 1987.

Hogdon, L. A. *Solving Behavior Problems in Autism.* Troy, MI: Quirkroberts Publishing, 1999.

Hogg, M. A. (ed.). *Social Psychology.* Thousand Oaks, CA: Sage Publications, 2002.

Holden, G. W. *Parents and the Dynamics of Child Rearing.* Boulder, CO: Westview Press, 1997.

Holmes, J. *John Bowlby and Attachment Theory.* New York: Routledge, 1993.

Hughes, H. C. *Sensory Exotica: A World Beyond Human Experience.* Cambridge, MA: MIT Press, 1999.

Hyde, M. O. and Setano, J. F. *When the Brain Dies First.* New York: Franlin Watts Inc., 2000.

Ingersoll, B. D. *Distant Drums, Different Drummers: A Guide for Young People with ADHD.* Plantation, FL: A.D.D. WareHouse, 1995.

Jencks, C. and Phillips, M. *The Black-White Test Score Gap.* Washington, DC: Brookings Institution Press, 1998.

Johnson, M. J. *Developmental Cognitive Neuroscience.* Cambridge, MA: Blackwell, 1997.

Johnson, M. H. and Morton, J. *Biology and Cognitive Development. The Case of Face Recognition.* Cambridge, MA: Blackwell, 1991.

Johnson-Laird, P. N. *The Computer and the Mind: An Introduction to Cognitive Science.* Cambridge, MA: Harvard University Press, 1988.

Jusczyk, P. W. *The Discovery of Spoken Language.* Cambridge, MA: MIT Press, 1997.

Kalat, J. W. *Biological Psychology (7th edition).* Belmont, CA: Wadsworth Thomson Learning, 2001.

Kaplan, H. I. and Sadock, B. J. *Synopsis of Psychiatry: Behavioral Sciences, Clinical Psychiatry.* Philadelphia, PA: Lippincott, Williams and Wilkins, 1994.

Karen, R. *Becoming Attached: First Relationships and How They Shape Our Capacity to Love.* New York: Oxford University Press, 1998.

Kirk, S. A. and Kutchins, H. *The Selling of DSM: The Rhetoric of Science in Psychiatry.* New York: Aldine de Gruyter, 1992.

Kinney, J. *Clinical Manual of Substance Abuse.* St. Louis, MO: Mosby, 1995.

Kleinman, A. *Rethinking Psychiatry: From Cultural Category to Personal Experience.* New York: Free Press, 1988.

Kosslyn, S. M. and Koenig, O. *Wet Mind: The New Cognitive Neuroscience.* New York: Free Press, 1992.

Kutchins, H. and Kirk, S. A. *Making Us Crazy: DSM: The Psychiatric Bible and the Creation of Mental Disorders.* New York: Free Press, 1997.

LaBruzza, A. L. *Using DSM-IV; A Clinician's Guide to Psychiatric Diagnosis.* St. Northvale, NJ: Jason Aronson Inc., 1994.

Leahey, T. A. *A History of Psychology: Main Currents in Psychological Thought (5th edition).* Upper Saddle River, NJ: Prentice Hall, 2000.

LeDoux, J. *The Emotional Brain.* New York: Simon and Schuster, 1996.

Levelt, W. J. M. *Speaking: From Intention to Articulation.* Cambridge, MA: MIT Press, 1989.

Lewis, M. and Haviland-Jones, J. M. (eds.). *Handbook of Emotions (2nd edition).* New York: Guilford Press, 2000.

Lowisohn, J. H. *et al. Substance Abuse: A Comprehensive Textbook (3rd edition).* Baltimore, MD: Williams & Wilkins, 1997.

McCabe, D. *To Teach a Dyslexic.* Clio, MI: AVKO Educational Research, 1997.

McCorduck, P. *Machines Who Think: A Personal Inquiry into the History and Prospects of Artificial Intelligence.* San Francisco: W. H. Freeman, 1979.

McIlveen, R. and Gross, R. *Biopsychology (5th edition).* Boston, MA: Allyn and Bacon, 2002.

McLachlan, J. *Medical Embryology.* Reading, MA: Addison-Wesley Publishing Co., 1994.

Manstead, A. S. R. and Hewstone M. (eds.). *The Blackwell Encyclopaedia of Social Psychology.* Oxford, UK: Blackwell, 1996.

Marsella, A. J., DeVos, G., and Hsu, F. L. K. (eds.). *Culture and Self: Asian and Western Perspectives.* New York: Routledge, 1988.

Matlin, M. W. *The Psychology of Women.* New York: Harcourt College Publishers, 2000.

Matsumoto, D. R. *People: Psychology from a Cultural Perspective.* Pacific Grove, CA: Brooks/Cole Publishing, 1994.

Matsumoto, D. R. *Culture and Modern Life.* Pacific

Grove, CA: Brooks/Cole Publishing, 1997.

Mazziotta, J .C., Toga, A. W., and Frackowiak, R. S. J. (eds.). *Brain Mapping: The Disorders.* San Diego, CA: Academic Press, 2000.

Nadeau, K. G., Littman, E., and Quinn, P. O. *Understanding Girls with ADHD.* Niagara Falls, NY: Advantage Books, 2000.

Nadel, J. and Camioni, L. (eds.). *New Perspectives in Early Communicative Development.* New York: Routledge, 1993.

Nobus, D. *Jacques Lacan and the Freudian Practice of Psychoanalysis.* Philadelphia, PA: Routledge, 2000.

Oakley, D. A. "The Plurality of Consciousness." *In* D. A. Oakley (ed.), *Brain and Mind,* New York: Methuen, 1985.

Obler, L. K. and Gjerlow, K. *Language and the Brain.* New York: Cambridge University Press, 1999.

Ogden, J. A. *Fractured Minds: A Case-study Approach to Clinical Neuropsychology.* New York: Oxford University Press, 1996.

Owusu-Bempah, K. and Howitt, D. *Psychology beyond Western Perspectives.* Leicester, UK: British Psychological Society Books, 2000.

Paranjpe, A. C. and Bhatt, G. S. "Emotion: A Perspective from the Indian Tradition." *In* H. S. R. Kao and D. Sinha (eds.), *Asian Perspectives on Psychology.* New Delhi, India: Sage Publications, 1997.

Peacock, J. *Depression.* New York: Lifematters Press, 2000.

Pfeiffer, W. M. "Culture-Bound Syndromes." *In* I. Al-Issa (ed.), *Culture and Psychopathology.* Baltimore, MD: University Park Press, 1982.

Pillemer, D. B. *Momentous Events, Vivid Memories.* Cambridge, MA: Harvard University Press, 1998.

Pinel, J. P. J. *Biopsychology (5th edition).* Boston, MA: Allyn and Bacon, 2002.

Pinker, S. *The Language Instinct.* New York: HarperPerennial, 1995.

Pinker, S. *How the Mind Works.* New York: Norton, 1997.

Porter, R. *Medicine: A History of Healing: Ancient Traditions to Modern Practices.* New York: Barnes and Noble, 1997.

Ramachandran, V. S. and Blakeslee, S. *Phantoms in the Brain: Probing the Mysteries of the Human Mind.* New York: William Morrow, 1998.

Ridley, M. *Genome: The Autobiography of a Species in 23 Chapters.* New York: HarperCollins, 1999.

Robins, L. N. and Regier, D. A. *Psychiatric Disorders in America.* New York: Free Press, 1991.

Robinson, D. N. *Toward a Science of Human Nature: Essays on the Psychologies of Mill, Hegel, Wundt, and James.* New York: Columbia University Press, 1982.

Rugg, M. D. and Coles, M. G. H. (eds.). *Electrophysiology of the Mind: Event-Related Brain Potentials and Cognition.* Oxford, UK: Oxford University Press, 1995.

Rutter, M. "The Interplay of Nature and Nurture: Redirecting the Inquiry." *In* R. Plomin and G. E. McClearn (eds.), *Nature, Nurture, and Psychology.* Washington, DC: American Psychological Association, 1993.

Sarason, I. G. and Sarason B. R. *Abnormal Psychology: The Problem of Maladaptive Behavior (9th edition).* Upper Saddle River, NJ: Prentice Hall, 1998.

Savage-Rumbaugh, S., Shanker, S. G., and Taylor, T. J. *Apes, Language, and the Human Mind.* New York: Oxford University Press, 1998.

Schab, F. R., & Crowder, R. G. (eds.). *Memory for Odors.* Mahwah, NJ: Lawrence Erlbaum Associates, 1995.

Segal, N. L. *Entwined Lives: Twins and What They Tell Us about Human Behavior.* New York: Plume, 2000.

Seeman, M. V. *Gender and Psychopathology.* Washington, DC: American Psychiatric Press, 1995.

Seligman, M. E. P. *Helplessness: On Depression, Development, and Death.* San Francisco, CA: W. H. Freeman and Co., 1992.

Shorter, E. *A History of Psychiatry: From the Era of Asylum to the Age of Prozac.* New York: John Wiley and Sons, Inc., 1997.

Siegler, R. S. *Children's Thinking (3rd edition).* Englewood Cliffs, NJ: Prentice Hall, 1998.

Simpson, E. M. *Reversals: A Personal Account of Victory over Dyslexia.* New York: Noonday Press, 1992.

Singer, D. G. and Singer, J. L. (eds.). *Handbook of Children and the Media.* Thousand Oaks, CA: Sage Publications, 2001.

Skinner, B. F. *Science and Human Behavior.* New York: Free Press, 1965.

Slavney, P. R. *Psychiatric Dimensions of Medical Practice: What Primary-Care Physicians Should Know about Delirium, Demoralization, Suicidal Thinking, and Competence to Refuse Medical Advice.* Baltimore, MD: The Johns Hopkins University Press, 1998.

Smith McLaughlin, M., Peyser Hazouri, S., and Peyser Hazouri, S. *Addiction: The "High" That Brings You Down.* Springfield, NJ: Enslow publishers, 1997.

Sommers, M. A. *Everything You Need to Know about Bipolar Disorder and Depressive Illness.* New York: Rosen Publishing Group, 2000.

Stanovich, K. E. *Who Is Rational? Studies of Individual Differences in Reasoning.* Mahwah, NJ: Lawrence Erlbaum Associates, 1999.

Symons, D. *The Evolution of Human Sexuality.* New York: Oxford University Press, 1979.

Symons, D. "Beauty is in the Adaptations of the Beholder: The Evolutionary Psychology of Human Female Sexual Attractiveness." *In* P. R. Abramson and S. D. Pinkerton (eds.), *Sexual Nature, Sexual Culture.* Chicago, IL: University of Chicago Press, 1995.

Tavris, C. *The Mismeasure of Women.* New York: Simon and Schuster, 1992.

Triandis, H. C. *Culture and Social Behavior.* New York: McGraw-Hill, 1994.

Tulving, E and Craik, F. I. M. *The Oxford Handbook of Memory.* Oxford, UK: Oxford University Press, 2000.

Vygotsky, L. S. *Mind in Society: The Development of Higher Psychological Processes.* Cambridge, MA: Harvard University Press, 1978.

Weiten, W. *Psychology: Themes and Variations.* Monterey, CA: Brooks/Cole Publishing, 1998.

Werner, E. E. and Smith, R. S. *Overcoming the Odds: High-Risk Children from Birth to Adulthood.* Ithaca, NY: Cornell University Press, 1992.

White, R. W. and Watt, N. F. *The Abnormal Personality (5th edition).* Chichester, UK: John Wiley and Sons, Inc., 1981.

Wickens, A. *Foundations of Biopsychology.* Harlow, UK: Prentice Hall, 2000.

Wilson, E. O. *Sociobiology: A New Synthesis.* Cambridge, MA: Harvard University Press, 1975.

Winkler, K. *Teens, Depression, and the Blues: A Hot Issue.* Springfield, NJ: Enslow publishers, 2000.

Wolman, B. (ed.). *Historical Roots of Contemporary Psychology.* New York: Harper and Row, 1968.

Wrightsman, L. S. and Sanford, F. H. *Psychology: A Scientific Study of Human Behavior.* Monterey, CA: Brooks/Cole Publishing, 1975.

Yap, P. M. *Comparative Psychiatry: A Theoretical Framework.* Toronto, Canada: University of Toronto Press, 1974.

Zarit, S. H. and Knight, B. G. *A Guide to Psychotherapy and Aging.* Washington, DC: American Psychological Association, 1997.

Useful Websites

Amazing Optical Illusions
http://www.optillusions.com
See your favorite optical illusions at this fun site.

American Psychological Association
http://www.apa.org
Here you can read a peer-reviewed e-journal published by the APA, follow the development of new ethical guidelines for pscychologists, and find a wealth of other information.

Association for Advancement of Behavior Therapy
http://www.aabt.org
An interdisciplinary organization concerned with the application of behavioral and cognitive sciences to the understanding of human behavior.

Association for Cross-Cultural Psychology
http://www.fit.edu/CampusLife/clubs-org/iaccp
Including a full-text downloadable version of their journal.

Bedlam
http://www.museum-london.org.uk/MOLsite/exhibits/bedlam/f_bed.htm
The Museum of London's online exhibition about Bedlam, the notorious mental institution.

Bipolar Disorders Information Center
http://www.mhsource.com/bipolar
Articles and information about bipolar 1 disorder.

Brain and Mind
http://www.epub.org.br/cm/home_i.htm
An online magazine with articles devoted to neuroscience, linguisitics, imprinting, and many other related topics.

Exploratorium
http://www.exploratorium.edu/exhibits/nf_exhibits.html
Click on "seeing" or "hearing" to check out visual and auditory illusions and other secrets of the mind.

Freud and Culture
http://www.loc.gov/exhibits/freud
An online Library of Congress exhibition that examines Sigmund Freud's life and key ideas and his effect on 20th-century thinking.

Jigsaw Classroom
http://www.jigsaw.org
The official web site of the Jigsaw Classroom, a cooperative learning technique that reduces racial conflict between schoolchildren. Learn about its history and how to implement the techniques.

Kidspsych
http://www.kidspsych.org/index1.html
American Psychological Association's childrens' site, with games and exercises for kids. Also useful for students of developmental psychology. Follow the "about this activity" links to find out the theories behind the fun and games.

Kismet
http://www.ai.mit.edu/projects/humanoid-robotics-group/kismet/kismet.html
Kismet is the MIT's expressive robot, which has perceptual and motor functions tailored to natural human communication channels.

Museum of Psychological Instrumentation
http://chss.montclair.edu/psychology/museum/museum.html
Look at images of early psychological laboratory research apparatus, such as Wilhelm Wundt's eye motion demonstrator.

National Academy of Neuropsychology
http://nanonline.org/content/pages/research/acn.shtm
A site where you can download the archives of Clinical Neuropsychology, *a journal that focuses on disorders of the central nervous system.*

Neuroscience for Kids
http://faculty.washington.edu/chudler/neurok.html
A useful website for students and teachers who want to learn about the nervous system. Enjoy activities and experiments on your way to learning all about the brain and spinal cord.

National Eating Disorders Society
http://www.nationaleatingdisorders.org
Information on eating disorders, their precursors, how to help a friend, and the importance of treatment.

Neuroscience Tutorial
http://thalamus.wustl.edu/course
The Washington University School of Medicine's online tutorial offers an illustrated guide to the basics of clinical neuroscience, with useful artworks and user-friendly text.

Online Dictionary of Mental Health
http://www.shef.ac.uk/~psysc/psychotherapy
The Centre for Psychotherapeutic Studies at Sheffield University, UK, runs this online dictionary. There are links to many sites offering different viewpoints on major mental health issues.

Personality Theories
http://www.ship.edu/~cgboeree/perscontents.html
An electronic textbook covering personality theories for undergraduate and graduate courses.

Psychology Central
http://emerson.thomsonlearning.com/psych
Links to many useful articles grouped by subject as well as cool, animated figures that improve your understanding of psychological principles.

Schizophrenia.com
http://www.schizophrenia.com
Information and resources on this mental disorder provided by a charitable organization.

Seeing, Hearing, and Smelling the World
http://www.hhmi.org/senses/
A downloadable illustrated book dealing with perception from the Howard Hughes Medical Institute.

Sigmund Freud Museum
http://freud.t0.or.at/freud/
The online Sigmund Freud Museum has videos and audio recordings of the famous psychoanalyst—there are even images of Freud's famous couch.

Social Psychology Network
http://www.socialpsychology.org
The largest social psychology database on the Internet. Within these pages you will find more than 5,000 links to psychology-related resources and research groups, and there is also a useful section on general psychology.

Stanford Prison Experiment
http://www.prisonexp.org/
A fascinating look at the Stanford Prison Experiment, which saw subjects placed in a prison to see what happens to "good people in a bad environment." Learn why the experiment had to be abandoned after six days due to the unforeseen severity of the effects on participants.

Stroop effect
http://www.dcity.org/braingames/stroop/index.htm
Take part in an online psychological experiment to see the Stroop effect in action.

Quote Attributions

opening quote

Each chapter in *Psychology* contains quotes that relate to the topics covered. These quotes appear both within the main text and at the start of the chapters, and their attributions are detailed here. Quotes are listed in the order that they appear in the chapter, and the page numbers at the end of each attribution refer to the pages in this volume where the quote appears.

What Is Abnormality?

Kessler, R. *et al.* "Lifetime and 12-month Prevelance of DSM-III-R Psychiatric Disorders in the United States: Results from the National Comorbidity Survey." *Archives of General Psychiatry*, **51**, 1994, p. 6.

Merriam Webster's Collegiate Dictionary (10th edition). Springfield, MA: Merriam-Webster, Inc. 2001, p. 9.

Miller, E., and Morley, S. *Investigating Abnormal Behavior*. London, UK: Weidenfeld, 1986, p. 12.

Widiger, T. A. and Trull, T. D. "Diagnosis and Clinical Assessment." *Annual Review of Psychology*, **42**, 1991, p. 15.

Mental Disorders

Kaplan, H. I. and Sadock, B. J. *Synopsis of Psychiatry:*

Behavioral Sciences, Clinical Psychiatry. Philadelphia, PA: Lippincott, Williams, and Wilkins, 1994, p. 24, p. 28, p. 42.

Weiten, W. *Psychology: Themes and Variations, (2nd edition)*. Pacific Grove, CA: Brooks/Cole Publishing, 1992, p. 26, p.27, p.40, p.42, p.45, p.52.

Szasz, T. *The Second Sin*. Garden City, NY: Anchor Press, 1973, p. 34.

Davison, G. C. and Neal, J. M. *Abnormal Psychology*. New York: John Wiley and Sons, Inc., 1994, p. 41, p.43.

Lezak, M. D. *Neuropsychological Assessment (3rd edition)*. New York: Oxford University Press, 1995, p. 58.

Abnormality in Development

Jolliffe, J., Lansdown, R., and Robinson, C. "Autism: A Personal Account in Communication." *Journal of the National Autistic Society of London*, **26**, 1992, p. 74.

Hoffman, D. to Kim Peek, the inspiration for Hoffman's role in Brian Morrow's movie *Rain Man*. 1988, p. 78.

Hornsby, B. *Overcoming Dyslexia: A Straightforward Guide for Families and Teachers*. New York: Arco Publications, 1984, p. 80.

Cooper, P. and Ideus, K. *Attention Deficit/Hyperactivity Disorder: A Practical Guide for Teachers*. London, UK: David Fulton Publishers, 1996, p. 87.

Psychotherapies

Greene, G. *Ways of Escape*. London, UK: Bodley Head, 1980, p. 96.

Wittgenstein, L. *Tracatus Logico-Philosophicus*. 1922, p. 99.

Descartes, R. *Discourse on the Method of Rightly Conducting the Reason, and Seeking Truth in the Sciences*. 1637, p. 107.

Voltaire (1694–1778). Unpublished quote, *c*. 1750, p. 109.

Boileau-Despréaux, N. *L'Art Poetique*. 1672. p. 115.

Physical Therapies

Osler, W. *The Principles and Practice of Medicine*. New York: D. Appleton and Co., 1892 p. 121.

Anon. "Understanding Depression." *At* http://www.prozac.com/, 2001, p. 125.

Kellner, C. H. *et al. Handbook of ECT*. Washington, DC: American Psychiatric Press, 1997, p. 134.

Phyllis, an ECT patient. Cited in C. H. Kellner,
  Handbook of ECT. Washington, DC: American
  Psychiatric Press, 1997, p. 135.

Mental Disorders and Society
National Alliance for the Mentally Ill, Press
  Release, 2001, p. 144.
Seligman, M. E. P. *What You Can Change and What
  You Can't*. New York: Knopf, 1994, p. 149.
Lee, N. On being confined to Bedlam mental
  institution. 1684, p. 156.
Holmes, O. W. (1809–1894). Unpublished
  quote, 1838, p. 159.
Brady, J. (born 1940) Unpublished quote,
  1982, p. 161.

Every effort has been made to attribute the quotes
throughout *Psychology* correctly. Any errors or omissions
brought to the attention of the publisher are regretted and
will be credited in subsequent editions.

Set Index

2:37–38, 92; **4**:22–23
epistemology **3**:14
equilibration **4**:74, 75
equilibrium **4**:74, 75–76
equivalence paradox **6**:117
Erber, Ralph **5**:32
Erewhon (Butler) **2**:141
Erikson, Erik **1**:57–58, 65; **4**:114,
116, 138; **5**:101; **6**:97
eros **1**:54
ERPs (event-related potentials)
1:98, 99; **2**:78; **3**:38–40, 42; **4**:27
ethics
of artificial minds **2**:162
of cloning **5**:144
of psychological studies **1**:163
see also morality
ethnic differences, in intelligence
5:138–141, 153
ethnic identity **4**:142
ethnocentrism **1**:153
eugenics **1**:24, 136; **5**:143; **6**:137
cloning and **5**:144
eustachian tube **2**:76
event-related potentials
see ERPS
evolution, theory of
1:23, 134–135; **2**:161
and behaviorism **1**:76–77
and the brain **2**:7, 14–19
and heritability **5**:147
and humans **1**:136, 139–140; **2**:7
and sleep **2**:130–131
virtual evolution **2**:161
see also evolutionary psychology
evolutionary psychology
1:7, 28, **134–143**; **5**:41
key works **1**:138
see also evolution, theory of
examinations, studying for **3**:106, 107
examples, mental dictionaries
and **3**:77–78
excessive daytime sleepiness
(EDS) **2**:131
exclusion, social **5**:43–44
"executive function disorders" **2**:27
exercise, law of **3**:52
existentialist psychology **1**:69
existential therapy **6**:115
exocytosis **2**:35
exorcisms **6**:7, 21
experience, effect on the brain **4**:9, 10
experimental science **1**:7, 45
experimental methods **1**:162
research methods **1**:**162–163**
subjective and objective
information **3**:13
expertise **3**:141–142
expert systems **1**:130–131;
2:156, 157–158
*Expression of the Emotions in Man and
Animals, The* (Darwin) **2**:87
externality effect **4**:53
extinction, of conditioned responses
3:47, 56
extinction bursts **3**:56
extroverts **1**:60; **4**:150
heritability of extroversion **5**:155
eye-blink response system **3**:48–50
eyebrows, communication with **5**:79
eyes **2**:9, 65
communication with **5**:79

rods and cones **2**:65–66
saccidic movements **4**:41
structure **2**:66
eyewitnesses *see* witnesses
Eysenck, Hans **5**:96, 123; **6**:101

face(s)
expressions **2**:87–88, 89, 91–92, 93;
5:81, 83–84
"facial feedback hypothesis"
2:92–93
hands mapped on the **2**:34
inability to recognize **1**:94
mother–baby interactions
4:132–133
perception by infants **4**:52–53
and personality **5**:34
recognition **2**:71–72
robot facial expressions **2**:155
facial nerves **2**:21
factitious disorders **6**:24, 29
Münchausen's syndrome **6**:29
factor analysis **5**:119
false-memory syndrome **2**:57
see also memory, and crime
familiarity **3**:97
families **5**:162
of children with developmental
disabilities **6**:90–91
family theories of eating disorders
6:49–50
and heritability studies **5**:149–150
violence **1**:136
family therapy **6**:115
fantasies, childhood **1**:62
fathering **4**:128, 129
fats, dietary, during pregnancy
4:12, 13
fear classical conditioning **3**:50
fear(s) **2**:86, 87, 88, 92, 105, 106
conditioned **1**:78, 79; **2**:106; **3**:50
and reinforcement **3**:57
see also phobias
feature-associative networks **3**:77
feature detectors **2**:70
Fechner, Gustav **1**:31–32; **2**:63, 64
feedback systems **1**:106
feeding disorders **6**:69
feminist therapy **6**:115
fentanyl **6**:55
Fernald method **6**:84
Festinger, Leon **5**:47, 59
fetal alcohol syndrome (FAS) **4**:13
fetus
development **4**:**6–23**, 56, 153; **5**:46
and language development
1:123–124; **3**:128; **4**:11
measuring habituation in **4**:153
spinal cord **4**:23
"fight or flight response" **2**:23, 93
filter theory **3**:24, 26
firefighters **6**:15
Fiske, Susan **5**:32
fixation **5**:98–99; **6**:96, 97
fixed interval schedules **3**:55
fixed ratio schedules **3**:55
"flashbacks," after LSD use **2**:36
flooding **6**:102–103
fluoxetine (Prozac) **2**:39;
6:41, 124, 125
flying, phobia **6**:121
Flynn, James **5**:132

Flynn effect **5**:132
fMRI (functional magnetic resonance
imaging) **1**:96, 102, 117;
2:29; **4**:151
combined with EEG **1**:103
compared to PET **1**:102–103
disadvantages **1**:103
fetal **4**:22
and language **1**:118
typical experiment **1**:103
Fodor, Jerry **1**:114; **3**:11; **4**:37
folic acid **4**:12
food, and taste-aversion
conditioning **3**:48
food poisoning **3**:48
forced-choice preferential
looking procedure **4**:27
forebrain **2**:25–26, 27, 100
see also hypothalamus; thalamus
forgetting **3**:96, 98–99
Foster, Jodie **6**:160
fragile-X chromosome **5**:154; **6**:74
frame problem **2**:156
*Frankenstein, or the Modern
Prometheus* (Mary Shelley) **2**:13
free association **1**:56; **6**:96
Frege, Gottlob **3**:64, 70, 72
frequency, sound **2**:75
Freud, Anna **1**:57–58, 59, 65; **6**:97
Freud, Sigmund **1**:6, 16, 21, 52–57;
4:114; **6**:93–94
current controversy over **1**:64–65
and defense mechanisms **1**:55–56;
4:95–96; **5**:98, 100
and developmental psychology
1:55; **4**:113; **5**:98–101
dream analysis **1**:56; **2**:134; **6**:42, 94
key works **1**:53
limitations of his work **6**:98–99
and mental disorder **6**:18, 37,
42–43
and resistance **6**:96–97
and social attitudes **1**:7
and the tripartite structure of the
mind **1**:54–55; **4**:113; **5**:97–98
and unhappiness **6**:93
Freudian slips **2**:119
friendship **4**:139, 144–149
maintenance **5**:48
and nonverbal communication
5:81
preadolescent same-sex
("chumships") **5**:95, 114, 115
and proximity **5**:47
Friesen, Wallace **2**:88, 89, 90
Fritsch, Gustav **2**:12
frogs' legs, electricity **2**:12
Fromm, Erich **1**:64; **6**:97, 98
Fromm-Reichmann, Frieda **6**:38
frontal lobes **1**:91, 93; **2**:27, 55, 58,
117; **3**:93, 109, 111
frustration **5**:69–70
fugue state **3**:112
Fuller, Thomas, quoted **3**:105
functional fixity (functional
fixedness) **3**:138–148
functional imaging
see brain-imaging techniques
functionalism **1**:6, 39, **40–45**;
2:43, 48, 141
"functional systems," in the brain **1**:94
fundamental attribution error

(FAE) **5**:36, 37
GABA (gamma-amino butyric
acid) **6**:121, 134
Gage, Phineas **1**:91; **2**:28, 58, 100
Galen **2**:7, 8; **6**:23
Galilei, Galileo **2**:10; **6**:14
Gall, Franz Joseph **1**:20, 37, 91–92,
118; **2**:7, 11; **3**:120
Galton, Francis **1**:23; **3**:64, 65;
5:126, 142, 143, 150
Galvani, Luigi **2**:12
gambling **6**:55–56
gamma-amino butyric acid
(GABA) **6**:121
Gandhi, M.K. **5**:56; **6**:12–13
ganglia, basal **2**:29
gangs, street **5**:44
Garcia, John **1**:26
garden-path sentences **3**:122
Gardner, Howard **1**:114;
5:119, 121–123, 125
gate-control theory **2**:80, 81–82
Gazzaniga, Michael **3**:88
GBL (drug) **6**:55
gender
and childhood histories of
shyness **5**:116
difference in abilities **5**:137
difference in nonverbal
communication **5**:86
difference in parenting **4**:160–161
early boy/girl differences **4**:139–142
gender-identity disorders **6**:66
and intelligence tests **5**:136, 138
and mental disorders **6**:17
gender dysphonia **6**:66
generalized anxiety disorder
(GAD) **6**:23, 25–26, 30
general practitioners, and mental
disorders **6**:146
General Problem Solver (GPS)
1:112, 130, 133; **2**:147, 156–157;
3:23, 141
genes **1**:135; **2**:15
alleles **5**:146
and the environment **5**:144–145
and heritable traits **5**:145–148
multiple effects **5**:159
"selfish" **1**:135–136
genetics **2**:15
and ADHD **6**:88
and Alzheimer's disease **6**:59
and anxiety disorders **6**:27–28
and autism **6**:74
behavior **1**:29
and bipolar 1 disorder **6**:46
and dementia **6**:17
and depression **6**:41–42
and dyslexia **6**:82
and eating disorders **6**:48
and intelligence **5**:134
of psychology **4**:153–155
and schizophrenia **6**:36
and substance abuse **6**:53
geniculate nuclei **2**:25
Genie (child) **3**:133
genome, scans **4**:155
genotype **5**:146
Gernsbacher, Morton **3**:68–69
Gestalt psychology **1**:6, 39, **46–51**,
105; **2**:43; **3**:22; **4**:50–51
Gestalt therapy **1**:49–51; **6**:115